color outside the lines

Let your inner
weirdo shine!

♡ Pià

color outside the lines

the lines

be who you are, do what you love,

and let your inner weirdo shine!

By Pia Edberg

ISBN-13: 978-0995814219
ISBN-10: 099581421X

Book editor: Catherine Turner, turnerproofreading.com
Cover designer: Ethan Scott, facebook.com/ethanscottillustration
Book designer: Hynek Palatin

Less of the Excess Media
www.piaedberg.com

To my younger self, who was perfect just the way she was
Here's to letting your inner weirdo shine

contents

part one

part two

part three

part one

introduction

"Normal is getting dressed in clothes that you buy for work, driving through traffic in a car that you are still paying for, in order to get a job that you need so you can pay for the clothes, car, and the house that you leave empty all day in order to afford to live in it."
~ ELLEN GOODMAN

Have you ever been told that you're a little weird? How did it make you feel? Depending on who you are, this was either a compliment or an insult.

Do you feel like you're a professional social chameleon? Are you an expert at changing your colors in order to blend into the situation yet seldom reveal your real self except to those closest to you? Maybe you don't even share yourself with anyone at all? Are you exhausted from trying to be someone you're not?

Maybe waking up every morning feels like being forced to board the Titanic while already knowing that the ship is going to sink. No matter what you do, the awareness of drowning in the criticisms of others leaves you feeling tired, lonely, and suffocated because your parents, coworkers, or community will never understand you. Every day is a struggle to fit in.

The problem with being skilled at altering your persona is that nobody ever really gets a sense of who you truly are. And neither do you.

It's so hard to be normal!

But what *is* "normal" exactly anyway? This is a question I've asked myself since the first time one of the "cool girls" in eighth grade pointed out that I should be very embarrassed about the music I listened to because it wasn't popular enough. Let's face it; normal is pretty much the opposite of being weird.

The funny thing is, being *called* normal isn't exactly the highest form of flattery either because then we wouldn't be our awesome and unique selves! Could it get any more confusing?! Which one is it then?

We all want to be accepted and liked for who we are, but sometimes expressing our true nature can get us into trouble. It can unintentionally cause conflict or push people away, leaving us feeling isolated and alone. Where do we draw the line between fitting in and being who we are?

Society expects us to conform to a dying system and live our lives according to a prescribed formula. It seems like so many of us are on autopilot, but life is simply not a grocery list of accomplishments to be checked off.

We're sold the lie time and time again that all we have to do is go to school, get a good job, get married, buy a big house and a nice car, have kids, work, retire, and then die—all by a certain age on top of that. Only then can we be seen as successful. But what if we don't measure up to or agree with those social standards? What if we want to do things differently, or not at all?

Are you tired of molding and twisting your personality so you don't push anyone's buttons? Are you exhausted by the end of the day and just want to curl up in your warm, cozy bed and fall asleep to escape it all? Do you feel like you're always the odd person out because your thoughts, dreams, decisions, desires, opinions, or appearance are different compared to your social circle?

That inner conflict can manifest in minor ways, such as trying to convince your coworkers to go to a vegan restaurant for lunch because you don't support the meat industry but joining them at the steakhouse anyway so you don't ruffle anyone's feathers.

But it can also manifest in more significant ways, such as hiding your sexual orientation in fear of being judged, ridiculed, alienated, or even worse, harmed, by your peers or community just for being who you are. How do you deal with these situations in a confident, healthy, and joyful way?

A common complaint I hear from people is they either don't know where to start or feel like they don't have the time or energy to work on themselves, even though they know it will benefit them in the long run.

However, this thought-provoking book will help you unleash the wonderful weirdo waiting within so you can live a more authentic life. It's filled with practical tools and exercises to help you align your internal and external worlds so that you gain back that energy to focus on what you love to do and the dreams you want to pursue. You will no longer feel like you're constantly trying to color within the lines drawn by someone other than yourself.

Maybe you're already great at being yourself and you have no problem wearing that thrifted hot pink bodysuit to work—you're an inspiration!

Or perhaps you are the friend who encourages all your less vocal friends to "Stand up for who you are!" and "Be yourself!" That is awesome! We need more of you in the world.

Then there's the group of you who don't understand why anyone would care so much about what others think. You may already have an excellent handle on how to manage yourself in these situations; however, you may find some insightful tips in these pages that can improve your life even more!

This book is for anyone who has ever felt like an alien on this planet—whether it's because you are constantly made fun of or criticized for being, looking, or thinking differently, or you just don't agree with what is expected of you. You may be socially awkward and a little unusual. Maybe you like it that way, but maybe you don't as it causes more trouble than you like.

Maybe you are the black sheep of the family because you are extremely creative and want to cover your body in piercings and tattoos when everyone else is conservative. Or maybe you prefer to reject the rat race and be a travel photographer for a living instead. Perhaps you're a little bit shy or sensitive, and you don't speak up for yourself when you should, and so you hide your essence in fear of being judged. Or, maybe you have a dream of going back to school to become an embalmer because you want to learn how to preserve the beauty of human remains. (Hey, someone's got to do it!)

Some of the greatest greats were eccentric folks as well, and their unconventional ways of thinking led to success in a big way. They embraced their way of seeing and trusted their inner voice whether it was to prove that the planets revolved around the sun, and not the earth (Copernicus), or to build one of the largest and most successful computer brands in the world (Steve Jobs). If they were able to contribute their talents for the greater good of humanity, then so can you, no matter how big or small.

If we haven't built a strong foundation of who we are, it can be isolating. It's frustrating; I know from experience. Often, we care so much about the happiness of others but forget to take care of our own happiness. Everyone deserves to joyfully live an authentic life, and this book will show you how. It will help you challenge normativity and live according to standards that are true for you.

Self-actualization is a lifetime work in progress. I'm nowhere near perfect, and I don't have the answers to everything; however, I've learned so many amazing things that I want to share with you. Just like you, I am also a strange and wonderful person who has struggled with being myself, but I saw this obstacle as an opportunity to learn and grow.

As a self-proclaimed self-help junkie, I have spent over fifteen years studying personal development through numerous books; a psychology degree; countless courses, workshops, and trainings; as well as a ten-year human resources career in the film, animation and tech industries. I have helped so many passionate people just like you who think outside the box and crave more meaning in their lives. It's been a bit of an obsession, but where is a better place than here to share my experience and knowledge with someone who may be looking for some answers?

I think being a human resources professional and having done a lot of career coaching, mentorship, and teaching has allowed me to be that person who people go to regularly to discuss what they can do to find the courage to be themselves and pursue their dreams. Usually,

7

they're in some sort of rut or realize that what they've accomplished doesn't make them happy anymore. Often, they believe that achieving what they want is impossible in their current situation.

It can be scary flipping your whole life upside down. But nothing lights me up more than to help someone through these unfamiliar times. After having spent thousands of hours helping friends, colleagues, family members, and acquaintances be themselves and live their dream lives, I have compiled everything I've learned into one book so I can share my knowledge with a wider audience. I have experienced the success of these tools firsthand as I have gone through my own journey of self-discovery, so I know that they can work for you too.

Thank you for picking up *color outside the lines*! This book will help you get to know yourself intimately and inspire you to figure out how to embrace that unconventional side of you that struggles to fit in, even in a world that expects you to follow a certain formula.

You will read through a collection of psychological, spiritual, and practical tools, exercises, and stories that I have accumulated throughout my journey. These tools are designed to help you resolve any issues you have around expressing your true nature, loving yourself, and living your purpose your way so that you can become a happier person. You'll be taken on an intense, introspective journey into your psyche and into places deeper than you've ever known. It may not always be easy, but it will definitely be worth it.

Some of the points written in this book might bring up a few reactions, but I also know that a trigger for one person has dramatically helped another, so I made the conscious decision to share them anyway instead of keeping them silent. The intention of this book is not to judge the old way of conforming to what society wants, but to help the world evolve and create a new way of living. Change happens at the individual level first—both internally and externally. Only then, can it happen collectively.

So, my dear friends, don't miss out on the life-changing opportunity to build your confidence to be the unique and awesome person that you are! We're here to close that gap between what the world sees versus who you really are. Why not be the type of person that people aspire to be by sharing your gifts with the world and inspiring others to do the same! All you have to do to change your life is to keep on reading. No matter your age, background, or experience, a journey of exciting *aha!* moments lies ahead.

Let's *color outside the lines*!

but first

*"You live most of your life inside of your head.
Make sure it's a nice place to be."*
~ UNKNOWN

What you read may raise some emotional issues for you, so be sure to practice proper self-care through adequate sleep, a healthy diet, exercise, journaling and any necessary pampering as you work through the activities. Also, I am not a mental health professional, so if you are currently dealing with any mental or emotional health issues, please consult a mental health professional as these exercises and techniques are not an alternative to professional medical treatment. The author and publisher are not responsible for any physical, mental or emotional distress or trauma that may occur from following the exercises in this book.

While I encourage everyone to live a life true to who they are, I don't encourage this behavior if it causes any harm to yourself or others. If you live in a community where you may be in danger for challenging what is accepted, please consider which exercises may or may not be appropriate for you. Your safety, as well as the safety of others, comes first.

A regular critique I come across in self-help book reviews is that there is no way some of us have the time or energy to focus that much attention on ourselves. That book *must* be for single people who have tons of spare time. I get it; some of us have to take care of children or elderly family members or have demanding jobs. Some of us think it's self-indulgent to focus that much attention on ourselves.

I would like to challenge you on this. I follow some incredible influencers and inspiring people in my life who have full-time jobs, children, health conditions, and busy social lives and still do all they can to fit in a little bit of personal time.

Just like the culture of a company is influenced by the leader, the happiness of a home also stems from those taking care of it. If a CEO is stressed out and angry, her employees will experience the negative result of that. So, if you don't put your relationship with yourself first, any stress or other negative emotions can trickle down to your children, partner, family, and so on. But if they can see that you take care of yourself and are a healthy and happy person, everyone benefits.

How can we be healthy and happy for our loved ones if we don't take care of ourselves first? Even if all you have is ten minutes every night to read or listen to something motivational, it will seep into your subconscious, and those little bits of information and growth are well worth it. Change is hard and sometimes it takes a midlife crisis to make that shift, but why not alter your life before you get to that point?

The structure of this book is broken down into three parts. Part one is an introduction to get you familiar with what it means to color outside the lines. It's created to prep you for part two, which is where the meat of the book is. Part two is filled with practical tools, techniques, and exercises to help you gain clarity on your passions and purpose; emotional tools to help you banish stress, anxiety, and depression from being someone you're not; goal setting and life-design advice; how to build self-love and self-expression; and how to break through any limiting beliefs and perceptions you may have.

Lastly, part three wraps the first two sections together with some overall thoughts on other unconventional lifestyles; inspiration from some of the most influential people who society thought were weirdos too, but they accomplished great things; the importance of connection; and some closing words of encouragement.

This is the book I wished was written when I was younger, and it contains ideas that have helped me in my life and that I hope will help you in yours.

Good luck!

what does it mean to color outside the lines?

> *"I feel it is the duty of one who goes his own way to inform society of what he finds on his voyage of discovery. To be normal is the ideal aim of the unsuccessful."*
> ~ CARL JUNG

Draw a box in the space below.

Now color in the box.

The box represents societal rules, norms, and expectations, and the scribbles represent *you* within these social boundaries. Did you consciously color inside the box, or did you color outside of it?

Do you remember being a child and been given a coloring book? Were you instructed to stay within the lines of the image and told which colors were supposed to go where?

Often, we are taught early on that our artwork should match reality and not to stray outside of it. We learned to listen to direction, but not to think for ourselves, and that was the end of it. But what did this do to our creativity and ability to think critically?

Life is like a coloring book. If we stay within the lines, we are following the prescribed rules of society—which ultimately, were made up by us, and in reality, can be changed by us. This social structure doesn't allow us to think beyond the collective confines we are used to. Instead, it teaches us control and self-discipline, which has its time and place, but what message does this send to a child? What happens to our imagination as we get older?

In a 2012 article in the Huffington Post, journalist Line Dalile wrote that schools were killing our creativity and that kids who were taught to color within the lines had trouble thinking critically and creatively later on in life. However, the need for critical and creative thinking is more important than ever.

Depending on how we were brought up, our uniqueness can get shoved down into the deepest parts of ourselves, never to be seen again. Some of us choose to remain within the social lines, while others rebel and choose defiance. Then there are some of us who are stuck in a state of confusion and live inside the lines because it feels safe but also want some freedom of expression at the same time.

You can still be creative when you color inside the lines and create new fantastic things. A car's general functionality and structure remain almost the same, but there have been massive improvements in the engineering and design over time, even though the car is essentially still a car. There are also survival benefits to being accepted by the majority and playing by the rules. You will likely have a lot of social support which means having a community around you who will always be there for you when you need them because you match the dynamics of the group.

But so much more is possible when we stray outside of the lines and pay attention to our contrarian side. Just think, we wouldn't have the internet or electricity if there hadn't been someone brave enough to shift the paradigm. And when people go to watch *Mary Poppins* or *The Wizard of Oz* and see their children's faces light up, the creator's magic was what enriched this experience. Amazing things can happen when we step into the universe of our minds!

It may not be easy being the artist in a group of accountants, but if we can't be who we are, then what are we doing here anyway?

You are great just the way you are, and you don't need to change in order to please anyone. You don't have to act like a successful person, think like the herd, or dress in a way that makes everyone comfortable. You have to be yourself, or this isn't going to work.

If you have dimmed your light, it's time to shine and travel on your own path. Are you ready to be yourself? Inner honesty will give you the freedom. Color with joy and creativity. Follow your heart and courageously pursue your dreams! Shift your paradigms and remove all the "shoulds" and limiting beliefs you were given from your parents and society and listen to your true nature.

Wear that wacky shirt, write that song that burns in your heart, tell someone you love them, take that acting course, see the pyramids of Egypt, and switch careers if your day job doesn't fulfill you.

And if you're afraid? Keep reading!

"You have to know what sparks the light in you so that you, in your own way, can illuminate the world."
~ OPRAH WINFREY

my story

"Never be bullied into silence.
Never allow yourself to be made a victim.
Accept no one's definition of your life; define yourself."
~ HARVEY FIERSTEIN

My fascination with human nature began in university, but the misfit in me started early on as a child.

I didn't notice or think that I was that unusual back then. It was only later on I realized that I didn't quite fit in. The herd was going one way, and I was running far away in the opposite direction.

I was a creative and sensitive child with synesthesia. **Synesthesia** is a condition where one sense (sight, hearing, touch, taste, smell) is experienced simultaneously with another sense. For me, all of my five senses are combined with colors, so I see colors in my mind's eye when I use my senses. For example, when I listen to music, I see colorful shapes and textures in pink, black, and yellow floating beside me depending on notes themselves. I can also "hear" movement, like the *swoosh* sound when the lines on the road zip by when driving. Being so sensitive, I felt emotions intensely to the point of constant meltdowns whenever my family would take me out of my comfort zone.

I was also an immigrant (born in Denmark) and an only child of mixed race (a Filipino mother and a Danish father), which meant eating meat and potatoes one night and rice and pancit (noodles) the next night. As a tomboy, I climbed trees and swam in ditches to catch frogs and salamanders even though I was ridiculously clumsy and always came home with a collection of bruises. I already didn't quite fit into a perfect box like the other neighborhood girls.

At age eight, I would spend many hours drawing, writing, and creating science and how-to books, similar to this one, so I could share what I learned with others.

When I was ten years old, my role model was a middle-aged transgendered woman down the street who owned (see definition of *hoarded*) over 400 small animals. It was because of her that my love of animals developed, as my true love as a child was my giant collection of pets (rats, voles, rabbits, snakes, hedgehogs, guinea pigs, hamsters, fish, and frogs). I had a lot of freedom growing up in my neighborhood in the '90s. Our parents were never too involved or minded what we got up to (within the limits of our safety of course). I expressed my full potential without holding myself back at all.

As time progressed, I started noticing that the way I interacted with people did not follow the social rule book. I discovered that my direct and exuberant style of expressing myself was often too passionate, which caused me to hurt people's feelings or make them feel uncomfortable, and they often pointed this out to me. This took an emotional toll on me and my close relationships. I was hard on myself as I felt so bad about it. Like anyone else, I just wanted to be liked and accepted. So, I grew up feeling misunderstood by my family and peers, and I couldn't understand why.

By high school, my quirkiness was not accepted at all aside from a few close friends. As a lanky, quiet, awkward teenager with long dark brown hair to the middle of my back, I was bullied for looking "disgusting" (whatever that meant), which caused a lot of anxiety and loneliness. I even had two of my best guy friends, who were big and strong twins, be my bodyguards in ninth grade. I was afraid to go to school on many occasions, and I turned inward becoming very shy and timid—mostly because I feared for my safety.

Bullies called me names, smeared butter into my hair, and spat on me just for being myself. Even my closest friends pulled me aside to tell me to stop being who I was because it made them not want to be around me.

The alienation I felt and lived with because of the different ways in which I thought or acted was the result of the depth and richness of my inner world. I didn't know how to deal with the pain of having to suppress who I was just so I wouldn't get beat up by the mean girls at school.

I slowly began to pull away from my true essence and changed who I was so that I wouldn't cause any conflict between myself and those I cared about. I had no idea I was even doing that back then; I just thought it's what everyone did to fit in. I decided I'd rather have friends than go through all the heartache. I became a pro at faking my social skills, whether it was to dress like the cool girls so I wouldn't get teased, go along with everyone's opinions even if they were unkind, or pretend that I was more extroverted than I actually was. I'm sure there are a lot of people out there who think I'm pretty good at communication, but it took a lot of practice!

Unknowingly, my habit of concealing my true nature carried on into my adult years. I already didn't quite fit into one group or another, and while I was great at blending in, this caused immense psychological stress on me.

PIA EDBERG

As I was first learning to navigate the dating world, I would try and mold myself into what the other person liked even though deep down I had unconventional beliefs about what a relationship should look like. For instance, I liked my independence and alone time, I was not naturally nurturing (except to animals), most of my friends were guys (which caused a lot of jealousy and conflict,) and I didn't want marriage or kids.

I marched to the beat of my own drum and figured out through trial and error that being someone I was not left me drained, depleted, and resentful. The arguments I had with my significant others were so painful that I vowed I would never lose myself in a relationship again. Luckily, I was eventually able to work through this problem and become more honest with myself so that my future relationships were healthier.

Fast-forward to my career in human resources (HR). Trying to work in an HR job where I was supposed to be skilled at doing the right thing at the right time, when my real self always saw things differently than what was acceptable at a job, was so hard! I was constantly playing the internal guessing game, wrestling with what was expected of me versus what I actually thought. The reality was that my real thoughts were often too unconventional, honest and blunt, but because I held these ideas back, coworkers usually thought I was too *nice*.

The few times that I did let myself slip ended up in multiple chats with CEOs and managers about how I "shouldn't have said that/done that/sent that" and how I needed to improve myself. I mean, there was that one time the company I was working for was being purchased by another company, and I asked the new CEO how many people he was planning on firing—right in front of the entire executive team. What a mess.

I honestly didn't see what was wrong with the question at the time, and it wasn't a loaded one. I asked because as an HR manager, I needed to know how much prep work I needed to do and how we should let the team go gently. (Having experienced company takeovers three times, I was familiar with the process.) Anyway, that's just an example of how I got myself into trouble without even trying. Lucky for me, people kept me hired because I did the other parts of the job well, and I was always positive and reliable.

It's fascinating how much the experiences we go through influence who we become and can help us discover who we really are, but it's also our responsibility to work through any issues that hold us back from being our best selves.

I have always loathed injustice and hated to be misunderstood. As I mentioned before, I've spent all of my adult years studying personal development. I had to heal my own wounds to help others through their process. I also regularly teach what I learn at work or at one of the local schools.

A few years ago, I was inspired to revisit my book writing journey professionally so that I could share the tools and techniques with others who want to live a more authentic life. After a lot of thought and consideration, I left my well-paid nine-to-five HR career to focus on my writing, embrace who I was, and live an untraditional life according to what I wanted to do. I told myself I would give it a year, and to this day, it's been more than two years since I made this decision, and I have never looked back. It was both scary and exciting, but I knew that I couldn't live with myself if I didn't try.

In my new-found freedom, I also discovered a love for the spiritual realm and took a certification in tarot card reading, so this is also a personal development tool I love to incorporate when meeting with people. When we work with tarot cards, we work with archetypes that exist within all of us. They present us with a beautiful way to see things that we wouldn't have thought of otherwise. This empowers us to be the causing agents of our lives, and not at the will of others or the external world.

Many years ago, my father gave me a quote from a newspaper clipping that is now framed up on my wall. It contains words that I live by today.

> *If you follow the crowd, you will likely get no further than the crowd.*
> *If you walk alone, you're likely to end up in places no one has ever been before. Being an achiever is not without its difficulties, for peculiarity breeds contempt.*

> *The unfortunate thing about being ahead of your time is that when people finally realize you were right, they'll simply say it was obvious to everyone all along.*

> *You have two choices in life. You can dissolve into the mainstream, or you can choose to become an achiever and be distinct. To be distinct, you must be different. To be different, you must strive to be what no else but you can be.*
> ~ PHIL WERNIG (a.k.a. ALAN ASHLEY-PITT)

We all have our own stories. My story inspired me to write this book. But stories can also pigeonhole us into a narrow view of our future, so I always like to challenge the assumptions of our histories. Try to remain as open as you can as you read onward.

What's your story? How is it helping or hindering your growth?

you might color outside the lines if...

Below is a list of sensitivities, interests, or traits that might make you feel unique in your perspective. Also, it does not mean you embody any or all of these attributes; you may even disagree with some of them. Just take a look and see if any of the points describe you! Have fun with it.

- You're creative.
- You're an out-of-the-box thinker.
- You have unique or unconventional interests.
- You pay attention to parts of the world that are different to where most people focus on.
- You're an artist, painter, or musician.
- You're highly intuitive and sensitive to your environment.
- You're psychic, clairvoyant, a witch, a mystic, or interested in the metaphysical or spiritual realm.
- You're a healer or a shaman and are connected with a higher source or energy.
- You're an outcast, misfit, or outsider.
- You constantly analyze the meaning of existence.
- You don't understand the purpose of small talk.
- You're a poet or writer.
- You love cosplay or are well-versed in geek culture.
- You're a heretic and teach the world to see through different eyes.
- You're untraditional.
- You don't want children.
- You prefer to be single.
- You believe in aliens or life on other planets and take a deep interest in learning what exists "out there."

- You're a dreamer, a drifter, or a wanderer.
- You want to live in a different world than the one you're in.
- You believe in homeschooling or unschooling.
- You're an atheist or extremely religious.
- You're part of a counterculture (gothic, punk, raver, skater, emo).
- You feel like you're from another world.
- You're passionate and obsessive about things and get so absorbed you forget about everything else, sometimes to the detriment of your relationships.
- You have an intense need to fulfill your purpose.
- You're vegan or vegetarian.
- You prefer to work for yourself.
- You want to live off-grid.
- You have unconventional sexual preferences or fantasies.
- You're too private or not private enough.
- You reject the structure of society.
- You don't understand social rules.
- You possess incredible talents or intelligence.
- You have a unique fashion sense.
- You live an alternative lifestyle.
- You're a Luddite, hermit, or recluse.
- You think for yourself.
- You routinely escape reality through fantasy, imagination, and daydreaming.
- You prefer solitude (or animals) over the company of people.
- You prefer spending time on your passions over socializing.

Maybe you saw yourself somewhere in this list, or maybe you didn't. If you didn't, what makes you feel like an outcast? Feel free to write your ideas down:

_____

_____

_____

_____

_____

By now you have a pretty good understanding of what it means to _color outside the lines_. You possess qualities that stand out from the crowd, and you want to figure out how you can embrace your inner weird! In the next section, we'll talk about how we got to where we are today.

"I, myself, am strange and unusual."
~ LYDIA DEETZ

how did we get here?

"A possibility was born the day you were born and
it will live as long as you live."
~ MARCUS SOLERO

Our past can have a profound effect on shaping us into the people we become. Who we are today is made up of a mixture of our genetics, our upbringing, our family, our environment, our diet, our home, our community, our schooling, our experiences, our friends, and even our thoughts. No matter if we grew up in a small town in the countryside or a high-rise in the heart of a busy city, these experiences and environments make us who we are. Now, I'm not going to get into a scientific nature-nurture debate and argue which came first or has the most influence; most scientists and sociologists agree that it's a little bit of both.

When we are young, our brains have not fully developed into the logical thinking brains we have as adults. This means when a significant (or traumatic) event happens to us early on, it leaves a deep impression in our emotional memory bank. These Pavlovian links or associations (like Pavlov's dog who instantly salivated when he heard the ringing of a bell which was associated with food) mean that we unknowingly carry these reactions into adulthood. We are basically all a bunch of grown-up children wandering this earth trying to do the best we can with what we know.

Think of your parents, your parent's parents, your parent's parent's parents, and so on. Think about where they all came from, who they were, where they worked or lived, and how it influenced their children and their children's children.

For instance, my father's family came from a small rural town in Denmark, and they didn't have a lot of money. His mother (my grandmother) was an unusual woman who mainly kept to herself, created journals with pictures and clippings inside, and made paper dolls for the neighborhood kids. My grandfather was a hardworking laborer. My father, following his parent's lead, ended up as an independent engineer/handyman, who preferred spending time alone and built mechanical inventions. This was passed down onto me (well, half of who I am), and I have inherited the individualistic and creative traits similar to my grandparents.

Maybe your parents were adventurous and went on month-long motorcycle tours across the country in the summertime. Or perhaps they were quiet and preferred to stay indoors. Maybe you grew up in a chaotic, negative household, or it could be you had a helicopter mom who watched your every move. Maybe your parents were either minimalist nomads or preferred to keep up with the Joneses. Perhaps you didn't grow up with your biological parents at all.

Nevertheless, your environment has influenced the creation of who you are today whether it's your school, your peers, your culture, or any other aspect of your life you could imagine.

But it doesn't mean that we are stuck with those reactions and beliefs we grew up with. Our past does not have to define our future. We have the power to change ourselves into whoever we want to be even though it can seem impossible at times. As adults with logical thinking brains, there are so many ways we can work on unraveling our built-in belief systems that are no longer serving us. We don't have to listen to everything that society tells us and take them to be the only truth. How we were taught to see the world through our parent's paradigms is not how we must continue seeing things if we want to grow.

In the next section, we will dig into some of the fears that control and hinder us from accomplishing what our soul is aching for us to do.

embrace the fear

We hear the message over and over again to "Be yourself!" But just not too much... that would make us uncomfortable.

What?

It takes a lot of courage to be who you are, and we all experience fear to some extent, it's just a matter of how much we let it control us. Our minds will do all sorts of things to try to trick us. It will shout out mean comments about how unworthy or afraid we are until it drives us absolutely bonkers.

Fear can also disguise as practicality. We are brilliant at rationalizing why we shouldn't go for our dreams because it's not the *wise* thing to do. We stay at our predictable, unstimulating nine-to-five jobs because we're afraid we'll fail miserably or are worried about our passions not making us any money.

But what are we really scared of? We're afraid of failure, rejection, criticism, judgment, or being ignored, and we're fearful of upsetting our families and friends, or our communities. However, deep down, all we want is love and acceptance of who we are.

I was initially terrified to write this book. It's not easy putting yourself out there. But I know that my message needs to be shared, no matter how hard it is. It may not be perfect or even a best seller, but it's a part of the expression of who I am, and it needs to be released. I want to help people who struggled just like I did, and that is what ultimately motivates me. I'd be dimming my light again if I didn't write this book. Even if I only touch one person's life, then I've done my job. I understand how difficult and scary it is to put yourself out there.

Below is a list of things we tell ourselves that prevent us from pursuing our dreams:

- *Everyone will judge me.*
- *People will make fun of me.*
- *I'm not good enough.*
- *I'm too young or I'm too old.*
- *I won't find a job.*
- *I won't find a partner.*
- *I'll be disowned by my family.*
- *What's the point?*
- *Nobody will take me seriously.*
- *I don't have anything important enough to say.*
- *I'm too embarrassed.*
- *My family won't support me.*
- *I have bad luck; this will blow up in my face.*
- *I am not talented enough.*
- *Nobody will care.*
- *Nobody will buy my art, idea, or product.*
- *I don't know where to start. It's overwhelming.*
- *I'm afraid to leave my job.*
- *I'm afraid to look deep into my shadows and deal with them.*
- *People will think I'm trying to get attention.*
- *I'm too scared.*
- *I have too much anxiety.*
- *I don't have the money.*
- *I don't have any time.*
- *I'm not motivated enough.*

These perceptions will hold us back from achieving greatness, but they don't have to. If we can learn to control our thoughts and know that they are just linked associations from past experiences and energy trying to escape our bodies, we will be better off.

Fear is so boring, and comfort is a lie! It's natural for us to choose the easy, comfortable thing when we expose ourselves to new things. However, if you're too afraid to push beyond your comfort zone, even if it means you can have the life of your dreams, you're just not living. It's okay to ask the universe for what you want!

Yes, you might run into obstacles, and there will be people who will shut you down, make fun of you, or ignore you, but there is nothing wrong with you at all. Just "do you" and what brings you joy. That's all that you need to worry about. And it's ok to be a little self-indulgent when you're carving out your life. If you're not happy and thriving, how can you be good to those around you or to those who need you at your best energy levels?

You will never be seen for who you are if you have an overriding need to be accepted. You will never really know yourself or experience yourself in this world. Closing that gap between who people see us as and who we really are will make us happier, more confident, and more peaceful.

Lastly, we can worry all we want about the future, but all we have is the present moment. If you see the world in your own unique way, and you have a message or a talent that your soul is dying to share because you know it will make this planet a better place, it's your responsibility to shine that light and share your gifts with the world. This is how humans move forward, evolve, and improve. This is how we inspire people to push farther than they ever have gone before.

31

When we have nothing left to be afraid of, there is nothing that can hold us back. Eventually, you won't be bothered by failure or what others think about you. What is the worst that can happen? You try something, and maybe it doesn't work out, but you may discover that you are more capable than you think you are and achieve great success because of it. Don't do the safe and easy thing if you have a burning desire that needs to be actualized. So many of us live a lie and don't break out of what's expected of us. You only live once (at least in this lifetime).

the universe is creative

*"My role in society, or any artist's or poet's role, is to try and express
what we all feel. Not to tell people how to feel. Not as a preacher, not as
a leader, but as a reflection of us all."*
~ JOHN LENNON

Our universe needs us now more than ever. Just like humans, it needs love, compassion, and creative expression so it can become its best self.

This is because the universe is constantly evolving and growing, and each of us is a unique manifestation of its creativity as we actively and passively participate in the evolution of the cosmos. While nihilists may disagree, it is no accident that our entire existence is perfectly structured and built from the tiniest atom to over one hundred billion galaxies. Even if we splattered a bunch of paint onto a canvas, we couldn't paint the Mona Lisa. Dumping a pile of wood, nails, shingles, and carpet from the sky won't build a house. It takes thought, creativity, structure, and purpose. There really is something incredibly magical about our existence!

When we were children, we used to play. We were open, carefree, and loving. As we grew up, we were repeatedly told what we could and couldn't do, what to buy, and who to marry, and while we may have chosen to color within the lines, our mind was the one place where we could be whoever we wanted.

Our psyche is where the universe of all possibilities exists, and it's our gift and our right to be able to share that with the world. In our hearts and minds, we know our truth, even when our truth is opposite to consensus thought. We are artists, musicians, or writers. We are inventors and explorers. Author, trainer, and shift disturber Monique McDonald says we all have sacred gifts within us that we must share with the world. Gifts such as compassion, knowledge, vision, teaching, healing, and craftsmanship should never be hidden. It's why we are here on this planet.

Art is the way we achieve freedom. And by art, I don't mean being artsy. You don't need to be a painter or a poet. It's about realizing you need to use your talents and commit to a life of expressing them, no matter how that manifests for you.

It could be as big as coming up with the next big invention or business idea that will end all environmental suffering, or as small as giving back to your community through volunteering for a cause you believe in. It doesn't matter what it is, as long as you're putting yourself out there and living your truth. And I know there are a lot of shitty things that happen every day. People, animals, and our planet are being harmed daily, but wouldn't it be better to inspire others and contribute to a positive change than to sit back and watch it crumble?

The more we create or work on that thing we are passionate about, the more we self-actualize. And the more everyone is free to do the same, the more we flourish and become a free, liberated society. Ultimately, the more we as a society can actualize, the more the universe actualizes as a whole.

When we choose to create and express our authentic selves, we communicate our subjective experiences to the outside world in a symbolic way. It's a representation of what it's like to be you, and it allows others to get a glimpse into your emotions, perspectives, and ideas. Art reveals the true nature of an individual's inner world for everyone else to see and experience, and it's such a beautiful thing!

So, don't spoil the opportunity you have on this planet. Be who you are and share your talents with the world. The universe wants us to contribute our greatness to the larger whole and to make this place better. It starts with one person at a time. It starts with you.

practice self-care

As we embark on the journey to becoming who we are, it may cause some additional stress and anxiety when figuring out how we become the person we've been hiding all our lives. It takes baby steps, but I promise it'll get easier as you go.

Remember to exercise regularly, have a decent amount of sleep, and eat a healthy diet. Take relaxation seriously (unplug from technology, take hot baths, listen to soothing music, and connect with your loved ones). If it's within your means, take a small vacation if you need to step back and reassess your life from a distance. I always find getting away for some "me time" without distractions helps me gain a new perspective. If a vacation is out of the budget, visit a nearby place that gives you inner peace such a favorite hiking spot, or a view overlooking the ocean.

Sometimes self-care is not just about pampering yourself with bubble baths, chocolate, and wine. It's also about getting strict about the kind of life you want to build such as doing a hard workout even if you don't like to exercise or letting go of the things that constantly cause you stress and disappointment such as toxic friendships.

Something I've learned to do lately is to let go of the guilt that I *should* be doing something, like eating a super strict whole foods healthy diet when it just causes me more stress. Everything in moderation. Sometimes you have to make choices that offend other people (any vegan knows this!), but you know it will make you happy. Also, if you need that alone time to recharge, be okay with saying no to events you are invited to.

Don't take yourself too seriously, remember to laugh and be flexible to whatever comes your way. Remember that nothing is permanent, and you will always move through the current state you're in. If you're someone who likes to keep busy, try volunteering and helping others who need you. Giving your time to those who have less or don't have a voice is a great way to cure the blues.

In the meantime, if you find that your current way of living is causing unhappiness and you're not in a place to make any drastic changes, focus on the aspects that do make you happy and your reason for doing them. For instance, if you hate your boring desk job but you need the money, you can focus on the fact that you get to help people each day. Focus on the positives.

> *"The greatest gift you can give somebody is your own personal development. I used to say, 'If you take care of me, I will take care of you.' Now I say, 'I will take care of me for you, if you will take care of you for me.'"*
> ~ JIM ROHN

are you a sheep or a wolf?

Do you want to be a follower (sheep) or a leader (wolf)?

You're probably already familiar with the sheep vs. wolf analogy, but if not, let me explain.

A sheep is a follower. She relies on someone or something else, such as parents, culture, or religion, to dictate her life and her mind. A sheep follows the herd. Maybe you've heard of the term *sheeple* before to describe this mentality. They give into the peer pressures of society and follow the crowd as if they don't have their own viewpoint. It's normal for us to want to belong and be a part of a group that accepts us. But who will lead the way and inspire us?

A wolf is intelligent, independent, and thinks for herself. She is powerful, intuitive, and lives freely, even within a social environment.

You have learned that those in power who control society don't want you to think for yourself because then you are no longer easy to control. Consumerism, gender roles, celebrity worship, religion, school, how many "likes" we get on social media, and other institutions flood our cultural upbringing so that we blindly follow along, instead of thinking for ourselves. Everything is prepackaged, ready and done for you.

Why are we never taught how to think independently and critically in school? Why are we not taught how to love one another and to make the world a more inclusive and better place?

Now is the perfect opportunity to start bettering yourself and carve out your own path. Lead the way and let out your inner wolf!

~

In part two of this book, we will look at the practical applications of *coloring outside the lines*. You will go through a process of undoing some of your core beliefs, which may be scary or lonely. Make sure you have someone to talk to if something comes up, whether it's to share a new discovery or you need someone to listen to you.

If you get confused or doubt yourself along the way, it's totally okay; it's part of the process of growth. You are getting rid of who you thought you were so you can become the person you are meant to be! One day, you will look back on your journey and wonder why you were ever scared in the first place.

I hope the exercises, tools, and activities in the next section will inspire you to live a more authentic life, free of worry, judgment, and fear.

"Unfuck yourself. Be who you were before all that stuff happened
that dimmed your fucking shine."
~ UNKNOWN

part two

1

be authentic

be authentic

Authenticity is a word that gets thrown around a lot, but what does it really mean? "Be yourself!" "Just do you!" they say. I've searched for other words and phrases that capture the same meaning (true self, real, pure, genuine), but *authenticity* seems to be the most accurate even if it's a bit overused. Here's a description I wrote in my first book, *The Cozy Life:*

> When you break it down, authenticity is the quality of being real. Genuine. Down to earth. I see it in relation to the idea of being your true self, following your bliss, living according to your values, and connecting with your pure essence or spirit no matter what the outside world tells you.
>
> Authenticity requires self-awareness. Once we know who we are, we can properly pursue a happy and fulfilled life, whether it's in our careers, relationships, hobbies, or goals. Take a moment in your day to write down your thoughts and feelings about things that you love and value. Write about what you are and aren't drawn to. Listen to your intuition and trust your inner dialogue. The journey to finding our inner voice is something we all go through, and as we grow and evolve, our personalities grow and evolve with us. Take the time to reflect; we learn and discover new things about ourselves every day.
>
> Remember, you can't make everyone like you. If you pretend to be someone else, you will attract the wrong people. If you choose to be yourself, you'll attract the right people and they will be your people. ~ PIA EDBERG IN *THE COZY LIFE*

Are you living your most authentic life?

For the longest time, I was great at being authentic in the privacy of my own home surrounded by my self-help books, a collection of '90s memorabilia, music recording gear, and hippie décor and fashion; however, I didn't always share this side of myself with others because I thought I was too weird. I was afraid to be who I was publicly and wanted to be like everyone else. But more importantly, I didn't share my honest thoughts, opinions, and beliefs and kept them hidden from my social circle.

In the early 2000s, many people were ashamed of reading self-help books and owning them was taboo. It was like admitting they were flawed human beings—*gasp*—so they didn't go around bragging about it. Whenever I spoke of '90s nostalgia, which was one of my interests, people would tell me I needed to stop living in the past.

And I know, my interests were not even that unconventional—today I think they are pretty cool—but I was a lot younger and insecure back then, and I was afraid of hearing other people's opinions.

There is a price we pay for not living according to our authentic selves. If we don't behave congruently with our thoughts and beliefs or are forced to live against our nature, we are prone to depression, burnout, and anxiety. Furthermore, we are at risk for compromised immune functioning or other physical illnesses such as heart disease according to Janice Kiecolt-Glaser, the chairperson of the college of medicine at Ohio State University. It's exhausting trying to be someone we're not, and to get rid of this internal conflict we need to work on building our confidence and aligning our inner world with our outer world.

Louise Hay, a renowned author and healer, dedicated her book *You Can Heal Your Life* to this concept, which is about taking responsibility for our thoughts and feelings so our bodies can be healthier. She explains that when we are dealing with physical illnesses such as back issues or eczema, it's strongly connected to an emotional or mental area in our lives that we need to heal, and once we heal that, we become healthy again.

If we are a highly sensitive person, or HSP, coined by psychologist and author Elaine Aron, we may be susceptible to fears of expressing our authentic self as well. Aron describes an HSP as someone who has a "sensitive nervous system, is aware of subtleties in his/her surroundings and is more easily overwhelmed when in a highly stimulating environment."

Our world doesn't always have sympathy for sensitive people (I know it was certainly cruel to me at times), so we have to find ways to cope with the harsh realities. The problem is if we keep shoving our genuine opinions and feelings down, when it is completely unnecessary, we start to lose ourselves and become *inauthentic*.

Some of us cover up our essence with overconfidence and ego, and some of us are people-pleasers, pretending everything is "hunky-dory" all the time. People-pleasers suppress themselves the most as they essentially have to lie to others, not because of malicious intent, but because of intense fear of conflict or losing someone they love. But this is why it's so taxing. Our self-confidence is shattered because we don't think we're good enough just as we already are, so we stop getting to know that amazing person who exists within us and eventually forget where we came from. Think about how damaging that is to our self-worth.

Relationships are also an area where choosing a partner who has opposite values to ours can cause a lot of grief. Arguments about the importance of quality time are exhausting and detrimental to our happiness if one partner needs a lot of space and the other craves constant companionship. Of course, it's important to be thoughtful of the needs of others—relationships are a two-way street after all—but sometimes both partners are not open to changing until the costs outweigh the benefits of the relationship.

Working in a job where the environment doesn't match your personality will feel like riding a bicycle uphill for eight to nine hours straight, five days a week. Doing repetitive work on an assembly line is a challenge if you crave variety and spontaneity. Taking a sales job where you have to talk all day long when you are introverted and dislike too much human interaction will leave you depleted by the end of the week. It's hard to live a life against your nature when deep down you know that you're moving in the opposite direction of where you're meant to be going.

Sure, maybe you'll have a prosperous career, your dream car, a house with a pool, a perfect wardrobe, and proud parents, but before you know it, you'll be sixty-five and look like you've aged a hundred years because of the emotional toll the sacrifice took on you (if it's not what you actually wanted).

These accomplishments aren't bad if they align with your personality, values, and desires, but if they don't, then they don't do you any good. You'd be living and measuring yourself by another's yardstick, and succeeding by their measure, but failing by your own.

Unfortunately, many of us are tricked into believing we *need* to have these things to feel okay with ourselves and trade our dreams for our self-esteem. But it just isn't worth it. I've sat in too many classes with retired men and women who regretted not paying attention to their own desires because they paid more attention to the needs of others. Only in their older age are they now getting back to what they once loved like art, writing, gardening, or photography.

So how about you? Do you ever experience any of the feelings or reactions below?

- You hate getting up in the morning.
- You feel exhausted most of the time.
- You're unmotivated.
- You keep thinking negatively about everything and everyone.
- Your brain is not processing information clearly.
- Your attention is slipping.
- You're having relationship problems with your spouse, friends, family, or colleagues.
- You're forgetting or not wanting to take care of yourself.
- You have constant health problems related to stress. (Please see a doctor if you do!)
- You feel overwhelmed with life and its responsibilities.
- You're escaping through unhealthy methods such as taking drugs or drinking.
- You're irritable and have no patience.

These signs are similar to burnout and depression, but that is because trying to be someone we are not *is* very stressful and depressing!

It's easy to blame others for our problems or even blame ourselves when life is not going to plan. It took me years to figure out that I could just do the inner work first, learn to love myself, and take responsibility for my actions and my life.

I knew what kind of life I wanted and I was ready to face the consequences. I was ready to leave jobs and friendships that were hurting me as I couldn't fake it anymore. The irony of it all is that the more authentic I became, the better my career and relationships became. While there was resistance and judgment from some, which was expected, I was also surprised at how much support and love showed up in my life tenfold.

Expressing your truth is healing. You will inspire others to do the same and attract people who are on the same wavelength.

So, dear student of life, I believe in you. If I was able to carve out my authentic life, I know anyone can.

live a life in line with your values

Values refer to a person's set of standards that they place the utmost importance on when it comes to life and their behaviors. These may come from our families, our upbringing, and significant moments in our lives. For example, you may have grown up watching your parents start from nothing and work very hard to achieve financial success, and so you internalized this as important and thus value hard work. Or perhaps, after a few failed relationships where your partners were unfaithful, you place a high value on honesty and trust first and foremost.

Our first step to getting to the heart of who we are is to figure out what some of our core values are because happiness occurs when our lives and our values match.

I want to make a quick note that while this is an exercise to get clear on what we value, it's equally important to question our values in case they are limiting us in any way. For example, if you value money or status, take a deeper look and make sure you are valuing these things for a reason that sits well with you, and not using them to cover up deeper rooted insecurities.

Your values also don't have to align with anyone else's values either; you may find they are quite different. Our personal values are part of what makes us all unique.

You might have done a similar exercise in the past, and you might be able to come up with them easily off the top of your head; if so, write them down. I know this task can also be challenging for some depending on how much time you have spent analyzing this part of yourself.

Below is a list of some common values, but it is only a handful, so come up with your own if you don't feel like any of them resonate with you. While some will have little or no importance, others will stand out and feel like they belong to you:

love, authenticity, success, peace, authority, balance, challenge, compassion, knowledge, truth, stability, security, happiness, friendship, kindness, leadership, fame, creativity, faith, competence, community, fun, harmony, learning, growth, adventure, curiosity, honesty, purpose, pleasure, respect, responsibility, status, trust, health, comfort, empathy, freedom, open-mindedness, spirituality, etc.

If you're still having some difficulty coming up with your values, try the following exercise. I ask these questions when I do career coaching with people who don't know what they want to do for work. It helps them gain massive insight into what is the most important to them.

This activity is best done with a partner or friend, as they will be able to listen and hear the stories behind the words you say and what is the most meaningful to you. Pay attention to your pain points. For example, if your least favorite thing about your job is that it is boring and repetitive, then you might value freedom and variety. If your favorite memory is that time you performed at a talent show and won, perhaps you value creativity and expression. Pay attention to the *why* behind your answers.

1. What do you like the most about your current job? Why?
2. What do you like the least about your current job? Why?

3. What is your favorite memory? Why?
4. What is your least favorite memory? Why?
5. Who do you admire? What traits do they have that you wish you had? Why?
6. If money wasn't an issue, what would your ideal day/life look like? Why?

List your top values here. Try to stick to no more than five or six, because anything more than that can lose its meaning. The words you place below may give you insight into the kind of lifestyle you want. If you are doing things that don't line up with these values, consider questioning if you are in the place you want to be or doing the things you want to do and how you can potentially change that.

_____

_____

_____

_____

_____

_____

declutter the clutter!

Another approach to living a more meaningful life is purging things that do *not* represent who you are or who you want to be. Clutter is more than just our material possessions. It is everything that exists in our internal and external environments from things, people, obligations, distractions, our digital life, and so on.

Decluttering is a large topic on its own. I spent years blogging about minimalism, and there are countless videos and books about it. It's at the foundation of how I enjoy living my life. Getting rid of material, digital, social, and other distractions help us get to the core of who we are, so we can gain clarity and peace of mind on where we're going. With less stuff, we focus on what is most important to us such as time spent with loved ones, our passions, and giving back. It allows us to live simpler stress-free lives. We live in a society where more is more, but we can be more with less.

A few years ago, when I was going through some changes and searching for more meaning in my life, I had the realization that material things could not make me happy. I had checked off everything I wanted to achieve. I worked in a well-paid management job in a creative industry and had everything I thought I wanted—including a cute bohemian apartment filled with all the home necessities—yet there was still an empty feeling inside.

I came across the minimalist movement and decided to get rid of almost ninety percent of what I owned and move into a studio apartment with only what I needed and cherished. It was a liberating experience, and it felt like a weight had been lifted off of my shoulders. I cut down everything that was unnecessary, including excess clothes and shoes, furniture, knick-knacks, time commitments, toxic friend-ships, and bills (which was awesome for the bank account!).

Living a simpler and more focused life makes us happier people and strengthens our relationships. It fuels our hearts to do what we love.

Here are some key areas to focus on when decluttering:

- Time commitments: Only say *yes* to things that bring you value.
- Finances: Make an effort to spend less money on things.
- Our digital self: Clear out excess files, unsubscribe from junk mail, and spend less time surfing the internet. Unplug.
- Clothing: Only keep what you love and wear.
- Food: Choose to eat healthy, whole foods. Limit caffeine, alcohol, sugar, and processed foods.
- Negative self-talk: Learn to control your thoughts and allow positivity in. (We'll learn exactly how to do this in later chapters on emotional tools and self-love!)
- Distractions/vices: Get rid of unhealthy habits.
- People: Cut out toxic friendships or contacts and surround yourself with people who lift you up.

Is there an area of your life you feel overwhelmed with?

Take the next few days to declutter and stop doing what is not serving you or the person you want to be. Start slow. You can go in any order or choose the areas that need the most work. If you have a partner or family members, you might need to discuss this with them first if it directly impacts them, especially when it comes to personal belongings. Explain why downsizing is so exciting for you, make a list with them of what you can and can't keep, or get them involved and work on decluttering together.

Either way, I promise you will feel lighter at the end of it. Also, don't forget that one (wo)man's trash is another (wo)man's treasure. Donate your old items to your local thrift shop or charity so that someone else can enjoy your previously loved things.

Look, we can't take everything with us when we go, and none of this will matter in the long run. Free yourself from the shackles of unnecessary possessions and streamline your life. Why not spend more time doing what you love, so you are no longer distracted by what is not serving you or doesn't represent the authentic life you want to live?

the real you vs. the fantasy you

To expand a bit more on decluttering, pay attention to any belongings that represent who you *wished you were* or who you *once were*, and see if they match who you are today. This false self can be called the *fantasy* self.

For example, maybe you have dreams and aspirations of becoming an avid yoga lover because you want to be fit and bendy. You have purchased top quality yoga mats, blocks, bags, cute fitness outfits, etc. but in reality, you can't even make it to one class per week because you don't actually find it enjoyable.

Or perhaps you have bought an entire collection of art supplies because you said you were going to start painting on a regular basis, but the materials are still sitting in your closet collecting dust.

Fantasy selves can also be from the past. Maybe you were once really into video games and owned all of the popular games and consoles, but now they are stashed away in boxes in your basement. You have no plans to dig them back up because they don't represent your interests anymore. Maybe you could sell them to someone who will enjoy them?

Realistically, does your lifestyle right now match the things you own? Where in your life have you accumulated too much and where can you reduce these things?

reconnect with your inner child

When we were children, we used to play because it was fun, just for the sake of it. Who were you before society had time to influence who you should be? What did you love doing when you were younger that you have long since forgotten about?

I used to spend most of my spare time creating activity books about space, science, and art. I was fearless, expressive, and a free spirit. A few years ago, I reconnected with that aspect of myself that had been hidden away for decades, and now here I am having published my fourth book! It's an amazing feeling to rekindle a part of you that has been tucked away for so long.

Some of us are lucky to know exactly what we want to do with our lives right from the get-go and continue to master our craft ever since. But some of us lose sight somewhere along our journey and have to reconnect with our passions later on. Lastly, some of us get caught up in the busyness of life and never make that reconnection or have no desire to.

Now, I'm not saying it's necessary to look for purpose in this manner; some feel a strong need to move away from childhood things. Some of us did not have a happy upbringing whatsoever, and these questions may even be triggering. But if you resonate with the idea of connecting with your inner child, keep on reading.

Check back in with yourself and reflect on what used to make you happy and how you can bring that into your life today. What brought you the most joy? What feelings do you want to bring back that you once experienced? Use these emotions as a compass to guide you.

Place a photo or two of your younger self on your workspace to remind you of who you used to be and let it inspire you to pursue your dreams. You would never tell that child they weren't allowed pursue their aspirations. Why would you ever say those things to yourself now? My photos remind me that I was always an animal loving, creative, happy, enthusiastic person who was never afraid to express herself. I want to remind myself that I am all of these things today, and I love that side of me.

Take time to express yourself through art and creativity, whether it's painting a picture, writing a story, or digging up those old arts and craft supplies and making something new. Get out into the wild as nature stimulates our senses and keeps us in the moment. Let your intuition guide you as you explore the world around you. If we brought more unstructured playtime into our lives, we would see a glimpse of what makes us come alive.

You could also write a letter to your inner child or younger self. What would you tell him/her? Or jot down the characteristics of your childhood self that you may have lost a connection with. Think about a favorite memory. Describe it. Describe yourself. Reconnect with who you once were and let it rekindle a spark of new beginnings.

_____

_____

_____

_____

take a personality test

If you're into that sort of thing, of course. I absolutely love them! They have helped me learn so much more about myself that I could have never figured out on my own. They have helped peel back the layers of why I did what I did and what motivated me at a deeper level.

Personality tests have also helped me understand why my relationships were or were not working and how I could improve them. Why did my partner need to go out and socialize all the time, while I just wanted to stay indoors and write songs? It's one thing to observe that your partner prefers being social, but understanding *why* helps you get to know the person at a deeper level and build a new appreciation for them. If they can understand you and you can understand them, communication goes much smoother as you both know where you're coming from. It also teaches us that our way of doing things is not the only way, as many people think everyone else should be exactly like them.

Furthermore, I have taught several personality type discovery workshops in my career, and they have been invaluable to improving communication and culture at work. It is always amazing to see people's perceptions shift when they find out information about their and their colleague's communication styles.

For example, I remember several executives and software engineers coming into a workshop with a skeptical point of view about personality assessments, thinking logic and reason were the only ways to do things in business. But when they learned that fifty percent of the population use feelings and values as their main filter for decision making and considered the impact of their choices on the people in their organization, they were much more open to a well-rounded decision-making process.

One of the first personality tests that I learned was the **Myers-Briggs Type Indicator (MBTI)** developed by Katharine C. Briggs and her daughter Isabel Briggs Myers, based on the work of Swiss psychiatrist Carl Jung.

The MBTI is a tool used to measure our personality preferences and how we perceive the world and make decisions. It's based on our four preferences:

- **Extroversion/Introversion:** Where we focus our attention and energy (Do we need to be around people or be alone?)
- **Sensing/Intuition:** How we take in information (Do we trust facts/details vs. our gut?)
- **Thinking/Feeling:** How we make decisions (Do we use logic or values to make decisions?)
- **Judging/Perceiving:** How we orient ourselves to the external world (Do we prefer structure or flexibility?)

After finding out my type, I had a starting point on where I could improve, and also explain why I was naturally inclined to like certain things over others. I loved it so much that I decided to get certified in teaching it to others.

These assessments are not meant to put people into a box but are used more as a tool to describe how we take in information and communicate. It's like left and right handedness, we use both but have a preference for one, or both.

If you want clarity on how your interests connect to your skills, the **Strong Interest Inventory** by psychologist John Holland may help you figure out your potential passions.

STRONG INTEREST INVENTORY		
CATEGORY	**INTERESTS**	**SKILLS**
Social	People, teamwork, community service, relationships	People, verbal, listening, understanding, teaching, counseling, empathy
Investigative	Science, ideas, theories, data	Math, writing, analyzing, problem solving
Realistic	Machines, computers, athletics, hands-on	Physical coordination, practical
Conventional	Organization, accounting, investing, order, structure	Working with numbers, attention to detail, efficient
Artistic	Self-expression, art, aesthetics, culture, communication	Creative, musical, artistic, imaginative
Enterprising	Business, leadership, entrepreneurship, risk-taking	Verbal, assertive, motivating/inspiring others,

Visit www.psychometrics.com for more information about MBTI and the Strong Interest Inventory.

Another one of my newer favorites is the Enneagram, which has lately been taking the spiritual and business world by storm. While its origins date back to 4,000 years ago, it has been modified to fit today's society and is an invaluable tool for understanding yourself and others.

The **Enneagram** describes the human psyche through nine personality types that are all interconnected. Taking the Enneagram was like reading my fortune! There are plenty of free online tests and resources so check them out if they spark some interest. www.enneagraminstitute.com is a great place to start.

Finally, a useful career assessment tool to try out is a Vancouver, Canada based company called **Sokanu**. It is a platform that helps people find their ideal career. Being in the career development field, I like this tool because it asks questions about who you are and assesses what you are naturally drawn to, using this information to offer the best career suggestions for you. It contains over 750 career profiles for users, and the results seem to be extremely accurate. I highly recommend it! Visit www.sokanu.com for more information.

go out and experience things

Sometimes we haven't learned enough about ourselves to be able to extract what we like or what we value. Maybe it's because we're young and haven't had enough life experience yet, or maybe it's because we haven't stepped outside our comfort zones. But when is a better time to try something new than right now!

Try out that hip-hop dance class you've been curious about; maybe dance will be your new thing. Learn to play the guitar. Try a new job working with animals. Volunteer for a cause you have always wanted to help out with. Try a new restaurant or cook a new recipe. Plant a vegetable garden. Take a money management course or learn a new sport. Discover what moves you and what inspires you.

Let your imagination run wild. The possibilities are endless. The worst that can happen is you learn something new about yourself!

it's okay to be selfish!

But of course, stay humble.

As you have gone through this first chapter in part two, how did it feel? Was it fun? Uncomfortable? Difficult?

If you felt any guilt about focusing on yourself too much, this is totally okay!

This book is focused on how to improve yourself, which requires a lot of inner reflection and work. To see a difference in our external outcomes, we need to do a bit of internal shifting.

Selfishness has negative connotations. We may associate this trait with the spoiled cartoon character Angelica Pickles from *Rugrats* (for any of you '90s babies out there!) She has no respect or regard for others, and she bullies her peers to get what she wants. She doesn't share, and she only thinks about herself and how she will benefit.

But in this context, I'm talking about being *self-full*, or being aware of your personal needs and tending to them. So many of us ignore what our soul is crying out for in fear of being too selfish. However, we can't take care of others if we don't take care of our well-being first. And we can't be in a healthy relationship if our foundation isn't solid.

I find that often women especially are taught to be giving, empathetic, and self-sacrificing, while men are taught to be the breadwinners, to find independence, find a job, and build their dreams. Some people will give so much of themselves to others and forget to pay attention to their own needs. They sacrifice their own happiness to make sure that others are more comfortable and end up feeling miserable and resentful.

Balance is always key. Women especially feel the pressure to "do it all" by taking care of everyone, working a full-time job while balancing a ball on the top of their head. You don't have to get to that point. You matter just as much as everyone else, and you can put yourself on the top of your priority list once in a while.

~

You've taken a deep dive introduction into living a more authentic life. Next, we will talk about what drives you and how to figure that out. What does your heart yearn for, and what would make you happier? Let's take a better look!

2

find your passion

find your passion

"Don't ask yourself what the world needs,
ask yourself what makes you come alive.
And then go and do that.
Because what the world needs
is people who have come alive."
~ HOWARD THURMAN

Some of us know exactly what we want to do or be from early on and go ahead and pursue it. But for those of us who don't, that is totally okay.

"Finding your purpose" is a loaded term, which can cause excitement in some, and anxiety in others. I want to stress that finding purpose is not the be-all and end-all. It can be overwhelming and scary, especially if we feel pressure from others that we need to find our true calling or we are not complete. But honestly, you do you. If it's not a big deal to you, it's okay to be comfortable without a big ol' plan.

At the very least, we can be happy as we are and feel we are contributing to the world in a positive way. What I have found helpful is to *feel on purpose*, a concept taught by author and personal development trainer Monique McDonald in her Sacred Gifts training. This means being aware of your strengths and weaknesses and allowing them to guide you so you can do more of what brings you joy. But it's not just about doing something well; it's also about using these gifts to give back to the world no matter how big or small.

When we think about purpose, what we are really asking is

69

What makes your heart burn so fiercely you would give anything to pursue it?

I recognize we don't all have the luxury to change our lives so drastically. Perhaps you need to keep your current job to support your family and pay your bills or stay in a relationship because too much is at stake. Maybe moving out of your city or country is not an option. However, I challenge you to keep reading with an open mind.

The following ideas may not be for you right now, but it never hurts to begin exploring in case they open up a new side to you, just like discovering you had a treasure chest hidden in your attic this whole time that was filled up to the brim with gold!

ikigai

The Japanese have a concept they live by that is said to be their secret to finding longevity and purpose in life. It is called **ikigai**. Ikigai combines the Japanese words *ikuru* (to live), and *kai* (the realization of what one hopes for) which together mean "a reason to live." It's a path to happiness and gives you a reason to wake up in the morning.

Japan is known for having the longest living people in the world. According to the Ministry of Health, Labor and Welfare, the average life expectancy is about eighty-seven for women and eighty-one for men, and while other lifestyle choices (i.e., diet) and genetics come into play, sociologists think that ikigai is one of the reasons for this long lifespan. Furthermore, older citizens are highly valued, so this gives them a reason to keep giving service to their communities.

What stood out for me about ikigai was the idea that there was no such thing as retirement like we have in the West. If you are doing what you love and using your talents, it won't feel like work, and you won't need to retire. It's a part of who you are. For example, if you love to paint and you built a career out of it, why would you stop painting once you hit sixty-five?

Ikigai can be found when the intersection of the four following questions overlaps:

1. What do you love to do?
2. What are you good at?
3. What does the world need from you?
4. What can you be paid for?

If you do what you enjoy, or at least find purpose in what you're currently doing, it leads to overall good health mentally, emotionally, and physically. Serving at a restaurant might not be your dream job, but in trying to find the good in it to keep you motivated, such as brightening someone's day or meeting new and interesting people, you will connect with your ikigai.

what are you obsessed with?

What's that *thing* you like to do that you know you just can't *not* do? What occupies your mind for most of the day? Do you daydream about writing a best-selling novel, or mentoring children to raise their self-esteem? Do you want to become a world-renowned documentary filmmaker who spreads the importance of a healthy diet or a famous DJ who produces their own dance music and psychedelic shows? Do you want to build beautiful furniture for people to enjoy? Do you love memorizing facts and lists about random subjects?

A great way to figure out your purpose is to think about what types of things you fantasize about. And yes, you will need to throw away any limiting beliefs you have about what you are capable of. Your parents or society may have told you certain things are impossible, but that's just bullsh*t. Anything is possible! Your fantasies can be as wild as you want.

If you love playing video games, for example, figure out what you enjoy about them the most. Is it the problem solving, the art, or the technology? Research the video game production industry and learn what it's all about. Maybe it will inspire you to go to school and eventually work at a game studio.

If you have a knack for taking risks and picking up on how things can be improved, maybe you're a natural entrepreneur. Maybe you have a passion for the environment and want to start up your own nonprofit to spread the message about the importance of sustainability and taking care of the planet. Go nuts; the world is your oyster. You just have to get creative and add a bit of courage.

Obsessions are not just limited to thoughts either. How do you spend your free time? What type of books do you love to read or what kind of movies can you not wait to watch? What hobbies or activities do you get excited about?

What are you obsessed with?

_____

_____

_____

_____

_____

_____

_____

_____

_____

_____

_____

what are you good at?

What would you say your strengths are? We usually aren't the best at noticing what we're good at, and some people will even say they are not good at anything. But everybody is good at something. You might just not notice it because it comes so naturally to you that you can't see it. Also, having a strength doesn't mean you have to be the best at that thing you do. We live in such a comparison-driven world, but this is not what we're aiming for here.

If you're still having trouble figuring this out, ask for feedback! Find five to ten people who can answer this question or who can tell you a specific story about when you were your best. Choose wisely; you want to ask people you trust and like, who know you well and who will give you an honest opinion. Try a mix of personal and professional contacts. Ask them what they think you're great at and what your gifts are. They'll have a better insight into you.

When you receive the feedback, look for common themes and see if anything stands out as they will point to your strengths. You can also ask your contacts what you could improve on. This will give you insight into areas of your life that may need your attention.

Once you have gathered the information, compile a list of the strengths and use them to figure out your purpose. For example, if people think you are great at teaching them new skills, where can you use that talent in your career? School is an obvious answer, but there are so many other businesses and institutions that can use someone with training abilities. Perhaps in a field that is also interesting to you like a yoga class if fitness is a passion.

List ten people you can ask about your strengths:

_____

_____

_____

_____

_____

_____

_____

_____

_____

ask yourself *why?*

Why do you like to do what you do?

I have a genius software engineer friend who really enjoys his work. I once asked him why he liked coding so much, and he said it was because he loved to help solve people's technical problems and make their work easier. For him, it was about other people's happiness.

I asked the same question to another software engineer, and he responded that he liked to code because he enjoyed the creative side of building a useful tool and seeing the results of his efforts turn into a useful application. For him, it was about the hands-on experience and using his brain to solve problems to create a product.

These are two different reasons for liking the same career. But these underlying reasons point to your purpose and the type of things that intrinsically motivate you. You could be inspired to help people, solve problems, work with technology, or use your hands. Ask yourself *why?* Once you figure out what drives you, how can you do more of it?

what have you overcome?

If you know you want to help people, but you don't know how or where to start, a great way is to think about an experience you had to overcome.

All of us have a story, no matter how big or small. For example, I have struggled with fitting in and owning who I was, so I decided to spend my life on self-improvement, and then teaching others how to do the same, so they could also lead a more authentic life.

Perhaps you have overcome depression, cancer, or a drinking problem. The world is ready to hear your story. How can you help others who have gone through, or are going through, something similar? How can you help their families? Maybe that means working in the field of your selected subject or writing a book.

One of the most common excuses I hear from people is that so many others have already done what they want to *do* or *write* or *make,* etc., so there is too much competition. But the thing is, you bring your own flavor to the mix. You're the only you there is, and only you can tell your story, your way. People who relate to you will be drawn to you. There can be a hundred individuals who want to become nutritionists, but they will attract the clients who like or relate to them the most. Start with an abundance mindset; there is room for everyone. A scarcity mindset will only hold you back and limit your success.

How many coaching books on authenticity or living your dreams are out there? If I didn't pursue my goals because I thought there were already too many books on the same topic, I wouldn't have written this one. Don't retreat into your shell; we need to express ourselves.

What are some things that you have overcome?

_____

_____

_____

_____

_____

_____

_____

_____

_____

what would you do with
ten million dollars?

If you won ten million dollars in the lottery tomorrow, what would you do with the money? You could quit the job you hate, move to the place you want to live (Italy anyone?), start your own dream business, and give back to any cause you believe in!

Many people say they would continue working even if they won the lottery because they would be bored otherwise. Of course, we want to spend our time doing something useful and meaningful, but now that you have the option to do anything, what would that be? Would you start up your own clothing line? Would you build an animal shelter? Would you use the free time to volunteer with seniors? Maybe you just want to build your own homestead and live off the land for the rest of your days.

What would you do if money wasn't an issue? This will point to your purpose. You might not have ten million dollars today, but it never hurts to dream!

_____

_____

_____

embrace the sh*tty situations

I had coffee with one of my oldest friends who gave me some great advice. If you're prone to suffering or complaining about your unfavorable situations, listen up.

He told me a story about a job he once had on a mushroom farm. His job was to, well, pick mushrooms. It wasn't the most glamorous gig, but he figured he'd make the most of it. Instead of spending his energy complaining about how boring it was to uproot plants all day, he made the conscious decision to be the best mushroom picker there ever was!

He plucked those fungi with the eagerness of a child catching grasshoppers in the summertime. He learned to be fast and efficient and was the top mushroom picker that ever worked at this farm. He even took it one step further and used his handyman skills to fix broken sheds and machinery. He made himself useful, built a great relationship with the owner, and now has an interesting story to tell his friends combined with a life lesson.

So, through my friend's experience, he learned that suffering was optional, and we can choose how we feel and deal with any situation. His motto? Don't half-ass anything, become your greatest version, and go big or go home.

How can you embrace your current situation and make the best of it?

do what you love dammit!

If all else fails, and you cannot come up with anything that excites or drives you right now, that is completely okay. Try to focus on what you love to do and listen to that little voice inside you. Own who you are and do what makes you happy right now. A simple life can be the perfect life.

Focus on your hobbies—play that guitar, take those photos, go hiking and enjoy nature. Spend time with your loved ones, bake cookies, and drink wine. Follow your likes and avoid your dislikes. But always try something once; you might discover something new.

~

In the following section, we'll talk about personal responsibility, reframing the past, and not allowing our circumstances, our fears, or other people to decide how our lives should be. I'm excited to share this information with you!

3
personal responsibility

personal responsibility

Whether we're aware of it or not, we are creating our reality in each moment. There are times when we are active participants such as planning our wedding or next vacation, and there are times when we are more passive or on autopilot such as when we are buying groceries or watching a movie. When things become a habit or too familiar, these passive moments can slip away so quickly that before we know it, the day/week/month/year is done, and we wonder where the time went.

As I mentioned before, we can either choose to keep doing things the way we've always done them, or we can begin to create new patterns and disrupt our old ones with something new and intentional. You will learn more about this in this chapter on personal responsibility.

take responsibility

To start taking steps to being more of the real you and designing your ideal life, you have to lay down the foundation of taking responsibility for things that happen to you. It's so easy for us to blame something in our external world when things go wrong whether it's another person, our past, our environment, our culture, our race, or our gender. The person driving in traffic in front of you stops suddenly, and you nearly have a fender bender, and you blame them for driving like an idiot. But perhaps you were also following a bit too close? How did you participate and how can this situation be avoided in the future?

It's easy to take the credit and internalize something when things go right, like after winning a game of hockey. You're asked by an interviewer why you won, and you explain that you and the team practiced very hard and that's why you won. Taking credit for something allows us to celebrate our achievements and push further next time around. But why do we blame external factors when things go wrong?

Of course, shitty things happen to all of us that are outside of our control. An undesired event absolutely might not be your fault, but how can you take responsibility for how you deal with the situation? Awful things occur that are outside of our control, and sometimes the only thing we can control in these instances is how we feel. Who can we reach out to for support? Who can we speak to?

Sometimes our situations can't be changed because they involve someone else. In this case, we again also have the power to take responsibility for how we react to the situation. Nobody can *make* us feel a certain way. We can do the inner work and shift our perspectives. We can forgive.

When we blame others, our power is diminished and we become the victim. To take responsibility is to take action. This is how we become proactive in shaping our lives into exactly what we want. Instead of blaming a person or situation for things going wrong, or living your whole life thinking you have bad luck, you can set some goals and take active steps to move forward. You have the power to change your life. Stop blaming, stop complaining, and be your own driver. If you've always wanted to get into shape or eat a healthier diet, but you can't find the motivation or information to get started, who can you talk to to help you?

List three areas below where you feel you can take more responsibility. Spend the next week being aware of when you complain or blame others, and then use your power of responsibility to change the meaning of the situation.

Example: You are notorious for complaining about how little time you have to start exercising more, yet you spend over an hour on social media every morning. How can you take responsibility for your choices?

_____

_____

_____

get out of the rat race

Ahh, the incessant **rat race**—the competitive way of life that is tiring and routine but allows us to reach an ideal level of status or power. It's about climbing the social ladder to finally "make it," but the cycle never ends as we are never satisfied with what we've got.

By the time we come home from our nine-to-fives we are exhausted and have no more energy to live the life we're trying to build. How can we build a *lifestyle* instead, full of creativity and connection?

The world is awakening. We're moving out of the Piscean age of structure, power, and hierarchy, into the age of Aquarius which is free-thinking and more egalitarian. Religion and government exist for you only if you allow them into your mind. Chasing the rat race will no longer be relevant, and we can even see it now with so many people fighting for fairness, love, and authenticity over money and power.

The only way out of the rat race is to connect within, realize what's truly important to us, and make a conscious effort to go against the grain. We have to stop blaming our parents, the government, and our educational systems and realize the power is within us to make changes. There will naturally be outside influences, but we can choose whether to accept them or not. We could change the world if more of us did this!

high love vibes

Have you ever met someone and thought, man, that guy has a really negative vibe? Or visited a new Mexican restaurant and thought that the energy is amazing there?

That's because human emotions have unique vibrations. Low vibrations (slow moving) are related to dark emotions such as fear, hate, and sadness. High vibrations (fast moving) are connected to uplifting emotions such as love, compassion, and peace.

When we live a life within the lower vibrations, we will encounter constant setbacks and negativity. We may feel apathetic, depressed, exhausted, unhealthy, angry, and see the world in a pessimistic light. Bad things happen to all of us, but they are always opportunities to teach us lessons and make us into better people.

If we choose to live in higher vibrations, we connect with our higher selves. We become self-aware, compassionate, grateful, healthy, and happy overall. These qualities help make the world a better place.

Of course, nobody is perfect and happy 24/7; however, whenever we find ourselves feeling low, it's an opportunity to take responsibility and feel the high vibes instead.

Choose love always.

reframe the past

Is there anyone in your life that you are still holding a grudge against? Has anyone done you wrong, and has this one person or incident shaped how you react to certain situations today?

I know that being bullied in school and then encountering toxic people at work who told me that I was not good at my job caused me to avoid anyone who was domineering and aggressive. It wasn't rational but I did it anyway. I didn't understand this side of myself until I dug deep to question where my fears came from which eventually caused my reactions to disappear.

It's so easy to resent these people and go on believing that you are not worthy of your successes. You go around thinking that you suck at your job, you're incompetent, not pretty enough, or not lovable enough. It's time to let go of these stories so we can move forward.

Start by writing down a list of everyone you hold a negative association to. It could be a friend, a family member, a colleague, heck, even a stranger. Then take the time to write out the story around this person, how they made you feel this way, and how it has affected your life.

_____

_____

_____

_____

_____

_____

_____

_____

_____

Now here comes the tough part: how were you responsible in these situations? Could you have confronted them about the issue and talked it through instead of allowing the situation to happen or letting the pain fester? Could you have asked for help from someone else? Try putting yourself in the other person's shoes as well. Everyone is always right in their own perspective, even if we completely disagree with it. If you had the other person's background, knowledge, and experience, would you have done the same?

I like the example that if you draw the number nine on the ground in chalk and have the other person stand across from you, they will see the number six. You will both argue your perspectives and nobody will win. How can you see things from their perspective?

Think about how your feelings and associations around these people or situations have triggered you. How has it hindered your progress? These events also affect our core beliefs. For example, if we had a terrible experience dating a certain type of person, we might never choose to date someone again who is similar because we were so hurt the first time around. How does this close us up to future connections?

As you write down the names, you may start to see a pattern. For myself, I noticed a pattern that I was bullied a lot, or perceived that I was bullied, and never stood up for myself. The reason I didn't do anything about it the first few times was that I was young and in high school and was more afraid of my physical safety because I had a small frame. Irrationally I carried this fear around with me into adulthood so that even if someone bullied me in the workplace, and I was not in physical danger, I behaved as if I was. I became paralyzed and timid in fear of my life (subconsciously that is).

Try to become aware of how you are being controlled by these fears and let them go. It's time to gain some inner peace and know that these fears are only your body's way of protecting itself from harm, even if it is not real anymore. We need to free ourselves from these past hurts so we can be more of who we are now.

quality vs. quantity

The ancient Greeks had two words for time. The first was **chronos**, which represented chronological time and was quantitative in measure. You know: you have ten minutes to get to work, or the day has twenty-four hours, or it is seven o'clock. Their other word for time, **kairos**, focused on embracing moments and is what we should be paying more attention to. It's qualitative in measure.

The first time I heard about *kairos* vs. *chronos* was during a free evening philosophy discussion in the city. The topic of the class was "What do I need to stop wasting my time on?" and so the topic of time obviously came up.

We discussed the phenomenon of how time seems to speed up the older we get, and our facilitator, a retired philosophy professor in his 70s, described the importance of *kairos*. He used to hate running errands in the city such as banking and grocery shopping and also despised performing other mindless tasks such as cleaning the house. But one day he actively decided he wanted to be more present and create more *kairos* in his life.

He proactively took the time to connect with people he would briefly encounter, such as the grocery store clerk or bank teller, and get to know them a little bit. He felt that it was an honor to learn about someone and have them allow you into their world; a place he didn't have access to before he started talking to them.

It was his way of slowing time down, and he described it beautifully. It was such a valuable lesson on seeing the world with new eyes, just like a child discovering the magic of the forest. It's so easy for things to become mundane when we've done them over and over again. But time is precious, and we deserve deeper and more present connections.

Where in your life can you start being more present? Perhaps you can turn off your cell phone and rely on speaking with people to get directions or walk a different route to work so you are exposed to new streets and buildings to explore.

Another concept that places a heavy emphasis on being present and enjoying the simple things is the Danish concept of coziness called **hygge**. As I'm half Danish, I centered my first book, *The Cozy Life,* around this idea. It's about an appreciation for the moment, connecting with those you love, and experiencing emotional coziness, as well as physical comfort. It's one of the main reasons Denmark is consistently rated the happiest country in the world year after year as it is built into their culture. *Hygge* is a giant lesson on joy and we can all learn more from it, so I highly recommend you check it out.

the fundamental attribution error

Imagine this situation; you're walking home from work or school, you hear a loud yelp and witness a man violently kicking his dog. How would you judge this situation?

If you're an animal lover, you'd probably react with rage and start yelling at the man about what a horrible person he is. But without all the facts, you may have made the **fundamental attribution error**. He may have been acting quickly because his dog was about to bite a toddler, and you only caught the tail end of the incident and saw it with your own filters. Don't get me wrong; I'm completely against animal abuse, as most people are, which is why this is such a disturbing example.

I first learned about the fundamental attribution error (FAE) in my first year of my psychology degree. The FAE refers to our tendency to explain someone's behavior based on their personality or disposition and to underestimate the influence that external events have on another person's behavior.

If that sounds too confusing, think of it this way. If we judge someone too quickly, without knowing all of the information, we are often and likely incorrect in our assumptions as we only see a piece of the puzzle.

We often make quick assumptions as we are busy people and it's our brain's way of simplifying all of the information available to us. However, if you can become aware of it, try to take responsibility and get as much information as possible before making snap judgments.

Ask more questions and even ask your friends to look at situations from another angle.

One benefit when we can stop assuming things about other people is we simultaneously stop worrying that people are assuming things about us. We'll talk more about projections later in chapter 5, but there is a world of difference when we change our perceptions.

> *"Never ASSUME, because when you ASSUME,*
> *you make an ASS of U and ME."*
> ~ THE ODD COUPLE

finances

Although this is not a book about money management, I know that money is usually at the top of people's minds when they are deciding whether or not to quit their jobs or simplify their lives, so I wanted to add some techniques that worked for me here.

We all have different financial situations; some of us have mouths to feed, or don't even make enough money to pay for rent. But there are those stories of people who were over $100,000 in debt, with a family to take care of and bills to pay, who were still able to get out of their circumstance. If they can make big changes, then I believe anyone can. I'm sure you've come across these stories on the news or social media from time to time, so it can be done!

Living a happier, more meaningful life is not only about having lots of money. Money can certainly buy us freedom to do the things we love, but even the richest and most successful people suffer from depression and unfulfillment because they crave something more than material things. The less materialistic we can be, the faster we can build our wealth through investing it wisely or simply have more freedom and time to focus on the things we love.

One way to save more money is to trim down our monthly expenses. It's common for us to increase our standards of living the more money we make, but do we really need all of those expensive things? Unless we're millionaires, the difference between buying that $5,000 purse versus investing the money and watching it grow is quite different. Who are we trying to impress anyway and why? Perhaps we can try to think about the utility of an object instead of the feeling it generates in us when shopping. Furthermore, how can we build our self-confidence so we can let go of what others think of us based on our appearance and possessions? Many of us are used to believing that as long the world thinks we're doing okay financially, then we don't have to deal with what's really going on inside. Let's shift that perspective and heal our need for acceptance and do what's right for us by exploring where we may feel lacking.

A few years ago, I was tired of working the nine-to-five because I wanted to focus on writing, so I knew I had to make a financial plan to get out of it. The first thing I did was get strict about my budgeting. It's obvious math that we must spend less than we make. Otherwise, it's a path to debt, and we don't want that.

I took a look at my monthly bills that were unavoidable—things like rent, car insurance (a car is not necessary, but I chose to keep mine), utilities, gasoline, food, internet (also not necessary, you can go to a coffee shop), cell phone, and any savings I wanted to put away every month. I made a budget to see what my minimum monthly cost would be to determine how much money I had to make at the very least to pay my bills.

Then I eliminated all of my extra expenses such as credit card bills, random monthly internet subscriptions like access to streaming online movies, and apps or business tools I never used. I also sold a bunch of my belongings, stopped mindlessly shopping, and moved into a studio apartment with cheaper rent so I could live minimally. If you don't mind roommates, you could move into a shared space and save even more money. Depending on the housing market in your neighborhood, this could be a very practical option. We all have different spending habits, so other areas where you could eliminate expenses might be things like cable television, car payments, student loans, etc.

Money is a tricky topic when other people are involved or when we need to consider a partner or family members. This goes beyond what we will talk about in this book, but there are many helpful resources out there at your local library or online. My suggestion is you can always start with your personal expenses and see where you can cut down first.

finance exercise

1. Make a list of **all of your current monthly bills** and how
    much they cost. Then add up the total. Include subscriptions,
    shopping allowances, entertainment, etc.

_____

_____

_____

_____

_____

_____

_____

_____

_____

Total: _____

2. Take the top list and see what expenses you think you could **eliminate or downsize**. Get creative. I saved a lot of money on car insurance by increasing my deductible. Do what you are comfortable with. Then add the expenses up.

_____

_____

_____

_____

_____

Total: _____

Now **subtract the total from question 2 from the total in question 1,** and you will have a new monthly budget that you can live on. This is the minimum amount of money you will need to make in order to not go into debt. I know not all of us want to live like a student again, especially if we've worked hard to achieve our current lifestyles. But if it's an option, knowing that your standard of living has only gone up because you made more money, see if you would be willing to trade that money for freedom instead so you can work less or grow your own business.

Q1 Total – Q2 Total = New monthly budget

_____

You've come this far. How can you downsize your current "must-have" monthly bills even more? Can you move into a cheaper place, sell your car, use the coffee shop for internet and get rid of your cell phone? It all depends on how far you want to take things and whether or not you are single or have other people to consider. Can you eat out a lot less and cook at home? Can you stop buying $6 lattes every day? Write these ideas down below and be sure to apply this new budget to your real life. Good luck!

_____

_____

_____

_____

_____

_____

_____

_____

_____

_____

_____

design your life!

If you want to be the star, you need to create the show! So to make money doing what you love, you need to take action and start creating something.

After learning the power of taking responsibility, we can begin to take charge of our lives, on our terms. We no longer have to be the victim of blindly following the rules on how things "should be done." If you don't want to work a nine-to-five job, then get a part-time job, or start your own business. We are not meant just to pay bills and die. What kind of existence is that? Our dreams can seem impossible to achieve, and we might even think we are not worthy of them. I know; I've been there. But this is your chance to challenge that.

~

In the next section, we will explore how our attention and filters shape our reality, and how we can change them so we have a more positive experience of life in line with the world we want to experience.

"The most important kind of freedom is to be what you really are. You trade in your reality for a role. You trade in your sense for an act. You give your ability to feel, and in exchange, put on a mask. There can't be any large-scale revolution until there's a personal revolution, on an individual level. It's got to happen inside first."
~ JIM MORRISON

4

energy flows where attention goes

energy flows where attention goes

"All that we are is the result of what we have thought.
The mind is everything. What we think we become."
~ BUDDHA

Our thoughts and feelings guide us like the northern star, and so we need to be careful about what we focus on. Like attracts like, and we attract what we become.

Some call this the **law of attraction (LOA),** which I'm sure you've heard about. This is the idea that we can attract anything we desire by believing as if we already have it. For example, if we need a couple thousand dollars to pay off a credit card bill, the idea is that if we believe and feel that this has already happened, the money will show up for us in an unexpected way, either through a refund, a check in a mail, or some other mysterious manifestation.

I know it sounds ridiculous, and you will encounter many people who will tell you that it is. However, I have tried this for myself when I needed money, and I would land book deals or receive some form of money deposited into my bank account, simply because I believed I already had it.

The LOA has existed for thousands of years since early religious teachings ("do unto others as you would have done to you"), but the phrase can be traced back as early as 1877 in an esoteric mystery book by Helena Blavatsky called *Isis Unveiled: Secrets of the Ancient Wisdom Tradition.* You have probably also heard of Napoleon Hill's book *Think and Grow Rich,* which also applies the practice of the LOA, and

Rhonda Byrne's *The Secret,* which brought the concept into mainstream culture.

Scientist, teacher, and author Joe Dispenza, who does a magnificent job of bridging the gap between science and spiritually, explains the LOA by using quantum physics. If we can let go of our past restraints so that we don't predict the future based on our previous experiences—which are often based on fear and worry—we open ourselves up to unlimited quantum possibilities so that whatever outcome we desire, feel, and focus on, we can attain. So instead of using all of our energy worrying about a future event, we can use that *same* energy to create our desired outcome.

This concept works well when we want to become someone we are not. If we are unhappy with our physical health, it's one thing to exercise and eat well, but if we believe that we are already that happy and fit person, we change our internal state and rewire our brain. We become that person who enjoys eating vegetables and running, versus someone who is struggling to get through their next exercise routine. The same goes for achieving your dreams or overcoming things that make you anxious. Behave as if you are already that ideal person you want to be, and your worldview changes and opportunities open up simply by attracting them and noticing them.

Back in university, before I knew about the LOA, I would apply this concept in my own life. I called it **the filter**.

the filter

When we're able to direct our outcomes, it's almost as if life is like one big lucid dream—a dream where the dreamer is *aware* that they are dreaming. In a lucid dream, we can control and shape our environment such as making our crush spontaneously appear out of thin air or teleporting ourselves to a tropical island.

While reality isn't *exactly* as magical as a dream, we do have the ability to shape our world by being proactive and consciously choosing our filters. If we choose what our thoughts and emotions focus on, that's the life we get. But if we choose to remain on autopilot, then that's the life we get. Our subconscious doesn't know how to discern what is real or not, so we have the power to create our best life—like the lucid dream.

Try it with something simple. If you're going for a run (or doing a difficult exercise), and your natural, lazy, passive state is to feel like you want to give up, try using an active brain and tell yourself that you love exercise and that you are strong, healthy, and in amazing shape. Believe you are already this person with all of your heart and soul and you will start to notice your resistance disappear and your physical ability begin to shift. You'll be able to push harder than you thought you could. As long-distance marathon runners often say, it's not our bodies that are weak; our mind is the thing we need to overcome to push past our discomforts.

Ever notice when you're shopping for a new car, suddenly you see it everywhere? You chose that filter. What would happen if you chose all of your filters on purpose? What if you decided to look for confirmation that you were lucky or had great coworkers?

It takes work. We are so used to being on autopilot, allowing our brains and bodies to do the driving, and then we believe that that is the reality we are stuck with. We believe these are our personality traits and live our entire lives this way. But it's not true. We have more control than we think. We can will things into existence if we just try a little harder and put in a bit of effort. We can decide to be someone else. If we choose to be proactive instead of passive, we will surely see the results.

Try it the next time you're feeling sad. Think of a happy memory to bring up positive thoughts and feelings, and you will feel yourself shift. Or apply Joe Dispenza's concept; be proactive the next time you have to go to a family gathering you don't want to attend and imagine the best possible outcome instead of fearing the worst. You're going to use the mental and emotional energy anyway, why not use it for something positive instead of your default setting.

Once we realize how powerful we are by filtering what we pay attention to, we are unstoppable!

manifestation

In order to manifest things into reality, thinking and feeling something isn't always enough. We need to be clear and precise with what we want and *ask* the universe for what we desire. As Earl Nightingale puts it, people are like sailboats. If we don't know where we're going, we will float along aimlessly. But if we know exactly where we want to go, we will eventually end up there. There is no other way.

Words have weight, so with words, speak or write your intentions into existence. It's helpful to start a manifestation journal where you can get specific about what you want and write in a way as if you already have that *thing* you desire. Write in as much detail as you can so the visions are clear.

Napoleon Hill, famous for teaching people how to attract wealth, also asks us what we are willing to give to the universe so that it will give us what we want in return. It needs to be something that impacts others or the planet in a positive way.

We also need to pay attention to our intuition and be aware of opportunities that present themselves so we can take action and grab them by the horns. So, when you have set the intention to sell your next award-winning screenplay and you notice a Hollywood film producer at your friend's birthday party, connect the dots and introduce yourself. Take every opportunity you can get and apply this to all areas of your life. Notice synchronicities and see if there are messages in them for you.

Manifestation works through repetition, so ask for your desires at least twice a day, morning and night. Put it as the backdrop of your cell phone or paste it up on your bathroom mirror on a sticky note, so you see it every morning when you get ready. Avoid using the word *try*. Don't say you will *try* to cook at home every weeknight. You either will or you won't. Our words are vibrations of energy commanding our subconscious mind. Commit to your word and the rest will follow.

Lastly, don't complain about what you *don't* want because then you will also attract these undesirable outcomes. If you hate your job, you will subconsciously attract that job to you and never leave.

We need to work hard to get what we want as it's not magically going to show up just because we want it to—even though that would be awesome! But sitting on the sofa, wishing for things to happen to us isn't going to cut it.

To summarize, here's how you can manifest things into your life:

1. Be precise and clear with what you want. Write it down.
2. Decide what you are willing to give to the universe in exchange for what you desire.
3. Be aware of opportunities that present themselves and take action.
4. Manifestation works through repetition. Ask for your desires multiple times a day.
5. Be patient and watch the magic happen!

you are not your thoughts

Buddhists have been saying it for centuries: "You are not your thoughts. You are the one who observes your thoughts." But what does this mean?

This is one of the most life-changing concepts I have ever learned. The books *The Untethered Soul* by Michael A. Singer and *The Power of Now* by Eckhart Tolle are great introductions to this.

Basically, the idea is that our thoughts are divided into our ego self and our higher self (or God or the universe, whatever you want to call it). Our ego is our conscious logical brain that helps us navigate day-to-day life, but it's also the one that gets scared or angry. It's the one nagging at you to get your errands done, or worrying about what someone thinks of you, or how you think of yourself.

On the other hand, the higher self is the one that observes our thoughts. When you speak to yourself, it is the one listening. This higher self has all the answers you're looking for, and it's connected to a higher source/God/universe/insert yours here. True freedom occurs when we are no longer wrapped up in our ego thinking or believing that the thoughts are really us.

The higher self knows what is right for us. It knows if we need to quit our addictions, and it knows if we should be paying more attention to our health. The ego needs validation from others, and it needs to feel satiated. It wants its comforts and only cares about protecting itself from danger—whether real or imagined. But once we can tap into the higher self and listen to her, we connect with what is truly important to us and can use it to guide our lives.

113

We can access this higher self through meditation (more on that later), consistently working on ourselves, improving our awareness, and not allowing our thoughts to take control. It takes years of practice, but it's worth all the effort. You could also check in with yourself multiple times a day by setting an alarm every hour and seeing if you're allowing your ego to take over, and then shift back to a relaxing state.

Think of it this way. Your ego is like the toddler who doesn't know any better and plays unsafely near the open ten-story window, while the higher self is the safe, comforting, loving, and nurturing maternal figure, who will always be there to protect us and provide us the guidance we need. If we pay attention to her, we'll have all the answers.

about being right

We all know someone who needs to be right all the time. They don't have to be as authoritarian and demanding as the wicked stepmother from the fairy tale *Cinderella;* however, someone who always needs to be right will fight for their life to not be proven wrong. Countries are politically divided because we think one viewpoint is more correct than the other, and religious beliefs have separated us.

It can be difficult to hang around someone whose entire identity is based on being right all the time. You probably know someone like this. No matter what information is presented, they have to pick it apart and argue their point of view to prove how smart they are. However, this need to be right is really about self-worth.

I used to be that person. Unfortunately, what happens is if we close ourselves off to other perspectives, we also push people away and live in a one-dimensional world according to our own filters and never get to experience all that the universe has to offer.

Why do so many of us need to be right all the time?

One explanation is that we have been taught in school that being right is rewarded and being wrong means you are a failure. You were not rewarded for getting an F on your math test. You were held back a grade or were grilled by your parents instead. No wonder we behave this way. So much of our self-respect is based on being accurate. When we're right and even praised for it, we receive a flow of feel-good hormones such as adrenaline and dopamine, and we get addicted to these feelings.

Some psychologists also think that being right has some evolutionary benefits, because if we were wrong—about the fact that a tiger might be hiding around the corner—we would die. Better to be safe than sorry!

But let me ask you this. What if your self-worth was *not* based on your ability to prove others wrong?

Other people are a gateway into another universe and this is such a beautiful thing! Think about it; there are billions of people on this planet, all with their own internal experiences and viewpoints, and by you needing to be right, you close yourself off from experiencing the beauty of humanity.

I'm not saying you need to agree with someone else's point of view because it may go against a value you hold. However, it's beneficial to put yourself in another person's shoes and see what they see. If you had the life experience that this person had, and the personality this person has, you would probably see things the way they do. So, ask questions, be curious and kind and have an open dialogue. Don't close yourself off to new perspectives.

When we can see another's point of view and learn to understand why they think the way they do, even if we disagree, they will be more open to hearing your side of the story in return, and the outcome will be a more effective, caring, and positive one.

How does this relate to *coloring outside the lines?* You will learn in the next chapter that when we shift the thinking of our own perspectives, we will perceive and live in a world that mirrors that, so this is a great place to start.

create a vision board

Raise your hand if you've ever made a vision board! It's usually one of those activities you do when taking any kind of personal development workshop, and there are many ways you can do them. Ultimately, it's all about being creative, so there are no rules. If you are familiar with vision boards, feel free to skip this section, but if you keep reading, you might learn something new!

A vision board is a collage of your goals and dreams. Some people don't believe that you can manifest anything just by having pictures up, but they are mistaken. Energy flows where attention goes, and you will subconsciously work toward the things you are dreaming of.

You can hang your vision board up somewhere in your home where you will see it every day, to give yourself the little reminder of who you want to become. I've got my vision board in my office next to my desk, so I can look at it while I write and remind myself that I am working toward being a best-selling self-help author who gives back to animal causes!

When creating your vision board, you mainly want to focus on how you want to *feel*. Try to find pictures that represent the experiences, feelings, and possessions you want to attract in your life. They should represent your purpose, the ideal person you want to become, and the life you want to live. Don't limit it to images either; you can pin small objects up as well that remind you of your goals such as dried leaves or feathers to remind you to spend more time in nature. There are no rules, so be as creative as you like, but try to keep it simple, only including exactly what it is you want to manifest. Put anything that inspires or motivates you but be as clear in your intention as you can.

As you work, write down the goals you want to achieve over the next year or five years. Consider areas of your life such as career, family, finances, hobbies, goals, relationships, travel, home, personal growth, social life, adventure, and education when cutting out images and words.

What you need:

- A board to stick your photos, quotes, and items onto. I personally like using a corkboard so I can switch things up. An inexpensive poster board or canvas from the dollar store is a great option as well.
- Scissors, tape, glue, and thumbtacks to stick everything onto your board.
- Photos, pictures, quotes, and affirmations either cut out from magazines or printed online. I like to be very precise, so I find the exact image I want on the internet and print that out in color.

How to put it all together:

- Vision boards are really fun to do with friends, so you can even make a date out of it.
- Set the tone. Turn off distractions, play some relaxing music, light a candle, and get everything ready to use.
- People have different working styles, but what I found helps is to place your items down first before committing to the glue or tape so that everything fits and looks the way you want it to.
- Get creative!

Don't forget to spend time with your vision board at least once a day to remind yourself what you're working toward. Visualize and internalize your dreams. Believe as if they are already a part of you.

~

You've now gone through several lessons about manifesting your dreams. Remember, it isn't always enough to keep our goals inside of our heads. We need to take action in order for things to start happening in our lives. Start doing some of the suggestions in this book, and you will notice your life start to shift and unfold differently than it did before! New opportunities will pop up, and you will notice synchronicities everywhere! Pay attention; the universe is always listening.

5

the world is our mirror

the world is our mirror

"People will love you. People will hate you.
And none of it will have anything to do with you."
~ ABRAHAM HICKS

The world is our mirror. What we experience as life is an external representation of our internal world and what we believe, think, feel, and do has a massive impact on what we experience. Our perception of reality is false because our assumptions and ideas mislead us to believe that we are separate from our external world. However, we are strongly connected to our outside world more than we think.

For instance, if you're taking a walk in the forest, you may notice the colors, the shapes, and the smells. However, if you're a professional arboriculturist (a person who studies trees and plants), you may be hyper-aware of all of the various species and what stage of development they're in. This person's perception will be vastly different to the regular person who isn't a tree expert. So, what is reality really when you observe something?

A **projection** is another related concept. Coined by psychologist Sigmund Freud, it's the idea that we attribute certain characteristics (positive and negative) onto others while denying they are also a part of our own traits. This can be good if the projection is a positive one, but if it's one that's based on deep-rooted fears, it can cause a lot of miscommunication.

For example, someone might accuse another person of being a liar, while being blind to how much they also lie in their own life. This is how interconnected our inner and outer worlds are. We can't even distinguish which traits belong to us. However, we can't recognize characteristics in others unless they are somehow a part of us.

Here is another example. You're at a party with some friends, and a young man introduces himself to the group. You have a quick conversation with him, and then he walks away.

One friend says, "Wow, he was really interesting! I want to get to know him more!"

Another friend says, "But he was so boring..."

And then you chime in and tell your friends that you thought he was conceited.

So, whose interpretation is reality?

Well, they are all true for each person as they all took their past experiences, beliefs, and values and viewed this man through their own filter. We make our own meaning out of every situation or interaction and create our own reality this way. Imagine how much of our entire world is missed because we only see things from a narrow point of view. It's mind-blowing!

Your first friend might have found this man very charming and attractive. Your second friend had nothing in common with him and found him boring, and lastly, you have insecurities around confident and gregarious people, so you found him narcissistic.

So, you can see, we can easily judge and project ourselves onto others—both the good and the bad—and it all has to do with our own internal crap. Not to mention, in Luigi Pirandello's book *One*,

No One, and One Hundred Thousand, he describes the idea that every single person has their own version of you inside their heads, from your family, your friends, coworkers, and acquaintances! You may not even really know yourself! So, what is reality?

Our interactions with people are like holding a mirror up to ourselves and looking at our own reflection. Whatever habits, beliefs, and behaviors you possess, value, or dislike will be reflected right back at you. Or as the saying goes, when you point at someone, there are three fingers pointing back at you.

Often, we are bothered by the negative traits in others because they remind us of things we don't like about ourselves. Or, their actions trigger one of our fears or insecurities that we don't realize we have. These negative traits point to our *shadow side.* (We'll talk about this next.)

However, let's not forget that we can also do a lot of healing when working on our projections as well. Notice the positive traits you love in others because these point to aspects that you appreciate and possess yourself or are qualities you want to work toward having. Admiral people are a window into the kind of person we want to become, and we can use this as inspiration to guide us. If you are ever hurt by someone, give them love instead. One by-product of offering a loving attitude is it will heal your own inner wounds as well. Judge less, and do more to build the world you want to live in.

"I think, therefore I am."
~ RENÉ DESCARTES

shadow work

"Shadow work is the path of the heart warrior."
~ CARL JUNG

Those who trigger us negatively the most are our greatest teachers. The person who makes our skin crawl or makes us want to explode in anger is there to show us where we need to be more compassionate with ourselves.

Swiss psychologist Carl Jung was a huge proponent of shadow work. He believed that we had to heal and integrate with our inner demons to become a full person. He encourages us to appreciate this side of ourselves instead of avoiding it or shoving it down.

Our **shadow side** is the part of ourselves that we are afraid to look at, qualities that we repress or judge, and that the world labels as ugly and negative. Qualities such as rage, deviant sexual preferences (when we judge them as bad), or addictions are often suppressed in order to adhere to our social contracts.

Shadow work is the process of exploring our inner darkness and uncovering the parts of ourselves we have hidden away. One of the best ways to figure out what our shadows are is to look at what we don't like about others. This reveals a lot about who we are.

It doesn't mean to say that because you despise a trait in someone, that you possess the exact same qualities. You may, but it might just point to a personal value you have around the personality trait you dislike. For instance, maybe you had early experiences with a family member who always told you to be quiet when you tried to express your emotions, and now you have a sensitivity around people who shut others down, causing your blood to boil. Either way, it's something you could look at and work on if you so desired.

What types of qualities do you criticize other people for? What makes you angry, distressed, or fearful? Do you judge others as too materialistic, or not materialistic enough? Do you hate controlling people? Are you easily jealous of others?

I was recently able to work through a trigger through shadow work. I had posted something important to me online about feeling like I didn't fit in with the world, and a follower commented that I was narcissistic and crazy. My face got hot and I was so angry. How dare they!

I brought it up with my significant other and explored where in my life I was quick to judge others in the same way. I realized that I needed to be more compassionate to people as I could be pretty direct and aggressive with my own opinions from time to time.

After realizing that I was just as guilty of criticizing people's viewpoints in a harsh way, I had a huge epiphany and saw the world with new eyes. I was free from my projection, and now I don't have an intense, heart-pounding reaction to offensive comments on my feed.

Make a list of traits that bother you or that you can't stand about others and then look at your own life and see where you might do the same. It might take some time, and you might need to talk to a trusted confidant to help you see yourself objectively. These traits are your shadows and likely areas you are hardest on with yourself, or traits you have abandoned because you didn't like that side of you. Be honest with yourself; there's no need to judge it or be ashamed of it.

_____

_____

_____

_____

_____

_____

_____

At one point or another, we had to protect ourselves emotionally, but sometimes these protective mechanisms no longer serve us. Facing our shadows helps us get honest with who we are and build more compassion.

We all get angry, depressed, jealous, and scared. This is part of the human condition. But once we identify what our shadows are, we can move from a place of judgment to understanding, self-love, and freedom. Moving forward, when we notice others exhibiting these qualities, we won't be so hard on them or ourselves.

Looking at our shadow side is a scary and vulnerable process. We will face denial, anger, shame, guilt, and fear, so be kind to yourself. It's part of the process. But try to sit in the feeling and work through it.

Too many self-help books and spiritual teachers tell us to look on the positive side of things. They focus on the lighter side of life, learning to be happier, inspired, and enlightened while ignoring the darkness.

But we need to look at our shadows to make lifelong shifts. If we don't look at our darkness, then we are ignoring an entire aspect of ourselves and will keep suppressing it in the future. Eventually, it will show up again in unwanted ways, like having a mental breakdown or sabotaging our relationships for no reason at all. How can we love ourselves more? We'll explore this more in chapter 7 on self-love.

"Be confused, it's where you begin to learn new things. Be broken, it's where you begin to heal. Be frustrated, it's where you start to make more authentic decisions. Be sad, because if we are brave enough we can hear our heart's wisdom through it."
~ S.C. LOURIE

it's not you, it's them

Some of us take things more personally than others. However, people can't possibly know all of your trigger points, such as what will make you angry, upset, or sad. So, if you are a particularly sensitive person, know that people are not deliberately trying to hurt you (unless they're actually assholes). They are just being themselves and are likely unaware of how their words or actions will be received. Their comments say more about how they experience their reality and have nothing to do with you or your personhood.

I have read some unpleasant reviews about my book, *The Cozy Life*, and I have seen very nice ones as well. These comments, both good and bad, have nothing to do with me but have more to do with the person writing them. It is how they perceive the world, the things they find important, and their experience of how my book impacted them.

If we do have a negative emotional reaction, again, this is our shadow side displaying itself. Refer back to that section and work on processing these negative emotions. Imagine the same "insult" being said to five different people. All five people would have different reactions. Some would be indifferent, some would be angry, and some would find it intriguing or maybe even funny. In order to change and stop taking things personally, it's up to you to look at how you handled it and why. Yes, the person might be an asshole anyway, but it doesn't mean you need to use up all of your precious energy sitting in the negativity.

reality testing

Another way you can deal with your reactions is through **reality testing**. Originally designed by psychologist Sigmund Freud, reality testing helps a person distinguish between their emotional response and the external event by seeing a situation for what it is. I learned about this concept years ago while taking a peer-counseling course, and it has been invaluable since.

For instance, you text your friend in the morning to hang out, and they still haven't responded by the end of the day, and now you think they must be mad at something you did.

The reality of that situation is they may have been too busy, were having a bad day and didn't want to speak to anyone, or maybe their phone just died. It had nothing to do with you, yet your fears led you to the worst-case scenario without you even finding out the facts first.

To reality test correctly we need to learn how to be objective and do a perception check. If a friend was telling you about the same situation, what advice would you give them? You would never tell your friend, "Oh Sally, Bob *definitely* hates you, that's why he hasn't called you back. You must have done something really bad to make him do that." No way!

When you find yourself reacting instantly, pause for a moment, be aware of the trigger, and think the situation through logically. If you're still confused, ask a friend what they think. I always try to ask as many people as I can, and it has always helped me feel better and gain other perspectives.

If we are the type of person who gets easily riled up, it's helpful to practice reality testing so we can learn to live calmer peaceful lives. The more we practice, the easier it gets, so we can get to the point where anything that anyone says or does will not bother us.

~

In this chapter, we've learned many helpful perspectives on how reality is shaped by our perceptions and how we can be more aware of them. The next chapter will give you an abundance of emotional tools to help you deal with any negative reactions you encounter in your day-to-day life because of these perspectives.

"We do not see things as they are.
We see things as we are."
~ ANAÏS NIN

6

emotional tools

emotional tools

"Everything that irritates us about others can lead us to an understanding of ourselves."
~ CARL JUNG

Depending on how you grew up, you've probably been told at some point that you need to develop a thick skin in order to survive in the real world. Maybe you've been told that your crying and emotional outbursts won't help you. This idea breaks my heart. I was definitely one of those people who believed I needed to be emotionally tough and keep it together when I was feeling something intense so that I wouldn't make other people uncomfortable.

The consequence of this is if we shut down our "bad" emotions like anger, sadness, or fear, we also shut down our positive emotions equally. We eventually get to a point where we've emotionally flat-lined, and life no longer feels colorful or interesting. We become apathetic and suppress our true nature.

Emotions are a natural part of human nature, and as I mentioned before, balance is always key, but complete shut-down is not.

How do you cope with emotionally intense moments? Do you scream at the other person? Do you walk away? Slam the door? Or stay silent? Maybe you don't react at all. We all deal with emotions in our own way, and some of us are better at dealing with them than others.

Our feelings make up a huge part of who we are. They help us decide whether we like or don't like a person, idea, thing, or situation, and if we shove them down, never to be seen, we will never fully get to experience ourselves. Sometimes we just need some coping strategies for those times when our emotions do take hold of us.

The goal for this chapter is to learn some tools and techniques to help us move from a place of reacting emotionally to discernment, which is the ability to judge a situation objectively, and not personally—with true wisdom. Using these tools, you will stop feeling emotionally stuck, and you will start to feel more freedom to become who you really are without fear or judgment.

mood-dependent memory

Our current emotional state will remind us of memories or feelings that are related to it. This psychological phenomenon is called **mood-dependent memory**. As **Hebb's Law** suggests, neurons that fire together, wire together, so if we get sucked into a negative train of thought, we can only imagine where we'll end up, emotionally speaking that is.

For instance, when we feel sad or lonely, our minds will wander to other sad and lonely situations we have experienced in the past and we may even end up in a depressive state and worry about how much our life sucks. The opposite is also true. Notice how when you're happy and having a great day, suddenly everything and everyone seem fantastic.

One way we can consciously shift our lower moods into more positive ones is through **attitude shifts**.

We do this by becoming aware of our language. Words have power and the way we speak about ourselves or a situation matters. If someone asks you how you're doing today, and you answer with, "Well, just trying to stay alive!" how do you think that impacts the rest of your day?

If you're annoyed by something like having to walk a long distance in the rain, shift your perspective into gratitude for having the physical health and the legs to carry you from one place to the next. Appreciate the idea that the earth is being nourished. Admire the nature and enjoy the sounds of the pitter-patter.

Another great way to change your state of mind and attitude is by listening to music that uplifts you. Put on a song you love and elevate your mood.

Dance if you feel compelled to get all of that stagnant energy moving in your body. One dance style that helps you get out of your head and into your body is called Ecstatic Dance. It's a freestyle dance where you let the music guide you and move however you wish, no matter how silly you look or feel! It's incredibly freeing! Or you can always just do jumping jacks instead.

You can also reminisce about a happy memory. Imagine all of the details, like the gorgeous landscape and sunset you saw that one time you hiked up your favorite mountain or remind yourself of a special person who fills your heart with joy. These will help shift your mood into a positive state.

Lastly, don't forget to smile. Studies indicate that even the act of faking a smile will trigger the physiological response of happiness in our bodies until we eventually feel the joy for real ☺.

affirmations

In addition to attitude shifts, **affirmations** are positive statements that can help us deliberately alter our current negative self-talk and change it to a positive. The point of affirmations is to repeat the statements often so they reprogram our thinking patterns into helpful ones. After a while, we start to believe the statements.

How to use Affirmations

Figure out what you want to focus on and come up with a positive statement that replaces the old thinking. Think about areas you are negative about and flip it into a positive. If you hate exercise, for instance, you can change it to "I love my body, and I enjoy my workouts. I am getting stronger every day" or "I love myself. I am perfect just the way I am." Make sure they are in the present tense and believe in what you say. This is key.

What do you want to change in your life right now? Write it down below.

_____

_____

_____

_____

You can also use an inspiring quote as an affirmation. For example, the affirmation I like to say to myself often is "I am more than I appear to be, all the world's strength and power rests inside me." This quote, by Robin Sharma, makes me feel powerful and inspires me if I'm ever feeling unsure about myself. I have it posted on my social media profiles and have it up on my wall.

Your affirmation should be realistic to you and once you come up with one, be sure to repeat it several times a day. You could even set up an alarm on your phone to remind you. It might seem awkward at first, but the words will begin to become meaningful and you will start to believe them.

emotional freedom techniques (EFT tapping)

I'm not going to lie, when I first heard about EFT tapping, I thought it was weird. I had never heard of it before, and I wasn't sure if I believed in what it could do, but I was open to giving it a try. EFT tapping ties into affirmations that we talked about previously, but it takes it a step further.

Developed by therapist and author Gary Craig, **EFT tapping, or emotional freedom techniques**, is a tool that helps heal emotional and physical issues by tapping on various parts of the body while simultaneously saying positive affirmations.

Like shadow work, it's about improving or mending any unresolved parts of ourselves. Clearing out our emotional blocks leads to freedom and happiness which is the goal of EFT. It works on any limiting beliefs, stress, trauma, chronic pain, relationship issues, or unhelpful stories we tell ourselves—pretty much anything—and the beauty of it is you can practice EFT tapping in the privacy of your own home!

Similar to acupuncture points in Chinese medicine, EFT tapping uses self-applied acupressure techniques combined with neuro-linguistic programming to deal with our problems; however, no needles are involved. We only need to use our fingertips. It's simple to learn, and anyone, even children, can learn the techniques. It helps to redirect negative energies in our bodies from past painful events into more positive ones. Eighty percent of people who try EFT tapping achieve lasting results.

There is also the option of seeing an EFT practitioner, but sometimes we can't afford it or are not ready to speak about our problems so openly, so this is a great tool to explore at home. There are also so many books and videos online on the topic that are available to anyone.

A few years ago, I met an EFT practitioner who invited me to try a session at her office. I had an issue with feeling anxiety and overwhelm when seeing how busy my calendar was and wanted to try EFT tapping on it.

We used the techniques below. At first, I thought it was useless and not doing anything, but after a few minutes and with the practitioner's guidance, I noticed my body become calm and relaxed. I felt an extraordinary release in my body and mind, and to this day, booked-up busy calendars don't bother me anymore. This is why I feel like I need to share this technique with you because it's not a healing practice that is often heard about.

How to Tap!

Note: This is a very basic introduction to EFT tapping, and I am not an expert. If you want to learn more, I encourage you to seek out a practitioner or pick up a book on the subject.

Tapping takes practice, but everyone can do it. There are ten tapping points on your body that you tap four to six times each, about as hard enough to hear a light sound.

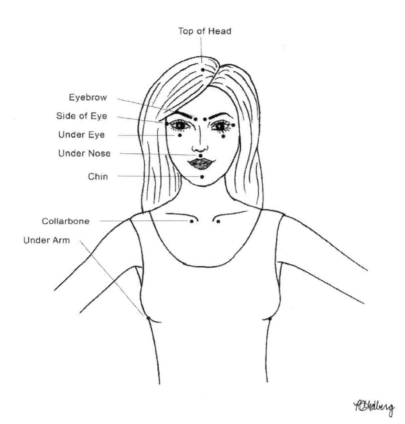

1. Top of the head
2. Beginning of eyebrow
3. Side of eye
4. Under eye
5. Under nose
6. Chin
7. Collarbone
8. Under arm
9. Inside wrist
10. Karate chop (outer edge of your hand)

The basic procedure is as follows:

1. **Choose the issue** you want to address with EFT tapping.
2. **Come up with a short Reminder Phrase** for the issue you're working on. For example, "I am afraid of flying," or "I'm craving junk food."
3. **Rate the pain or intensity level** between 0 (no intensity) to 10 (maximum intensity).
4. **Perform the Set-Up Affirmation** while tapping on the Karate Chop point. The statement is set up like this: "Even though [Insert Reminder Phrase here], I deeply and completely accept myself."
5. **Using your fingertips, cycle and tap through all ten tapping points** while saying your Reminder Phrase and Affirmation at least twice through. Stay focused on the memory or emotion you are trying to heal.
6. **Reassess your level of intensity** from 0 to 10.
7. **Repeat** the tapping cycle until you get your desired result and your intensity level has greatly decreased, if not disappeared! It can work immediately for some issues, or it can take a few cycles for others. Go ahead and give it a try!

change your posture

Emotions are displayed physically by the body. Just look at someone who is depressed. Their shoulders are slouched and their head is down. However, if we see a person who has just won the lottery, their head is high, their body is wide open, and their energy is soaring.

It doesn't matter what comes first, the body language or the emotion—it's like the chicken and the egg problem. But what this does mean is we can shift our state by changing our posture as our body language is tied to our physiology. Change your position, and you will change your mood. Whenever I need a boost of confidence, I like to stand up tall, smile, and keep my arms uncrossed. While it may feel vulnerable, it displays a sense of self-assurance, and you'll also feel the benefits internally.

The position of our head also shifts our focus. For instance, if our head is pointed downward, our focus is internal and reflective. If our head is facing straight ahead, we are more present. And finally, if our head is looking up, we are probably dreaming about the possibilities of something. Do a quick check-in with yourself. Where is your head pointing to at this moment? How do you feel?

practice gratitude

Gratitude is an emotion focused on appreciating what you have, rather than always wanting more. It's the quality of being thankful and returning that kindness to others. What sort of things are you grateful for? Do you take time in your day to appreciate what is in your life?

If we can cultivate more gratitude, we will increase our happiness and general well-being so we can live our best lives. A study in *Psychology Today* also found that gratitude is associated with increased energy, optimism, self-esteem, and empathy, and it helps us deal with stress, anxiety, and fear.

Just like starting a new exercise routine, if practicing gratitude is not our natural state, we have to make the conscious decision to build and maintain that habit. For example, keep a gratitude journal, even if it's just a note on your mobile phone. Or start a gratitude jar, filling it up with notes about things you are grateful for.

You can also take it a step further and give back to others if you aren't already doing so, whether it's volunteering for a cause or helping a friend or family member with a task they can't do on their own. Give compliments too!

Practicing gratitude is not only for the positive things in our lives. We can also think about how we are grateful for the people we dislike and negative events that have occurred. This allows us to connect with ourselves at an even deeper level, seeing how every event is an opportunity to learn, grow, and become more understanding. Gratitude helps us forgive others who have wronged us and free us to focus on the positive outcomes we long for.

look at the stars

I remember one night when I was just three years old, living in my country village house in Denmark. It was the middle of winter and snow sparkled on the ground. I stood on my front doorstep looking up at the stars, and I remember thinking about the vastness of the universe and how small we were. It has stuck with me ever since, and I still look up at the stars at night and think about how tiny I am compared to the infinite cosmos.

Sometimes we sweat the small stuff when they shouldn't matter so much. If someone says or does something we don't like, thinking about the universe helps us see that we don't need to spend our precious energy on worrying about it. When we think about how massive the universe is and compare it to the size of our problems, it is humbling.

Try it out. If you're ever feeling overwhelmed, stressed, angry, or anxious, look up. How much does your problem matter in the grand scheme of things? You have this one precious life. Let the universe, and your heart, guide you.

Never stop looking up.

emotional transmutation

Another great way to center yourself is through **emotional transmutation**. Emotional transmutation in this context is defined as the act of changing from one state of emotion to another by shifting where our attention is coming from.

Let me explain.

Thoughts are energy. That internal chatter is our brain trying to deal with excess energy bouncing around. The more attention and emotion we give our negative thoughts, the louder the chatter gets, and the more energy builds up. Before we know it, we're caught up in the moment, completely emotionally worked up about an issue.

It's like gardening. A thought starts off with the seed (the event/situation/feeling). If we keep watering that seed with our worries and fears, it will eventually grow into a plant and keep spreading out until it takes over our entire mental garden. Eventually, it might become such a huge forest that we can no longer even see beyond the trees.

With emotional transmutation, we don't allow the seed to grow and we stop it in its tracks. It's like taking that seed and smashing it before it can spread (don't smash seeds, guys). But how do we do that?

If you ever find yourself triggered, anxious, worried, or angry about something, the first step is awareness of the event. Then you consciously take your attention out of your ego mind (the mind that is talking too much) and bring it to the observer or the higher self like we talked about before. You do this by choosing to observe your thoughts instead of getting wrapped up in the emotional energy of the thoughts.

If that is still too difficult, you can try talking to yourself from your higher self. Say things like "Hi [your name], I know you are having a hard time with [negative event], but I know you are just trying to protect yourself. I love you; you are perfectly safe." See if that helps calm you.

And just like that, this stops the energy flow, and the emotional reaction and racing mind dissipates and *transmutes* into a feeling of peace. We become quiet, tranquil, and more present. The body lets go of the energy because we've opened ourselves up to the higher self.

Remember these thoughts are not you. You are the observer. Notice how quiet it gets once you shift your attention from the one who has gone out of control and talks too much, to the one who watches from a loving place.

silence & meditation

Silence in any capacity does wonders for our mental health and happiness. In today's modern world, we are inundated with information overload whether it's on social media or having everything available to us at the click of a button. No wonder we are all so stressed out!

When was the last time you took some time to be still? When did you last take a walk in the forest, or light some candles and listen to relaxing tunes, travel within and rediscover who you truly were and what you wanted in life?

Meditation is a relaxation technique used to help us focus our minds on a particular thought, object, or activity so that we gain a clearer mental and emotional state, and it's one of the best tools for combating stress and connecting with ourselves. Eastern cultures have been practicing meditation for thousands of years, and it's now quite popular in the West.

There are several ways we can meditate, and certain techniques work better for some than for others. Some people prefer to move or dance as their meditation practice (it shakes up all that stale energy), while others prefer to sit still with their eyes closed. You'll only know what is best for you if you try out different styles.

Traditional meditation while sitting still in an upright position is always something I've struggled with. It's so hard when you're such a fidgety person! However, I recognize the benefits and have learned that I don't have to do it the "proper" way in order to get the benefits. If I'm going to be still, I prefer to lie down and turn on some meditation music. I'm not the type of person to fall asleep easily, so this works for me.

I can also get into that meditative state when I ride my bicycle and feel that gliding forward motion and the wind on my face. Maybe that's something that would work for you too.

A few other types of meditation are

- **Classic meditation** which requires concentrating all of your attention on one particular thought, image, or mantra.
- **Mindfulness meditation** which is about practicing awareness of the moment and the absence of busy thought.
- **Guided meditation** where one listens and follows along with an audio-recording or healer.

The goals, however, are the same—to slow down and quiet our minds. It's about being aware of the present moment and cultivating a state of profound, deep peace and calm.

It's no wonder it's so popular today as there are several benefits. It decreases stress and anxiety, improves concentration, clears and calms the mind, improves communication, increases self-awareness, increases happiness, improves energy levels, slows aging, improves overall cardiovascular and immune health, lowers blood pressure, increases creativity and intuition, and it connects you to your higher self on a spiritual level. Meditation has even become more common in schools and workplaces.

Below is a quick "meditation for beginners" guide. If meditation interests you, there are several apps (I recommend *Headspace* to start), classes, videos, and books available. So definitely dig deeper if it appeals to you!

1. Find a comfortable place to sit or lie down. You can sit on a chair or cushion.
2. Close your eyes.
3. Breathe as you normally would. Pay attention to your breath and observe how your body moves and reacts with every inhalation and exhalation. Pay attention to every single body part from the top of your head to your toes. What are your shoulders/stomach/legs/hands doing?
4. Your mind may start to wander, just allow the thoughts to pass without judgment and remember to bring your focus back to your breath.
5. Try this for five minutes a day, increasing it up to twenty to thirty minutes a day, and you will be well on your way to the benefits of meditation!

spend time in nature

Don't underestimate the healing powers of nature! So many of us spend way too many hours in front of a computer screen and never get enough time outside. We forget to connect to where we came from and experience how healing our natural world can be.

In Eva Selhub's book *Your Brain on Nature,* she talks about how spending too much time in front of a screen can cause depression, anxiety, fatigue, and difficulty concentrating. And so, the opposite is also true. If we spend more time outdoors, we will have fewer health issues and experience less stress and anxiety. Natural sunlight is also an excellent source of vitamin D, important for reducing diseases such as diabetes, the flu, and cancer.

Practice the Japanese art of **shinrin-yoku** or **forest bathing** and soak in the forest atmosphere. Pay attention to the senses, think, reflect, and breathe in the fresh air.

Even a twenty-minute walk can benefit you. Pets and other wild animals are also very healing. Go camping or on a nature retreat. Put plants around your home. Don't forget to also put plants into your body by eating more fruits and vegetables. They are nature's gift after all and are great for our health.

journal for emotional healing

Journaling is one way I like to get out my thoughts and emotions. I've been writing in them since I was nine years old. Writing is such a cathartic process. It's also great for personal growth and developing our self-awareness as reading back on our entries gives insight into our patterns and helps us process our emotions. Make sure you keep your journal in a private place or keep an online journal that is password protected if you prefer so that nobody can read it.

If it's new or uncomfortable for you, start with five minutes and don't overthink what you write. You are literally just transferring your internal thoughts onto the page, so it doesn't need to be grammatically correct or even that coherent. Don't censor yourself.

Try to end with jotting down things you are grateful for. It's great to get all of our negative feelings out, but it's equally important to acknowledge what we do appreciate. Make a list of things that make you happy if you want.

So, give writing a shot if you haven't already!

feel all the feels

You can have all the tools in the world, but sometimes it's just as important, if not more important, to just feel the feelings and move through them. You may have been taught to "suck it up" and "get over it," and these phrases can have detrimental effects on our emotional well-being. Feelings are nothing to be feared.

You can feel your feelings without judgment; sit in them, process them, and move through them. There's no need to let the ego get in the way. Feelings are what make us human, and we should never deny that.

When negative emotions come up, don't try to push them away. Dig deeper and ask yourself why you feel this way and what caused it? Try journaling your thoughts onto paper. Get everything out and don't filter the words. Your feelings are your feelings, and they are allowed to release.

And just remember, feelings are not forever. You might feel like absolute garbage right now, but the moment shall soon pass.

talk to a friend or seek a healer

If you're feeling blue and you don't know how else to deal with it, reach out to close friends or family members whom you trust. Social support is vital for our emotional well-being as it reduces feelings of depression, isolation, and anxiety. It doesn't make you a weak person. Sometimes we just need to vent, and we feel much better afterward. Don't allow the emotions to bottle up. Getting another person's perspective can also get us out of our heads and into a new way of seeing things. But make sure you talk to someone who lifts you up, not someone who brings you further down.

Social support is even more important if you don't feel like you fit in with most people around you. The more people we connect with who accept us just as we are, the safer we will feel. It makes a huge difference in our lives when we find people who believe in us.

If you don't have anyone to reach out to, there are several options when you're really feeling down. You can join online groups specifically targeted to your interests or talk to online counselors. You can even find a local support group or talk with a therapist or life coach in person. But don't give up if you're feeling down. Help is available all over the place no matter your budget or where you live. You aren't meant to go through life all alone.

~

You have learned several techniques to help you deal with your emotions, all the way from EFT tapping and meditation to journaling and emotional transmutation. Some might feel more useful to you than others, so use what resonates with you and leave the rest. They aren't all for everyone.

If you have ever struggled with self-hatred of any kind, keep reading. In the next section, we will focus on building a strong foundation of self-love.

7

love yourself

love yourself

"We accept the love we think we deserve."
~ THE PERKS OF BEING A WALLFLOWER

When we feel unworthy of love, it affects so many aspects of our lives. Our relationships suffer, our confidence plummets, and we can feel so alone.

The teenage years can be especially bad, as we're learning and growing into our unique individual selves and seeing where we fit into the whole equation of life. We want to be liked by our peers, and when we aren't, we feel isolated.

When it all comes down to it, everyone just wants to be loved and accepted for who they are. It's such a simple concept, but so difficult in practice. We are constantly being judged by our peers, our families, and social media. The younger generations are becoming more attached to how many "likes" they get online as a reflection of their personal worth. But why? Why do our flaws need to be pointed out when they don't affect anyone? Who cares about how much we weigh, what clothes we wear, or how much money we have?

Our need for social approval comes from an evolutionary need for survival. In 1995, social psychologists Roy Baumeister and Mark Leary discovered that human connection and belonging was just as important as food and water. For thousands of years, people lived in hunter-gatherer communities, and without these ties, they would not have survived in the wild. Most of us in the Western world no longer live in these types of communities, but our nature longs for acceptance.

Insecurities are the shadow that never leaves our side. Our self-doubt will show up at an important job interview and on a nerve-wracking first date. We can be our own worst enemy, questioning our every move.

Many of us love ourselves conditionally, meaning once we've lost the weight or have achieved financial success, only then we will be good enough. But if you've ever experienced achieving that thing you were working hard toward, without doing any of the inner work, your level of self-love doesn't improve. Having the perfect life with the perfect body, job, partner, house, or car doesn't guarantee happiness. Several of my friends and people I follow online got rid of the life they had built just to start over again because they wanted more meaning.

Outside success can never make us happy if it doesn't come from within. We need to learn to love ourselves now, just as we are, because our relationship with ourselves is what matters the most. Only then can we make positive changes and attract the life we want.

If we can learn to be gentle and love ourselves more, everything else will fall into place. We will stand up for ourselves when we're being mistreated, and we will take care of ourselves emotionally and physically.

One way to love ourselves more is to look at how we're speaking to ourselves. As I've mentioned before, words are powerful. If we spoke to our friends the way we speak to ourselves in our heads, they wouldn't want to be friends with us anymore!

What words are you using when you talk to yourself? Do you treat yourself with love and respect? How often do you allow your mind to run away with itself, telling you how stupid, unlovable, ugly, or fat you are? How can you become more aware of the words you're saying and catch yourself fast enough to change them?

What would you say to yourself as a child if he or she were with you now? You would never tell her she wasn't smart enough, pretty enough, or good enough. Why would you say that to yourself as an adult?

Make a list of all of the things you do love about yourself below and recognize that you are a lovable, beautiful person, inside and out.

_____

_____

_____

_____

_____

_____

_____

_____

get out of the rut

We all have down days. Not every day is going to be sunshine and rainbows. It's normal for us to get into a rut once in a while or feel unmotivated. Sometimes we want to stay in bed all day, and there might not even be an explanation for it.

Sometimes, when we've been working too hard or socializing too much, our bodies crash and need some downtime. Other times, doing the same thing day in and day out will make us feel bored or stuck. We may feel depleted, useless, and depressed like there is no point in life except the mundane repetition of it all. We start to feel worthless and might even isolate ourselves from our friends and family. We ask ourselves, *isn't there more to life?*

This is the perfect time to allow ourselves to feel our feelings and practice self-care. It's okay not to be busy all the time. It's okay to be alone, to feel tired and sad. In fact, it's often necessary when we're in these dark moments so we have an opportunity to heal.

Use this space to meditate, breathe, read, or go for a walk outside. Quiet time is necessary once in a while. Drink your favorite tea and relax or take yourself to a different location to find new inspiration. We're so used to constant stimulation and information overload with the internet, television, work, family, and people in general.

If you're afraid to take action, pay attention to the words of Dale Carnegie: "Inaction breeds doubt and fear. Action breeds confidence and courage. If you want to conquer fear, do not sit home and think about it. Go out and get busy."

This is a powerful quote. Think about it, when you're sitting at home, depressed or bored about how much your life sucks, it might be the inaction that is causing you to feel this way, and it only gets worse over time. Luckily, it's the action that builds us up again.

One of the downsides to inaction is that you may feel threatened by other's achievements. We've all had that jealous friend who puts other people down for having more or doing more. They walk around feeling hurt and betrayed, holding grudges, and it's a struggle to be around them.

We need to shift this mindset. I'm a firm believer of being happy for others when they achieve success. Because if they can do it, so can we. You can hold onto your anger, fear, and insecurities, or you can take responsibility and take your life into your own hands.

"Don't think about it, just do it. Most of your stress is in your thinking about what you have to do, but if you just do it, you find the doing is easy. It's the thinking that's hard."
~ AJAHN BRAHM

body image, exercise & diet

Let's let go of perfection and try to focus on health, loving ourselves more, and on the things we do like about our bodies instead. I know how hard it is. I struggle with it as well. We're constantly bombarded with beautiful models on social media or magazine covers and wonder why we don't look exactly like them, even though we know the photos are heavily digitally enhanced. We want to have that perfectly toned beach body and wish the cellulite would disappear.

Body image refers to how we feel and think about our, well, bodies. How we perceive our physical selves depends on our ideas of attractiveness and acceptance developed in childhood and the feedback we received from family, friends, and peers. Sometimes a negative body image can lead to eating disorders such as anorexia, bulimia, or emotional overeating. Body image is also tied to our mental health and self-esteem. If we hate our bodies, our self-esteem is also affected, so we need to do the inner work first.

A healthy body image means that you have learned to accept yourself and all of your flaws. Anything negative that anyone says about you will wash over you. You recognize that your body is your temple, and you take good care of it. You appreciate that it helps you get around, run, sit, walk, dance, jump, and pick things up.

How do we build a more positive body image? I know for myself, the more I eat unhealthy foods (chocoholic here!) and skip my exercise, the worse my body image gets. But when I do put effort into taking care of myself, my body image and self-esteem are so much higher! Even if nothing has changed physically, just knowing that I'm eating well and moving my body impacts me psychologically in a positive way.

When our self-care comes from a place of love and not fear, we become more compassionate to other people because they are a mirror of our internal world. Love and compassion for ourselves help spread this to others.

A diet full of processed food and sugar can degrade collagen in your skin (which keeps you looking young), kill off beneficial bacteria in your gut, disrupt your hormone levels, and may even lead to depression as it chemically affects the health of your brain, according to an article in *Eco Watch*.

Eating a clean whole foods diet (for me that means limiting processed foods, dairy, sugar, alcohol, and caffeine; although I realize that may be too restrictive for some) helps your body to function at its optimal level. According to an article in *Organic 4 Greenlivings*, a clean whole foods diet decreases heart disease, improves your mood, strengthens your bones, increases your IQ, improves your overall physical appearance, and makes you look younger (glowing skin anyone?). It's also great for the wallet! And don't forget to drink at least eight glasses of water a day to stay hydrated. Water is perfect for flushing out toxins and boosting weight loss if that is what you're looking for.

One thing to note, any extreme is never good for us and can make us go crazy, so don't feel guilty if you do decide to indulge once in a while. The hormones that our bodies create when we're stressed out about a poor decision can cause as much harm to our bodies as the food itself.

So, treat your body like a temple. It's the only one you've got. We all struggle with wanting to choose comfort and laziness over the hard, uncomfortable thing, but why would we take better care of our cars and pets than our own bodies? It's easy for us to take our health for granted until one day it's too late.

Take equal care of your mental and emotional health. Notice when you are feeling stressed, depressed, or anxious and how it affects your internal dialogue. Assess what is going on in your life. Nurture yourself and speak to yourself in a way that you would speak to your best friend or child.

Surround yourself with positive people who would never put you down because of how you look. Also, try not to judge others according to how they look either. Focus on who they are as a person and show respect. To help improve your own body image, choose clothing that makes you feel good and flatters the parts you love the most. Feeling attractive starts within and getting healthy is a great start.

stop caring about what people think

Many of us care way too much about what other people think, and it can prevent us from reaching our highest potential. However, one, we can't control other people's thoughts, and two, it's none of our business. We can only control how we approach the situation and how much power we're giving someone. The secret is not to allow anyone to take away our focus on improving ourselves. Focus on your own development and not on others.

Perfection Doesn't Exist

Stop trying to be perfect. Perfection doesn't exist. We all have our faults. Just because somebody seems to have it all together on the outside doesn't mean that inside they are flawless. For all you know, they are struggling to get up in the morning because they are dealing with crippling depression or anxiety.

Julia Cameron, an American teacher, author, artist and filmmaker who wrote *The Artist's Way,* says that jealousy is just a map masking a fear of what you really want to do or be (such as criticizing another filmmaker's work, when all you want to be is a director), and once you start producing the work you love, this feeling dissipates. If someone triggers that stomach-plummeting head-spinning sensation of envy, think about why this is happening to you and if there is something you can improve on.

Get to Know Yourself

Spend more time getting to know yourself, because the more you do, the less you will care what others think as you will have built a solid foundation of who you are. Do things that make you happy and fall in love with who you are. Spend quality time alone and take yourself out on a date. Want to see a movie and nobody wants to go with you? Go solo! Or take yourself to that funky middle-eastern restaurant that just opened up if you have the budget or time. Focus on your journey and stop comparing yourself to others. We owe it to ourselves to cultivate our relationships with ourselves.

Reflect on your goals and where you see yourself in the future. Generate your own opinions on various topics so you won't be swayed by someone else or need their validation. Once you are not dependent on the acceptance of others, you will be a force to be reckoned with!

You Can't Please Everyone

No matter what you do, whether you try to do what everyone wants you to or not, you can't make everybody happy. And to be honest, everyone's opinion of you is really their problem, and not yours. Even if you decide to give up on your dreams because you're afraid of disappointing others, there's always going to be someone who judges you. You might as well be as authentic as you can because you're going to disappoint people anyway. Put your happiness first. When we achieve this, we will attract like-minded people. It may not seem like it now, but there are individuals out there who will love and support you just as you are.

Nobody Cares

The truth of the matter is that most of the people you are concerned about judging you, don't care about you. They are too busy worrying about their own lives to worry that much about yours. Sure, people might say a few things if you do something they don't like, but they will quickly move on. The irony is, sometimes *we* don't move on. We replay our insecurities over and over again. But is it really worth not pursuing our dreams just because of a few words of gossip? We are not the center of someone's universe. We are the center of our own.

Constructive Criticism

If you're going to listen to the negative comments anyway, do consider the source. Is the person offering tangible examples on how to improve? Or are they just sharing their opinion for the purpose of insulting you? Are they someone you look up to or respect? Are they someone who possesses qualities you want to have, or are they doing the things you want to do?

set boundaries

Dr. Phil always says, "You teach people how to treat you."

This is true, and it's a quote I've carried with me for years. If we allow people to take advantage of us, we will pay the price. Boundaries are essential to our psychological and emotional well-being, but for some of us, it can be difficult to vocalize our needs because of how we interpret the situation. You might be afraid to let others down or cause any conflict, or you simply may not know what your limits are and haven't identified them yet.

A great example is when we start dating someone new. Many of us want to please our potential partner and put our best selves forward, so we might go along and breach our morals so we don't lose them. For example, someone might sleep with their potential partner too early in the relationship when they know this is not what's right for them. However, later on, this will kick us in the butt, and we may end up resenting the person when it was our fault in the first place for going along.

If you are a giver, and you focus too much on others and not enough on yourself, this can be very stressful, and it's another reason why boundaries are so important.

Boundaries are also crucial in our work life. For example, if your boss asks you to work overtime the whole weekend for three weeks in a row, and you know you need downtime to recuperate and have the mental energy to do your job safely, voice your concerns. I know this is a tough one because we want to impress our bosses but know your limits. Self-care should come first. Otherwise, you will pay the price later on.

Sometimes we need to set boundaries around our time. I had a recent experience where I kept saying yes to every job or social event that came my way until I was so burnt-out, I couldn't get out of bed and I was irritable toward everyone around me. I realized that I was not the type of person who had infinite energy to socialize, so I had to start cutting my commitments. It meant quitting a few gigs and not catching up with friends, even though I wanted to.

These moments of discomfort are the most important times to pay attention to your body and to how you feel. Is your stomach churning, are you feeling dizzy, or is your face beginning to flush? If someone takes advantage of you or says something that offends you, you have a choice. You can either let it slide or speak up. Without standing up for ourselves verbally, we signal that it is okay to treat us that way when it isn't okay at all.

There have been times when someone had said something offensive to me, and by the time I came up with a comeback, the moment had passed. It's okay to sit in your feelings and process your thoughts so you can come up with what you want to say later.

Once you have figured out what it is you want to say, make sure that you clearly express your needs assertively. Write it down if you need to. How you go about that depends on the person receiving the message as well—whether they prefer direct communication or a softer delivery. Be mindful of this so you can achieve the desired outcome.

Start small if you are not used to standing up for yourself. It takes practice, and it may not come naturally at first, but it gets so much easier the more you do it. You'll soon realize it's not as scary as you thought it'd be.

"No one is you, and that is your superpower."
~ DAVE GROHL

let go of toxic people

Sometimes boundaries aren't enough. If someone is being especially unkind to you, to the point of causing extreme distress and anxiety in your life, it might be best for you to let these people go. All relationships have their occasional pitfalls, but sometimes we need to draw the line for our own sanity.

A toxic person is fueled by their insecurities and has an intense need to control others by making them feel small or worthless. They lack empathy and respect and cannot see how their actions affect others. It may have come from traumatic childhood events, and it's the best way they have been able to cope with life. We've all experienced our fair share of toxic people, and they are not good for our happiness and can leave us emotionally crippled.

Compassion is always key, but sometimes no matter how much work we do on ourselves or express how we feel, it isn't enough.

Letting go of people is difficult. Especially if they have been a close part of your life or even if they are family. But maybe it's time to be honest with yourself and get clear on how unhappy they are making you. Let them go gently and then focus on the people who do lift you up. Focus your energy on your passions and life goals and surround yourself with people who are on the same page.

~

No matter where you are on the self-love spectrum, I hope that this chapter motivated you in some way, whether it taught you to be okay with down days, set personal boundaries, stop caring what others think, or inspired you to get healthy. In the next chapter, we'll dig into self-expression and what it means to show the world who we are.

"Go and love someone exactly as they are. And then watch how quickly they transform into the greatest, truest version of themselves. When one feels seen and appreciated in their own essence, one is instantly empowered."
~ WES ANGELOZZI

8

self-expression

self-expression

"Never forget that you are one of a kind. Never forget that if there weren't any need for you in all your uniqueness to be on this earth, you wouldn't be here in the first place. And never forget, no matter how overwhelming life's challenges and problems seem to be, that one person can make a difference in the world. In fact, it is always because of one person that all the changes that matter in the world come about.
So be that one person."
~ R. BUCKMINSTER FULLER

When we were children, we naturally expressed what was on our minds and didn't hide our true nature. Society hadn't tainted us yet, and we had not experienced the social consequences of being too honest.

To **self-express** means to convey our individuality through thoughts, feelings, fashion, and creativity so that others get a sense of who we are as a person. We already talked about authenticity in chapter 1, so in this chapter, we will expand on it and talk more about how to bring our inner world out.

Positive things occur when our unique worldview is validated by others. Self-expression is the way we can invent new technology, create beautiful art, come up with new designs, and solve difficult problems.

An interesting thing happens when we express ourselves. We change; we become more confident and more of who we are. When we can put our ideas to use creatively, we show the world a projection of our inner essence.

question your beliefs & values

According to Deepak Chopra, a belief is a "thought that is true for you." The reality we live in is based on our beliefs. How many times do you go through life assuming things are the way they are without asking yourself if what you believe is even true?

I grew up with the belief that if I had an alternative look with piercings, tattoos, and unnatural hair color, I would never get a job. It wasn't exactly a logical conclusion, but it was ingrained in me because when I was growing up in my small town, the adults around me would judge those who looked different and tell me they would never hire anyone who appeared that way.

It was not until I dyed my hair hot pink earlier this year that all three of my employers said things like, "It looks so great! Don't ever change it!" or "I'm so glad you're expressing yourself!" It wasn't even an issue. Even in the most corporate job I had, I received compliments. My deeply ingrained belief had been shifted.

I know that this is an exaggerated example and a sign of the times as so many people have funky colored hair and tattoos today, but this is why our beliefs are not logical. They are a part of who we are because of our past and the meaning we place on them.

Where in your life do you think you are holding back that may be the cause of a deeply ingrained belief?

Our beliefs can also impact our health. According to Louise Hay, our thoughts, feelings, and beliefs could influence our health. Of course, genetics, diet, habits, and our environment come into play, but so do our thoughts. Be mindful of your beliefs and how they may be limiting you.

Question EVERYTHING!

express your truth

Sometimes it can be scary, even debilitating, to speak our truth when we care too much about what other people think or feel unsure about how they will react. But how do we stop being so afraid?

I used to be afraid to tell other women that I didn't want to have children. In my experience, when I shared this information, I was told I was either going to change my mind later, I was weird and selfish, I hated children, I'd be lonely when I got older, or that I was missing out on the one thing that life is all about. That's not to say I won't change my mind later, but nonetheless, these responses were aggravating.

I stopped sharing this side of myself because I was tired of the feedback, but I didn't like that I couldn't express my opinions. I was judging myself and felt like others were judging me for not living up to the socially acceptable female standard. The pressure mainly came from family members, and I hurt a lot of feelings when voicing my disagreement. I want to mention that I do care deeply about mothers and children—I did write a children's book after all! But this is not the point I want to make. What we do with our bodies is personal and our own business—not anyone else's.

One day, I attended a writing workshop led by a friend of mine, Danielle Rondeau, who is an author and life coach of Write Your Soul Story, a weekly workshop that brings creatives together to write and connect with their inner voice.

I decided to focus on the subject of not having children as we explored what was holding us back and why we needed to share our story. I realized that as a principle, I just wanted everyone to feel free to be themselves and not fear being judged, so it angered me to hide who I was.

She asked us if we wanted to share what we wrote with the group. I was nervous and shaking. And I know it may not seem like a big deal telling this story, but it was one of my limiting beliefs that I couldn't share my unconventional views without upsetting other women.

I shared it anyway, and the results were eye-opening. About half of the group felt the same, and they were all accepting of my view. When I broke through my limiting belief, it became easier to share who I was with others so that now I have no problem sharing my thoughts on having (or not having) children.

I had made the issue into a mountain when it was a molehill. We think our problems are so big, but we close ourselves off in order to protect ourselves. Speaking our truth allows us to have deeper, meaningful relationships. It's our stories that connect us all, especially the less than positive ones. It's what makes us human. Being perfect is boring anyway!

So, what are you holding back right now? Why do you need to tell your story? What truth is hiding deep inside you that needs to be expressed?

Are you open to confiding in a trusted friend or family member something you're afraid to share? All it takes is that one time of openness and acceptance to make it so much easier to share a part of yourself again.

express your individual style

Our appearance says a lot about us whether it's the way we style our hair, do our makeup, what we wear on our feet, our clothes, our weight, and our age. There's a lot of pressure in our society to *look* a certain way in order to receive positive attention, whether it's appearing wealthy when we walk into a high-end store or dressing professionally enough for a corporate office.

The older we get, the more we get to know our tastes. Some of us like to wear what is currently trendy, some of us prefer a uniform wearing the same thing every day (think Steve Jobs), and some of us want to branch out and develop our own styles.

Some people love comfort over high heels and want to be able to move freely in what they wear. Some people prefer to wear neutral tones, while others are happiest in bright shades of pink, blue, and green.

Do you dress how you like, or do you feel pressure to wear what is currently acceptable in whatever circle you're in? How about dressing in a way that you like regardless of what is popular? Of course, sometimes there are dress codes—you usually can't wear a tank top with an exposed bra strap and flip-flops while working at a bank (even though I think dress codes are a bit antiquated, but that's another conversation!).

If this is something you struggle with, what would happen if you didn't give in to the pressure of wearing what was "cool" or "proper"? What styles are you drawn to when you're in shops or people watching? Try things on and notice which items make you feel the most confident and attractive.

Dressing the way we want doesn't mean we have to go out and spend hundreds of dollars on a new wardrobe either. Make do with what you already own. Shop your closet, your sibling's, or your friend's. Host a clothing swap (an event where you bring your friends together and unwanted clothes, pile the clothes in the middle of the room and trade). Shop at thrift stores where you can find unique pieces for great prices. Don't be afraid to experiment.

express your interests

Is there something you've always wanted to try or learn? Do you have unexpressed passions just dying to be pursued?

If you are intrigued by the study of herbology (making medicine out of herbs), but your social circle thinks it's a bunch of spiritual woo-woo, why stop yourself from learning it anyway? Take a class or read a book and start doing what you love. This is what makes you you.

Decorate your space the way you want to or get rid of everything you own if it's your preference. Don't worry about what is trendy or what your friends think. If you are into black witchy décor and your family is weirded out by it, who cares. If you want to paint your walls black and hang up your dead insect collection, go for it!

find your tribe

You've spent a lot of time finding your vibe; what about finding your tribe?

Surrounding yourself with people who love and accept you does wonders for the spirit. I spent many years masking my real self so that I could have people to spend time with, but in the end, I was never fulfilled and never really accepted. People could see right through me. It wasn't until I started expressing who I was, that the people who were on similar wavelengths started appearing. The more I got into tarot card reading and learning about spirituality, the more I attracted friends who were into similar subjects. The more I told everyone about my business endeavors, the more entrepreneurs I connected with, and so on.

As I mentioned before, our outer world is a reflection of our inner world. Only until I did the internal work and figured out who I was, was I able to see an outer image of myself.

If you are having trouble finding like-minded people, try taking a class or attending a meetup on a subject you are interested in. If you're passionate about music production, take a recording class. You will meet others who feel the same.

Also remember, it's the differences that make our friendships unique. I used to think I only had to hang around people who thought the same as me or were interested in the same stuff as me, but the beauty of other worldviews is they open us up to the full experience of reality. Don't be afraid to reach out. You may learn something new.

~

Up until this point we have done a lot of self-exploration and digging deep. The following chapters will focus on the practical side of life-design skills; things that I have learned in my career development profession and education that are sure to have you moving forward in no time!

9

goal setting
&
staying motivated

goal setting

*"The difference between who you are &
who you want to be, is what you do."*
~ UNKNOWN

Whether or not you have any goals that you are currently working toward, no matter how large or small, do not feel the pressure to have any just because people talk about it all the time. However, if you do have an idea for a dream that will fulfill you, but you're feeling a bit stuck, then this chapter is for you.

It's best to find a goal that motivates you. There's no point setting a goal to climb Mount Everest if you don't even like the outdoors (unless your goal is to push yourself outside of your comfort zone). Maybe you want to save a certain amount of money by a specific date. Maybe you want to start your own business and quit your day job. Or perhaps you're trying to get fit for your wedding day. Look back to your notes on chapter 1 (authenticity) and chapter 2 (find your passion) for some inspiration.

s.m.a.r.t. goals

There are countless goal-setting techniques available out there, and I would never be able to explain all of them. But for this section, I will talk about the S.M.A.R.T goals technique as it's one of the most common goal-setting systems used today.

Originally conceptualized by Peter Drucker's Management by Objectives principle, S.M.A.R.T. goals were first used in the November 1981 issue of *Management Review* by George T. Doran, and then eventually by Professor Robert S. Rubin who wrote about it an article in *The Society for Industrial an Organizational Psychology*.

S.M.A.R.T. Goals are

Specific: Your goal should be very clear so you know which direction you're going. Ask yourself who, what, why, when, and how.

Measurable: You should be able to measure your goal so you can track how far along you are, as well as be able to break your goal down into measurable steps.

Achievable: Your goal should be doable and realistic. Stretch yourself.

Relevant: Your goal needs to make sense and mean something to you.

Time-bound: Set a date that you will achieve your goal by.

For instance, saying "I want to be fit" isn't going to cut it. You need to be more specific, whether it's to get to a certain measurement or weight and by what date, or if you are going to start meal planning to help you get there.

If you are overwhelmed by the size of your goal and feel like it's impossible to reach, try breaking it down into smaller digestible pieces such as dividing your one big goal into smaller weekly or monthly goals.

One of the world's top business and life coaches, Tony Robbins, says, "A major source of stress in our lives comes from the feeling that we have an impossible number of things to do. If you take on a project and try to do the whole thing all at once, you're going to be overwhelmed."

Don't forget to connect with your *why* to stay on track. Why do you want to achieve your dreams? You know you have to write and record ten songs to complete your album, but if you forget why you want to finish it in the first place, finding the motivation will be difficult. Try to remain connected to the bigger picture. This is where vision boards and personal statements come in handy.

staying motivated

When we begin a new endeavor, we are excited and motivated. But sometimes, after some time has passed, we lose that initial passion and feel unmotivated or bored. Sometimes we even give up on what we were once so stoked about. It's hard to stay motivated every moment of every single day. Our passion dial isn't always turned up to one hundred percent every waking moment, so it can be a struggle to keep up the good work. We run into hurdles, and even if our vision board has photos of the dream home we want to purchase, we need to continue to take actionable steps to get to where we want.

This is where self-discipline and persistence come into play. Persistence builds character, and it's all about taking action when we don't feel like doing what we set out to do. But if we stick with it long enough, we will achieve our goal.

Try not to give in to comfort or impulses that take you off track. They will only leave you feeling disappointed in the long run.

A 2013 study by Wilhelm Hoffman discovered that people who had high self-control were happier than those who didn't. This was because those who had more self-discipline were able to deal with problems along the way easier than others. They didn't give in to their emotional impulses but stayed on track to their initial goals.

Discipline can be hard, but here are a few more ways you can be more productive and stay on track with your goals:

1. **Remove distractions** like social media if you are trying to get something done. Close the door. Turn off your cell phone. Get up earlier than everyone else in your home if it means having a couple of hours all to yourself.

2. **Stop multitasking** and focus on one thing at a time. Prioritize your to-do list and put the most important tasks at the top. Make it results oriented and be specific about what you want to accomplish at the end of the day.

3. **Be realistic with your schedule.** Don't fill your calendar with things to do for every minute of the day. Pace yourself. Consider things that also fill up your time such as meals, relaxation, and getting to and from places. Don't set impossible standards that you won't be able to meet.

4. **Don't be hard on yourself** if you fail. Pick up where you left off and keep moving forward.

5. **Don't give into your feelings.** There will be days when you don't feel like doing anything. Try to keep the bigger picture in mind and do the task even if you don't want to. You will be glad you did.

6. **Reward yourself.** Treat yourself to your favorite meal or buy yourself that thing you've been wanting to buy.

Choose a simple activity and commit to doing it every day for one week (or month if you're feeling adventurous) even if you don't feel like it at all. It could be as easy as doing twenty sit-ups per day or writing in your journal every evening. This will build your ability to stick to a promise you made yourself so you can move on to bigger goals.

What will you commit to doing every day this week?

_____

_____

_____

_____

_____

_____

_____

_____

_____

_____

_____

_____

(dis)comfort & the bigger picture

How do we motivate ourselves to start taking action toward what we truly want? It's hard, it's scary, and we often come up with all sorts of excuses to not move forward.

Comfort is a lie. I don't mean the cozy type of comfort like wrapping yourself up in a fleece blanket in the wintertime with a cup of hot tea and a good book. I wrote an entire book on this type of comfort in *The Cozy Life*.

I'm talking about the sort of comfort that is based on an underlying fear that prevents us from taking action. It can manifest as laziness, procrastination, or addiction. Some of us shop too much, sleep too much, eat too much (or too little), drink or do too many drugs, or spend too much time on the internet.

It's okay to indulge in creature comforts to an extent, but if it's preventing you from going for your dreams, it's time to dig deeper and maybe look at what feelings you are trying to cover up. Try sitting in the discomfort instead and see what thoughts come up the next time you find yourself wanting to indulge.

Comfort can also camouflage itself as being "fine" or "okay" with life. A dog who is stuck indoors every day is *fine*. He has food to eat and a bed to sleep in. But his real self dreams of happily running around outside in the fields, chasing a ball with his owner. Fine can be a dangerous word if we are afraid of pursuing more.

the obituary

A few years ago, when I was working with a life coach, he had me do an eye-opening exercise where I was asked to write two obituaries. One where I continued living my comfortable "fine" life, and another version where I expressed my full self and accomplished everything I dreamed of.

The results were shocking. My comfortable life was average at best. Life was mediocre, but my basic needs were met. I had food to eat and a place to live. I didn't try to make any new friends or explore the world. I stayed in my comfortable nine-to-five job; it paid well, and I liked the security. I didn't go for my dreams and inspire anyone because I didn't think anyone would listen to me. Then I retired, played board games with the folks at the retirement center, and died. The end.

Then I wrote my alternate-life obituary where I eagerly strived for my dreams, fearlessly colored outside the lines, and it was like a lightbulb went on! The obituary was exciting and full of life. I wrote many inspiring books to help people live more authentic lives. I was so successful at it that I was able to donate millions of dollars to support animal causes and save thousands of creatures, buy my dream home, and travel the world. It was exciting, and I left my mark on the planet.

Try it for yourself! Don't let the fear of change get the best of you. You have this one precious life to live, and you can do anything you want with it. Dream big and write it all down.

Write out your **Comfortable Life Obituary**:

_____

_____

_____

_____

_____

_____

_____

_____

_____

_____

_____

_____

_____

_____

Write out your **Dream Life Obituary**:

_____

_____

_____

_____

_____

_____

_____

_____

_____

_____

_____

_____

_____

the front porch analogy

Sometimes when I'm too scared or too lazy to do something, I think about myself as an old woman, sitting on her front porch on a rocking chair sipping tea and reflecting on life. I'd think about all the things I had done or hadn't done and if I was satisfied with it.

Bronnie Ware, an Australian nurse of palliative care, said that the top regrets of the dying were wishing they had the courage to be their true self, not having spent so much time working so they could be with their loved ones, having the courage to express their feelings, staying in touch with friends, and allowing themselves to be happier.

Let's say you have committed to living a healthier lifestyle by meditating more. You have every intention of meditating at least once a day, but you're too lazy. Will you have wished you had done it anyway if you knew that you could have prevented a heart attack?

No matter how hard something is at the moment, try to step back and look at the bigger picture. You will be happier for taking care of your health, spending time with your loved ones, being true to yourself, and creating meaningful memories, than to have chosen the comfortable option of staying home and sleeping (unless you really needed it).

.

10

build a career you love

build a career you love

"We're not on our journey to save the world but to save ourselves. But in doing that you save the world. The influence of a vital person vitalizes."
~ JOSEPH CAMPBELL

I'm hesitant to use the word *career* in this context, because when you're doing what you love, it's more of a *lifestyle* than a career. But for ease of use, I'll use the term to talk about the way we make money.

Having spent over ten years researching, teaching, and coaching others as well as designing my career path, I wanted to share some of my best career hacks in this chapter. I love helping people come up with ways they can achieve their dreams.

Of course, I can't cover every possible career-building strategy but take what resonates with you and leave the rest. Most of the suggestions below relate to working for someone else, but some of them may also be helpful if you want to start your own business.

So, with no further ado, below are some tips and tricks on building a career you love!

you can be picky

Be picky and stick to what you love. Going against your grain will cause a big ol' mess and stress. If you have taken any personality tests yet, you will know that going against your nature can be difficult, or at the very least, an annoying endeavor. Of course, we are malleable human beings, so we are more than capable of learning new skills and enjoying them. However, when we interview for jobs that are completely opposite to our strengths or interests, trying to convince our potential boss that we are genuinely intrigued or good at the job when we're not will come off as fake.

Okay, I know what some of you are thinking: we don't all have the luxury to choose what we do. It's true. In some circumstances, we are not lucky enough to be choosy. But that doesn't mean you should stop trying. Take what you can for now but keep your eyes and ears open to new opportunities that better suit you. Let your network, friends, and family know what you are searching for so they can also keep an eye out. Many people get their dream jobs by staying focused and persistent. We must believe we are worthy of something for us to allow the opportunities to show up. Believe in yourself and the rest will follow.

Here's a practical example of using your values and strengths to guide your job search. Imagine that you love helping people and are interested in the health-care field. You know you want to become a nurse or doctor one day, but you don't have any experience or education yet. Try to get an entry-level job related to this field so you can gain experience and start building your résumé for the future. For instance, get a job as a medical office assistant or receptionist at a doctor's office if health care is your passion.

Sometimes our careers develop naturally over time in a roundabout way. I had no idea where my career path would take me. All I knew was I loved learning about people and helping them, and I had a psychology degree. What the heck does one do with a bachelor of arts degree in psychology? I decided to apply to all the open entry-level human resources jobs in the city and convince them that I wanted to learn more about the field. I got a job at a giant tech company, and as the years went by, I grew my network, which led me to more jobs in creative film studios and eventually to my own businesses and writing.

So, dig deep and think outside the box. Sometimes a position at a glance appears unrelated, but the skills you use or can build, such as communication, customer service, or problem solving, are transferrable. Home in on those aspects.

By now you know a bit more about your values and strengths, so start there and use them as an internal compass to guide you.

make a list of companies

Having worked for several years in recruitment, I can assure you that the statistics don't lie. Eighty percent of jobs are not posted, so you never know what is out there until you actively search for them.

The technique below is one I have used many times over the years to gain more experience in a job or field I was interested in and it has worked well.

First, you create a list of every local company that is related to the field you want to get into, no matter how big or small. It could be the mammoth headquarters of a well-known company, or a small retail or mom and pop shop. Use search engines and list them all. If you want to move away from your current residence, feel free to expand your location search.

Your spreadsheet should include

- **Company name**
- **Contact name** of owner if it's a smaller company or human resources department if it's a larger one
- **Contact email**
- **Location**
- **Status** or **comments** section so you can keep track of when you last contacted them

Once you've compiled a list, draft your email. Here is the exact template that I have used; feel free to copy/use it.

Subject:

Job Inquiry – **[First & Last Name]** – **[Company Name]**

Email:

Hello **[Contact Name/Human Resources]**,

My name is **[First & Last Name]**, and I am a **[Title]**. *(i.e., if you went to school for animation, you are an animator or an aspiring animator if you have not done any previous work)*

The reason I am writing to you is because I am looking for full-time work in the **[Insert Field Name]** field, as I have always had a passion for **[Insert Passion(s)]**.

Having **[Insert Related Accomplishments, Education, Training, Volunteer Work]**, I would love nothing more than to work directly with a local **[Type of Company]** company and learn even more about the industry.

I would be an excellent candidate because I have also **[List Past Accomplishments/Skills]**. I am **[Strengths]**.

There may not currently be any openings, but if there are, I am positive I can put my skills to use for you and help with the success of your company. I would love to speak with you more about any potential opportunities.

You can see my résumé here. **[Insert Hyperlink to your Résumé or Attach File]**.

Thank you for your time and consideration.

Sincerely,
[First & Last Name]

This strategy has worked for me several times, even back when I barely had any work experience. Passion goes a long way! Show how dedicated you are to the industry/career path/company and what you are willing to give to help the business succeed. Businesses love to hear how you can benefit them.

Even if it doesn't work out for you the first time, keep trying. Don't forget to follow up a week later if you have not heard back from anyone. People's inboxes can get clogged and your email can get lost in the mix. Sometimes a job opening isn't available the first time you reach out, but something opens up later on when you try again. Don't give up.

network, network, network

For some, the word *networking* can bring up some uncomfortable reactions. I know there are lots of people who enjoy social functions and making new connections, but because of my introverted nature, I always cringed when I was invited to one—I can't even do parties.

Anyhow, face-to-face professional networking is a powerful tool. You don't have to meet people at events either as you will organically meet people at work, life, and other social get-togethers. A recent article on *Payscale.com* said that about seventy to eighty percent of people are hired through a connection they made. This is why having a good reputation is valuable. If you leave a good impression throughout your career, you are more likely to get referred to a job down the road. I've seen it over and over again in my HR career.

You can network with past or present coworkers, managers, clients, customers, social media contacts, influencers, friends, friends of friends, teachers, family members, and just about anyone you cross paths with!

Doors open when we network. I have personally been offered several jobs, without an interview, simply because I worked with the hiring manager in the past, or I had met them previously through career fairs with other companies. The artists I hire today for film studios are almost ninety-five percent through people I have worked with in the past, or through a contact with another former colleague.

I know it's not everyone's cup of tea, but if you use social media on a regular basis, it is a great way to network with different people without having to schmooze in person. Social media platforms are excellent for setting up coffee chats if you want to do any informational interviews or meet up with potential customers if you are growing a business.

Lastly, you need to give to get. If you have anything to offer to your network contact, help them in any way that you can. They will appreciate it. Buy them a coffee or make an introduction that will land them more business.

find a mentor

If you can find a mentor who has done what you want to be doing, this is a wonderful thing. Finding a mentor will depend on your current network, how much work experience you have, and who you've met. Sometimes it takes that one special job, with an amazing supportive boss who sees something in you and wants to help you succeed.

Finding a mentor is not about directly asking someone if they can *be* your mentor. That's just awkward. It's about organically building a relationship. Find someone you admire and who you see your future self in. Find an opportunity to meet with them, or ask them out for coffee and tell them you'd love to get advice on how they got into their career and pick their brain a little. Usually, people are pretty open to talking about their experiences to help someone else who is just starting out. If they aren't, they probably aren't a good match anyway.

Through your interaction, you'll find out if you connect or not, and if things go well, you can ask if they'd be open to continuing to meet or chat if you have more questions later. If they liked you, you might have a new mentor!

Don't force anything though. You'll be able to determine if the connection is genuine or if it was just a one-off. If you have trouble finding anyone, there are more suggestions below such as learning more about your heroes.

take courses

Taking continuing education classes or workshops is excellent for building your résumé and for networking. I like to take a self-improvement, spiritual, or business course at least once or twice a year. It keeps me inspired as I am always building upon my previous skills. I meet some great people along the way, and we end up in each other's lives somehow. There are also several free tutorials online or inexpensive classes in your local post-secondary institution depending on your budget. Watch free videos or listen to podcasts. They are all available to you.

Taking in-person workshops is a great way to meet like-minded people. They usually occur within a short time frame, are relatively inexpensive, and you get to speak with others who are either working in the field you're interested in already or want to be.

do it as a hobby or volunteer

If you can't get paid work yet, be sure to continue working on your passions in your spare time or volunteer in the same industry if your interests are more hands-on or service based. If you have the option of teaching a skill to others or have friends you can collaborate with to host an event or workshop in your field of interest, it's a great way to get involved in your community, inspire others, and build your experience and network.

sign up with a recruitment agency

Depending on where you live, there may be several recruitment agencies in your town. They're always looking for people to add to their roster so that when jobs come up that you have the skills for they will hire you. Tell them what you have to offer. Agencies will generally specialize in particular sectors or look for a certain level of experience, from entry-level to executive, so make sure you do your research and choose the one best suited to you.

build a lifestyle from your creativity

Not to point out the obvious, but if you want to build a lifestyle out of your creativity, you need to start getting creative! It's one thing to tell your friends that you *want to write a book,* you need to actually write the book! This is how we build a lifestyle from our creativity. The rest will follow.

Learn how to produce more than you consume but remain focused on your goal. Creatives tend to be full of many brilliant ideas, but we also tend to get stuck because we have too many projects on the go. You know who you are!

There will definitely be times you have to do things that you don't love to do but are necessary for building the life of your dreams in the long run. Whether it's administrative paperwork, heavy lifting, or dealing with finances, they need to get done. You can always delegate the tasks to those who enjoy them when you have the budget. Just keep on grinding.

Stay persistent and consistent. Many people don't have the grit and audacity to keep pushing on their goals for five or ten years, so you'll already be way ahead. Move past any failures; know they are just learning opportunities and stay focused.

personal branding & social media

Social media can be a blessing or a curse depending on how you use it or how you view it. We live in such an incredible time where we can connect with people across the globe and keep in touch with them wherever we are. It is also an incredible business tool. If we learn how to use it intentionally, we can build an audience and online brand or persona.

It needs to be used authentically as people buy who you are, not the product itself or the talent you possess. In fact, you don't even need to be that talented these days to build a following. If you are likable, relatable, and provide valuable content, it will do wonders for building an online presence. We now live in a time when if we don't share a little bit about our stories, people have a harder time connecting with us and becoming our supporters. People connect with our hearts and how we make them feel.

In order to build a personal brand online, you also need to have a clear vision of what it is you want to convey and provide consistent, valuable content. If you can do that, then money becomes a by-product.

Lastly, don't forget to engage with your followers regularly by replying to comments or liking other people's content so they can get to know you and you can get to know them.

blog/website/portfolio

It's helpful to have your own website, blog, or portfolio to show future employers, clients, or followers how passionate and knowledgeable you are about the field you're interested in. Skills can be taught, but the love of an art, science, philosophy, or lifestyle comes from within and can't be fabricated.

Blogs are a great option if you want to start making money online through affiliate links, sponsored posts, or selling your own products (digital or physical).

If you're stuck, there are unlimited resources online that can teach you how to get started and it's become easier than ever!

look to your heroes

I used to score as impulsive and overly emotional on personality tests. When I was a kid, if someone picked on me for my size, I would have ended up crying like a baby. I didn't know how to handle my reactions. And as a teenager into my early twenties, I would have uncontrollable emotional outbursts if I was upset about something.

It was always something I wanted to work on so that I could have a better grasp on my relationships, work, and business. I eventually learned to love my sensitivities, but I knew that the logical side of me could have used some development, as I often blew things out of proportion. I didn't know what "logic" actually meant. It's always great to have some balance in our thinking.

One thing I did (subconsciously) was choose romantic partners who had qualities that were missing inside of me that I wanted to have. I chose mates who were logical, scientific, business savvy, and serious. I found this attractive and wanted the same skills.

Let me emphasize that the way I chose my significant others was not on purpose, because once I was able to build those traits within myself, I no longer felt like I needed them. I came to notice a pattern that if we lack confidence in certain areas in our lives, we often choose partners who have characteristics that are missing within us, versus someone who complements us and is our partner in crime.

The great thing about dating people who had qualities I admired, was that I spent hours and hours asking their advice and figuring out their thought processes so that I could learn how they saw the world.

Now, I don't recommend doing what I did; however, the lesson is that a great way to improve your weaknesses is to seek those who are doing what you wish you already could. It could be a mentor, a boss, or an influencer you look up to. There is unlimited information on the internet, interviews, and autobiographical books you could also review if you are curious about someone specific.

If you admire someone that you know in person, ask them if you can pick their brain. I always try to get to know local entrepreneurs so I can get insight into how they deal with setbacks and decision making because I value that skill set. Maybe you want to learn how to get into a creative industry such as acting or filmmaking. Take time to meet with people who are already doing this, who can help you gain insight into a world you are unfamiliar with.

Sooner or later, when you surround yourself with people who have the skills you want to have and with the information you want to learn, it becomes a part of you. Bit by bit you will learn the skills and apply them. Whether consciously or subconsciously, if you are obsessed enough, you will eventually develop the expertise that the person you admire has.

share your accomplishments

This might take some courage, but don't forget to share your wins with people who care about you. Hearing their feedback can motivate you to keep going, and it also helps you acknowledge when things are going well and improve your confidence.

just take action

Stop overthinking about all the things you have to do or are afraid to do. There's no need to worry about perfection. It will only keep you stuck. You're either working on your career and passions, or you're not. All the other excuses or fears we come up with are our own stories, and they don't serve us. As they often say in the entrepreneur world, "Done is better than perfect!" So don't worry about getting the ideal logo, website, or experience, just do, do, do. You can change everything later as you go. The rest will follow.

And finally, don't let the Negative Nancy's out there deter you from pursuing your dreams either. It will take hard work and persistence, but it's worth it. Keep trying, fail, and try again. Learn from your mistakes and keep moving forward. Don't take no for an answer.

~

There you have it! I hope that these techniques and tips have inspired new ways of approaching your career development. Networking doesn't have to be hard. All we have to do is put ourselves out there.

In part three, we will close out the rest of this book with some inspiring stories from those who *colored outside the lines*, look at some other unconventional lifestyles, and talk about the beauty in the simple things.

part three

failure & success

"Those who dare to fail miserably can achieve greatly."
~ JOHN F. KENNEDY

As you grow into your authentic self, you may find yourself coming up against even more people who will question or judge your every move. You'll need to keep pushing even when the times get tough.

I once asked my old boss, the CEO of a tech company, what he thought about failure because I noticed that he would keep pushing even when things didn't go as expected. He replied that he never looked at defeat or loss as failure. It was an opportunity to learn about what went wrong, or what didn't work, and a chance to fix it for next time.

We can't do everything perfectly all the time. But if we can try, try, try and get back up again, we can push our boundaries and test out the results. To hold back because of fear would be the real failure. Imagine being on your deathbed, knowing you didn't try hard enough only because you were afraid? Would it not be better to give it your all than to forever wonder "what if"?

There are going to be people who will not want to see you succeed because it triggers their own insecurities. But learn to embrace failure and use it as an opportunity to learn. Mistakes teach us valuable lessons about ourselves and reality. Even if you feel like you've tried your hardest and it still hasn't worked out for you, there is no reason not to keep trying. Success might be just around the corner. If you keep bumping up against a wall, try asking for feedback and seeing if anyone can offer some helpful advice. Or seek a coach or mentor who has done something similar to what you are trying to do.

Also, it's helpful not to get too emotionally invested. I know that creating anything is a vulnerable process as it's a reflection of who we are, but we shouldn't take it so seriously as it can damage our ability to keep moving when things don't work out perfectly.

Once we can release ourselves from the fear of failure, we are free. Failure is necessary for success. Anyone who has ever done anything great has experienced failure, and likely multiple times.

Here are a few of my favorite examples:

- Well-known stand-up comedian, actor, writer, and producer **Jerry Seinfeld** was fired from the TV sitcom *Benson* because his performance wasn't very good. (*thoughtcatalogue.com*)
- Musician and actor **Elvis Presley** was told he was better off driving trucks for a living by the concert hall manager of Nashville's Grand Ole Opry. (*snopes.com*)
- **Thomas Edison**, the creator of the electric lightbulb, spilled acid on the floor at a Western Union job and decided to become an inventor instead. (*facts.net*)
- Best known for her leading role in the popular 1950s sitcom *I Love Lucy*, **Lucille Ball** was considered a failed B-list actress. (*thoughtcatalogue.com*)
- American actress, model, and singer **Marilyn Monroe**, who was the iconic sex symbol of the 1950s, was told over and over again by modeling agencies that she should forget about modeling and just become a secretary or get married. (*mydomaine.com*)
- Dutch impressionist painter **Vincent van Gogh**, whose paintings are now worth millions of dollars, was unsuccessful when he was alive, having only sold one of his paintings to a friend. (*biography.com*)

- **Steven Spielberg**, who is one of the world's most successful film directors, was rejected three times from the University of Southern California School of Theater, Film and Television, and then dropped out of another school he was accepted at to give directing a go. (*time.com*)
- **Albert Einstein**, a German physicist, best known for his theory of relativity, couldn't speak until he was four years old. He also couldn't read until he was seven. He's one of the most iconic scientists today. (*huffingtonpost.ca*)
- **Charles Darwin**, an English biologist and geologist, who was famous for his contribution to evolutionary science and published the well-known book *On the Origin of Species,* was called lazy, dreamy, and lacking intellect by his family and was never thought of as the smart one. (*medium.com*)
- **Abraham Lincoln**, sixteenth president of the United States, didn't do well in the military and also had multiple failed businesses. It also took him running in five elections before he won. (*abrahamlincolnonline.org*)

You see, even the most successful people in the world had to deal with naysayers or failure a few times to make it to where they got. Failure is not a bad thing!

the proof is in the pudding

In contrast to embracing failure, I wanted to share a few examples of people our society celebrates who have chosen to live outside the box or *color outside the lines*. Some of the most influential, creative, and successful people had an insatiable need to pursue their dreams no matter how crazy they seemed. They were the ones who led revolutions, created beautiful art, and invented new things because they valued and loved their differences and passionately pursued their dreams. They trusted their intuition to guide them to achievement and happiness, no matter the obstacles they faced. Below are some more inspiring and famous people who did not follow social norms.

- **Albert Einstein** (again, because I think he's cool!) would eat grasshoppers in front of his friends to shock them and kept a disheveled hairstyle. He also refused to wear socks. (*thoughtco.com*)
- Pacifist **Mahatma Gandhi** was India's leader in the nonviolent independence movement against British rule. When he was imprisoned in India in 1932, he chose not to eat for six days to "protest the British decision to segregate the 'untouchables', those on the lowest rung of India's caste system." Starvation was Gandhi's way to preach nonviolence and get his point across. He thought outside the box and stood up for what he believed in, even if his life was in danger. (*biography.com*)
- **Mozart**, an influential composer of the classical era, was a child prodigy, composing music from the age of five. He wrote over 600 works in his lifetime. (*wikipedia.com*)
- **Stephen Hawking** was a British author, scientist, and professor who contributed revolutionary work in physics and

cosmology. At twenty-one, he was diagnosed with ALS (a progressive neurodegenerative disease that affects the nerve cells in the brain and spinal cord) (*alsa.org*). His many books about cosmology have inspired people around the globe. Hawking used his illness as fuel to help him focus on doing something worthy with his life. Before his diagnosis, he was never as disciplined. (*biography.com*)

- American artist, producer, and director **Andy Warhol** was the leader in the pop art movement in the 1960s (*wikipedia.com*). He was a bit of a packrat and collected all sorts of trash from airplane menus to pizza dough. He also wore over forty wigs and had a bit of a foot fetish (*inktank.fi*).

- **Rosa Parks** is most famous for refusing to give up her seat on the bus to a white passenger on a segregated bus in Montgomery, Alabama. This led to the 381-day bus boycott that helped end segregation of public services and amenities. It was because of her bravery and determination, standing up for what she believed in which was not the way things were, that she was able to make a positive historical change. (*biography.com*)

- **Kurt Cobain**, an American singer, musician and songwriter, influenced pop culture through his individual approach to clothing and angsty rocker musical style, a sound that didn't exist until he came along. He did end up committing suicide because he couldn't take the pressure of fame, but his unique contributions to music have stayed with us today. (*mtv.com*)

- **Robin Williams**, an American comedian and actor famous for his leading roles in *Mrs. Doubtfire*, *Hook*, and *Good Will Hunting*, changed the world and made it a happier place through his brilliant comedic style. He had a joke for every situation and could become a variety of characters through his many voices and physical acting. His diverse approach to comedy inspired a new generation of comedians. (*cbsnews.com*)

The people featured above all had their own experiences. For some, their uniqueness helped their careers, and for others, it took extreme bravery to stand up for what they believed in.

Sometimes our logic gets in the way, especially if we have been brought up to believe that rationality is a higher value such as getting a reliable education so we can end up in a steady paying nine-to-five job. But if we keep choosing the safe option because it makes the most sense when we know deep in our hearts it's not what we want to do, it will only move us further away from who we are. If we can embrace our inner weird and choose relentless, unstoppable irrationality, persistence, and devotion, we are sure to achieve success. We must keep growing and pushing ourselves.

Unfortunately, the reality is that often if someone isn't already famous, they'll be medicated for displaying their eccentricities. Doctors or family members will assume they have a mental illness and so these people may hide their true nature so they aren't institutionalized. Being different from the norm is not a reason to cover it up with drugs, and I hope one day we can accept all neurodiversities for what they are.

Please note, I know there are instances when someone's mental health is detrimental to their everyday life or the safety of other people. In these cases, you should seek medical expertise. But if you're a little bit different and perceive the world in your own unique way, why can we not look at these as gifts instead of abnormalities that need to get fixed just so everyone else feels comfortable?

unconventional lifestyles

Coloring outside the lines also applies to out-of-the-box lifestyles. My favorite life coach and dating expert, Matthew Hussey, talks about living an unreasonable life. This means going for that wild and crazy idea or dream that you have, regardless of what people say or think. So what if you want to build your own hobbit-themed backyard or live a polyamorous lifestyle? If you're not hurting anyone, go for it!

Dan Price, a modern-day Peter Pan, in his own words said he never wanted to grow up and has been living in the hills of a field on rented land in Oregon because it reminds him of being a child again. He built his own hobbit house underground and lives with few possessions and grows his own food. He gets to express his full creativity and is not hindered by society. Of course, this lifestyle is not for everyone, but my point is if you crave a particular lifestyle, it's doable. Also, let me reiterate that you don't *have* to have lofty goals to live a full life. I'm just saying if you *want* to, but you are *afraid* to, don't hold yourself back.

One movement I enjoy following is the tiny house movement. It's becoming increasingly popular as more and more people want to quit the rat race and downsize their lives and belongings. A typical tiny house is around 100–400 square feet and is often on wheels so it can be transported from place to place.

One of the most common reasons people are choosing this lifestyle is because of environmental and financial concerns, and also so they can have more time and freedom to focus on what they love, whether it's art, or being in nature, or quality time with their loved ones. With the rising costs of the housing market today, especially in many bigger cities, people simply don't want to be paying huge monthly mortgages until they retire. I've seen a tiny house built anywhere from US$10,000 to US$50,000 for a more luxurious one.

This summer, two friends from Australia came to stay with us for a few weeks. They had spent the last couple of years saving their money so they could travel the world for an entire year. They have successful careers in the tech and marketing industries but have a deeper passion for exploration, and they chose to do things a little differently, ditching home-ownership and large monthly bills. Travel gives them joy and a sense of freedom. They are doing what they love, regardless of what is expected of them.

Do you know or admire anyone who lives an unconventional lifestyle? Think about the people who intrigue you, whether they are friends, family, actors, musicians, scientists, leaders, entrepreneurs, and so on. Do they inspire you to try something new?

"It is impossible to live without failing at something, unless you live so cautiously that you might as well not have lived at all — in which case, you fail by default."
~ J.K. ROWLING

community & the simple things

We've spent a lot of time on our individual growth, but let's not forget the importance of community, love, connection, and enjoying the simple things. Just because we spend time working on ourselves, doesn't mean we should ignore all of the other wonderful things that life has to offer.

Unfortunately, the more individualistic and independent our society gets, the more alienated we become. We are facing a social epidemic of loneliness and crave human interaction more than ever. However, if you think back to your favorite memories, they usually involve other people. We are naturally social creatures who have needed each other for centuries in order to survive. Connecting over our stories, dreams, and sorrows brings us closer together and gives us a sense of belonging.

Don't forget to get out of your head and into the world. Reach out to a loved one. Appreciate the simple things like the smell of freshly cut grass or a great conversation. A holistic approach to life is well worth living.

encouragement

"I said to myself, 'I have things in my head that are not like what anyone has taught me'... I decided to start anew—to strip away what I had been taught—to accept as true my own thinking."
~ GEORGIA O'KEEFFE

Congratulations! You've made it to the end! You've read through many soul-inspiring chapters of self-discovery, exercises, and new ways of thinking. You've spent countless hours learning how to get more comfortable with your inner weird so you can pursue your dreams! You have explored the deepest and darkest parts of yourself so that you can get more in touch with who you truly are and who you want to become.

I'm so proud of you!

Don't ever give up on your dreams just to make someone else happy. Your uniqueness and ways of seeing the world belong to you and you owe it to yourself to express them. Don't let your talents go to waste.

There is no such thing as "normal," so don't let your fears keep you from *coloring outside the lines*. Be brave, grab that big red marker and scribble it everywhere! Then add some blue and some green and some yellow!

Change is never easy. It can be the hardest thing in the world, and sometimes it takes hitting rock bottom for us to take action. It's confusing, it's intimidating, and it's frightening, but why not start right away? You now know that you are worth it; comfort is just a lie, and failure is not a bad thing.

Let go of everything you ever knew—those old fears, beliefs, and patterns—and embark on your new journey. Discover who you are meant to be and do what you love with unabashed authenticity. Love the world and everyone around you, but most importantly, love yourself.

Now go out there and share your gifts with the world! Never forget that your life is your canvas and you can create anything that you dream of.

You have about eighty years on this planet. How do you want to remember them?

"Here's to the crazy ones.
The misfits. The rebels. The troublemakers.
The round pegs in the square holes. The ones who see things differently.
They're not fond of rules, and they have no respect for the status quo.
You can quote them; disagree with them; glorify or vilify them. About
the only thing you can't do is ignore them. Because they change things.
They push the human race forward. And while some may see them as
the crazy ones, we see genius. Because the people who are crazy enough to
think they can change the world are the ones who do."
~ ROB SILTANEN

about the author

Pia Edberg is the best-selling author and illustrator of *The Cozy Life* and *Charlie the Cat*. Her work has been featured on Buzzfeed.com, MindBodyGreen.com, and Lavendaire.com.

Bridging the gap between her self-help books and spirituality, Pia is also a certified tarot card reader, specializing in personal growth, simplicity, and life design. She has a degree in psychology from Simon Fraser University, as well as numerous certifications in personal development fields. Over the past ten years, she has also worked in human resources and career development for the film, visual effects, animation and tech industries.

Pia was born in the tiny island city of Nykøbing Falster, Denmark. She currently lives in beautiful Vancouver, British Columbia, Canada.

Visit www.piaedberg.com to learn more.

thank you!

Thank you for reading *color outside the lines*! I really appreciate all of your feedback and love hearing what you have to say. If you enjoyed reading this book, please leave a review!

Thank you so much!

With love,
Pia

98631022R00139

Made in the USA
Columbia, SC
29 June 2018

LIBERATED
by LOVE

Finding Truth Beyond Lies and Pain

CANDACE "CANDY" THOMPSON

Trilogy Christian Publishers
A Wholly Owned Subsidary of Trinity Broadcasting Network
2442 Michelle Drive
Tustin, CA 92780

For information, address Trilogy Christian Publishing
Rights Department, 2442 Michelle Drive, Tustin, Ca 92780.
Trilogy Christian Publishing/ TBN and colophon are trademarks of Trinity Broadcasting Network.

For information about special discounts for bulk purchases, please contact Trilogy Christian Publishing.

Manufactured in the United States of America

10 9 8 7 6 5 4 3 2 1

Library of Congress Cataloging-in-Publication Data is available.

ISBN 978-1-64088-884-5 (Print Book)
ISBN 978-1-64088-885-2 (ebook)

DISCLAIMER

In order to convey the truth, the ideals, and the core message of my memoir, I have tried to recreate events, locales, and conversations from my memories of them. My desire was to maintain the anonymity in some instances of those who have impacted my life, so I have changed the names of some individuals and places. I also may have changed some identifying characteristics and details such as physical properties, occupations, and places of residence.

My book is, first of all, dedicated to my husband, Vernon. You encouraged me from the beginning and all along the way to get out my story and did not consider the shame and criticism that could come on you by association. You've always believed in me and loved me and saw Jesus in me. You taught me how to love and had amazing patience for my shortcomings. I love you more than when we were first married, and I look forward to every day with you.

Next, I dedicate this book to all of our children, grandchildren, great-grandchildren, and all of the generations to come down the line, especially to the girls and women in our family. You have a great inheritance that will not perish—true liberation through God's love and plan. I want to inspire, encourage, and lead all of you to choose Christ above all else for meaning and purpose in your lives. I pray that you will carry on the great heritage we have in Christ from generations of Christians in our family who fought the good fight of faith. I love you and pray for you.

I also dedicate my book to my four children who are with Jesus who were restored to me. I know I shall see you again, and we will have a joyful reunion. Peter John, Mary Hope, Joseph Paul, and Sarah Noel, your eternal purpose has been interwoven with mine for good to those who hear our story and come to know the reason for my hope.

Last but not least, I dedicate this memoir to my parents. You loved me and raised me with hearts of love and forgiveness, never reminding me of my failures and shortcomings. I will ever be thankful for the life you gave me and for having you as my parents. I look forward to seeing you again in a promised reunion as believers in Christ.

CONTENTS

PREFACE

*L*iberated by Love: Finding Truth beyond Lies and Pain was written out of great pain and suffering from the consequences of believing the lie of feminism. Instead of promised equality and self-fulfillment, I found pain, deception, and heartbreak so deep that I feared a lifetime of misery was my fate. Miracle of all miracles, my story tells of my true liberation. Being liberated *by* love first. Up from the dregs of doing it my way, out of a dark place where there seemed to be no way out, having been betrayed and discarded, alone with no purpose or vision for life, I was found lovable and valuable. I found truth and true liberation and have written my story out of my passion to tell others a miraculous, exciting, unbelievable story of restoration and redemption. It is my story—but one that I believe could be the story of many women.

I also tell about the one special man who came in to my life, willing to become a part of who I was, who I am, and who I am becoming—and the process of becoming the woman who finally gave her heart to him. Above all, my book is about love—love that looked beyond my condition, my situation, all my failures and pain, and didn't leave me where I was. This greatest love, the love of Jesus who died for me and saw me as a new woman, who defended me and gave me a life worth living, was the love that truly liberated me to be able to love others and be finally liberated. I tell about the process of being transformed into someone better than I imagined in my fantasies or dreams. In writing about her, I came to love her. But my greatest love is for the One who didn't leave me where I was but rescued me when I was too far down to pull myself up once again.

The transformation I experienced in my heart and thinking is the main part of my story, and I've tried to describe that process as best I can describe something that goes beyond our natural understanding and my scientific mind. It goes beyond my emotions and my reasoning and originates in a place that I can only understand by faith—my spirit. I am a new person, totally new.

I've footnoted the truths that set me free. What I hope to convey to you in my book is that this is not an inclusive, discriminating, unloving, judgmental, only for the rich, unreachable, based on performance blessing. It is for you—for everyone, men and women— and it's free. But especially, for women who, like I was, still have hope of finding the love she was created for and believes the impossible is still possible. I hope you too will be liberated by love and come to know the truth about the One who truly loves you as you were created to be loved—unconditionally, unreservedly, eternally.

ACKNOWLEDGMENTS

First, I want to thank my husband, Vernon Thompson. Since a great deal of my book includes him—some of which isn't totally favorable—I especially thank him for allowing me to expose parts of our lives that were painful to him as well. His input, approval, and support—financial, emotional, and every other way—were essential to my story, but it was his love that gave me a reason for never giving up. He is the man God gave to me to show me the love of a husband and to share this life—to fulfill my destiny and purpose as his wife.

Next, I want to thank Peter Lundell, my first editor, who took me from that first draft and taught me so much about writing. I especially appreciate his kindness and gentleness with my insecurities and his persistence throughout the process to keep believing that I could write my own story.

I also appreciate Trilogy Publishing group, especially Mark Mingle, who thought I had an important story to tell and encouraged me to get it out.

Much gratitude to my friend, Judy Ackerman, who reads my book several times through the various changes and developments, giving me invaluable input. I especially appreciate that she understood my spiritual journey and walked through many of the most difficult years with me, praying and encouraging me on this journey.

I am thankful for Christian friends who saw me as Christ sees me and loved me through it all. Thanks to Pat Werner, who encouraged me and gave me valuable input and was one of many in my church who prayed for me; Pastor Johnny Herndon at Jubilee Church, who wouldn't compromise his teaching of abortion, feminism, marriage, and other controversial subjects; his wife, Keri, who was an example of a true helpmate to her husband, a mother, and grandmother. I thank them for standing up for my covenant marriage and counseling me to honor and respect my husband and not divorce.

With immense appreciation, I thank my Christian leaders of the churches we attended who taught me the Word of God and didn't back down from the truth. Thank you all for your faithfulness to Christ and your calling.

I am ever grateful to my parents who loved me and gave me a wonderful life, who loved Jesus and are with Him now, and whom I will forever love with all my heart and will see them again.

Above all others, I acknowledge the wonderful God who created me and has faithfully and consistently never given up on me but has continued to make me into the woman He created me to be and bring me into His place of immense blessings through Jesus Christ, His Son, my Savior.

1

How Did I Get Here?

At thirty-three, my life was not supposed to end up this way. I was always told I was smart. I was the first in my dad's family to finish college with a degree in science teaching from a large university—very impressive. Mine was the generation of women who were supposed to have it all—careers, families, and marriages with equal respect and responsibilities. We were liberated. And we would not be bound to the traditions of our mothers and grandmothers.

Now the declarations I had believed to be true sounded hollow against the reality of the past nine years that had destroyed any hope for my marriage. Equality had always sounded good, and sharing responsibilities was a good thing. So why did I feel like a victim? I felt trapped with no way out. I was anything but liberated.

Hope for a home in the suburbs as a stay-at-home mom wasn't very feminist of me, but to my own disbelief, I *had* hoped for that. To no avail. Even the worn-out furniture in the townhouse apartment cried *failure*—failure as a woman, a wife, and a mother.

The rental house would never be ours if it meant my income supporting us. I would no longer be a slave to that man's whims, his desires, and his habits. I had already done that. No more sacrificing unborn children for him. We had no purpose or vision for family or for the future. The fall of our house divided would be inevitable.

"I don't need a man to take care of me!" went the ranting of anger at getting what I wanted. I deserved my pain. I didn't know who I was or wanted to be.

And unwittingly I had agreed with my tormentors and given them access, actually an invitation. I was who that man said I was—and more, even a murderer. But he never said it, and I never allowed my mind to go there.

I had not a single friend. No one truly knew me. All I had were secrets hidden by a façade that was now crumbling. Only this man knew my darkest secrets. If I exposed him, I exposed myself. I'd sooner die, so I kept quiet. But the guilt and the pain were too much to bear. My silence made me an accomplice. I had built a wall of anger and denial so strong that it seemed nothing and no one could ever penetrate it.

I frantically searched books on psychology. There had to be answers. I *could* figure myself out. What was wrong? Why was I so incapable of feeling love? Why so much anger? Dead ends and deadness sent me to a psychiatrist who didn't help.

Maybe I *was* crazy. Was the woman being stabbed on the television really me? Fear was one of the few things I knew to be true. The anger between this man and me was palpable, and any little thing might set him off.

On trips to the grocery store, I could have been someone else. All my attention went to my children, but on trips to the park or the swimming pool, I was disconnected. I hated myself, at least the self I denied. And I didn't know who the rest of me was.

I would go through years of getting better and worse and better. When I hit bottom, I didn't stay there. I didn't crumble and die. I had already died hundreds of times.

I wanted to live and be free, to laugh and love. If I said love "again," I'd have a hard time remembering whether I had ever really loved—or been loved—by a man. Feminism, which at first had sounded so good, misled me and failed me. And in the process, it destroyed part of me, along with what I held to be most dear.

My story is the answer to my heart's cry to be *truly* liberated—and to be loved unconditionally and unreservedly. This answer painfully freed me to be able to love, respect, and honor one special and imperfect man, the man who finally found me and pledged his love to me. This is a story of overcoming the past, of restoration and redemption, and of finding the truth that sets us all free.

2

A Tomboy Named Candy Kane

orn with a bald head shaped just like my grandpa's, I was
almost two years old before a few blond sprigs finally
appeared. "She looked like a boy with no hair," Mom would
later say, not meaning to hurt me, just unaware of the power of
words. "Sticks and stones..." isn't true. Words *do* hurt. Mom didn't
mean to hurt me. She just didn't build me up like she did the boys. I
don't know when I began to think that being born a girl was a disad-
vantage, but it was well after those early years.

My parents had hoped for a girl, and my first act in life was to
make them happy. The first of three children, I was born Candace
Kane Keaver on December 1, 1943, while Dad was off fighting in
World War II. Everyone called me Candy, but later I was careful to
keep my middle name a secret.

When Dad returned as a war hero, we moved into one of my
grandparent's houses on what had once been North Carolina farm-
land. We cousins played together, went to the same church and
school, and visited from house to house, always finding a welcoming
smile. Life couldn't have been happier.

No one questioned Mom and Dad's love for each other. They
were openly affectionate and fun loving. Both were good in sports,
enjoyed family games, picnics, growing flowers and vegetables, and
a swing around the dance floor. Their hard work and optimism for
a brighter future were characteristics that inspired others. Like all

our friends and family, they were satisfied in their traditional roles of Mom's taking care of us at home and Dad's bringing in the paycheck. No one questioned this pact. We could have been the subjects of a Norman Rockwell painting. I took so much for granted.

* * * * *

Growing up in the South in the fifties was full of adventure and challenges. I idolized my dad and loved following him around in the yard as a toddler. Dad's chickens and Grandpa's hogs were much more interesting than dolls and girly things.

We were allowed to roam all over the neighborhood without fear. Mom called me a tomboy because of the way I played. Even as a three-year-old, I was a daredevil, playing rough and tough, loving the outdoors and giving Mom reason to fret that I was going to get badly hurt. No one tried to discourage me or shame me for playing rough. I loved those summer evenings chasing fireflies with glass jars in the backyard while the adults caught up on the day's news, wishing the call to bed wouldn't come so soon.

Jumping off my grandmother Keaver's backstairs was more of an attempt to fly than to jump. Unfortunately, breaking my collar-bone was a reality check for this tomboy. Superman had made his debut about eight years earlier and must have been an influence, but Tarzan movies were the prime impression on me. Swinging on ropes over a ravine and creek in the woods was a Saturday adventure that older kids had going, and this six-year-old wanted to give it a try. Running as fast as I could and swinging all the way out over the creek, I felt for a short time the exhilaration of flying like Tarzan, not giving second thought to the idea that I could fall and meet with serious injury. I didn't think I was limited by being a girl.

Candy Kane was not afraid to jump off the diving board at Bible camp into the deep water without knowing how to swim after faking the swimming test or ride a full-size bike when it was still too big for her. My cousin Judy said, "Candy isn't afraid of the devil himself." She didn't know how true that statement would later become.

* * * * *

My parents thought I was ready at five to start school, which should have been the beginning of a happy and prosperous life. Since there was no kindergarten in the public schools, they paid for me to go to a private school. I would get up in the dark and dress myself for the long drive across town to Ms. Nettie Schaffer's two-story brick house. It seemed like a mansion compared to our little two-bedroom home.

That winter of 1948, when I turned six, Mom had what she called a "nervous breakdown," whatever that was. I later understood that it may have ensued from postpartum depression after my youngest brother, Peter, was born, three years after my second brother, Stan.

But she blamed it on the childhood diseases *I* brought home from school. That winter, we all three had mumps, measles, and chickenpox, and Mom was prone to let her mind go in every fearful direction. I shut my ears so I wouldn't hear her crying. Mom didn't die that winter and soon was her happy, loving self. I learned in later years Mom learned fearfulness from her dad, who would round up the kids and go to the cellar when a storm was approaching. His fear was transmitted to most of the children and came down to us. "Don't get near the window." "Get away from the fireplace. Lightning might come down the chimney." "Get off the phone. It's lightning," Mom would warn us, her voice full of fear. Unfortunately, her fear translated weakness, and I didn't want to be like her, so I rejected even the good things I could have learned.

Yet under the tough exterior was still a girl who loved fairy tales about Cinderella and Rapunzel and wanted to be beautiful like them, with a prince coming to the rescue. On Sundays, I tried being the reserved, mannerly, sweet Candy, feeling pretty in black patent Mary Janes and frilly dresses.

Mom had been a beauty queen and was runner-up in the city-wide beauty contest after high school, vying for the coveted "Miss" title. The winner clearly wasn't as pretty and seems to have won unfairly because of connections. We loved looking at all of Mom's pictures and reimagined how beauty pageant history should have been as she relived those proud moments. I wanted to be pretty too.

* * * * *

When I was seven, Dad bought an old white frame four-room farmhouse on ten acres, and later eleven more, in a rural community called Oakdale, about five miles from our enclave of friends and family in Hoskins. My dream for a pony didn't materialize our first Christmas at the farm to my great disappointment.

Roughing it was no problem to me during those early years. I liked the outdoors more than inside anyway. My second Christmas on the farm, a pony waited for me in the barn, the prettiest brown and white pinto I'd ever seen. Along with that came a full cowboy outfit with double holstered silver cap guns. I spent the next three years exploring every nook and cranny of that twenty-one acres and most of Oakdale. Inspired by watching *The Lone Ranger* and Roy Rogers every Saturday morning at our grandparents, I could be a cowgirl, an explorer, or an Indian princess. Wherever my pony and I could go, I would go. My dolls mostly sat on a shelf.

My skirmishes with the neighborhood boys became dangerous when I responded to their vulgar teasing by shooting at them with my bow and arrows and hitting one in the head. That resulted in Dad taking my "weapons" away permanently. I was strong and as big as most of the boys, and once I slugged two of my tormentors down a hill, where they met their fate in a row of rose bushes. To my mother's chagrin, I frequently came home with torn skirts and shredded dresses from jumping over barbed wire fences.

It didn't help that my nickname was Candy. "What kind of candy are you? I bet you taste good," they taunted.

"Sour balls," I yelled, running after them. It was true. My sweet name belied who I was. I was anything but sweet. Thankfully, no one knew that my middle name was "Kane."

* * * * *

The other side of the tomboy was the young girl who dreamed of being pretty like her mother and loved wearing pretty dresses and girly things. The spring of my fifth grade, our county 4-H club announced a contest for a Junior and Senior Dairy Queen, and my friend, Nelda Helms, and I were encouraged to participate. I won, and Nelda took second. My parents and I attended a breakfast in a fancy hotel downtown where the mayor crowned the Dairy Queens and awarded us gold pins with the key to the city. My parents were proud of me.

The whole month of June, the Senior Dairy Queen and I went to luncheons and events throughout the city and county. She was friendly and confident giving me the assurance I needed. Every meal was a challenge for this little country girl, but I learned to eat chicken with a knife and fork instead of my fingers and how to be friendly to strangers and smile a lot.

* * * * *

We were Christians. The center of our lives was church and family, which were practically one and the same. We all got baptized, dedicated, and educated at the little Presbyterian church with most of our large, extended family. At twelve, I joined the church, professing the requirements of the denomination. If only that had set me up to solve all my future problems. "Be good," Mom would remind us. I learned early, somehow, I had to make myself good. It was up to me. The problem was I felt there was something in me that wasn't good, and religion didn't help me.

About the same time, a visiting evangelist herded me straight to the altar with his hellfire preaching. I was afraid of God and hadn't heard much about the devil, just Mom's threats that the devil or the boogeyman would get me if I stepped out of line.

I memorized Bible verses and the catechism, and I tried to make myself good enough for God. But I doubted I'd ever fully measure up, especially since I never had a sudden zap of spirituality. Not understanding faith, I thought I had missed out—a hopeless case. I didn't know the grace side of God that wiped the slate clean with forgiveness if I repented. Neither did I know what it took to go to hell, but I thought I had crossed the line by the time I was twelve because of something so horrible I must have done. Even so, church was a place where I felt the love of family and friends who encouraged me and where I was accepted. As I grew older, I began to question and doubt what I had learned and been taught. If only I had gotten good answers.

* * * * *

I was in all the church and elementary school plays, sang in talent shows, and even took piano. In the fifth grade, John Lee, the class clown, and I teamed up. I belted out the lyrics of Patti Page's hit "Let Me Go, Lover" behind the curtain, while John pantomimed a tormented lover on stage. The audience, and especially my parents, loved it.

In junior high school, I played sports and was in all the talent shows, the forever performer. Slipping cigarettes, my friend and I challenged the status quo for women before feminism hit in the sixties and Virginia Slims told women how far they had come. By high school, I had the habit. My parents disapproved, but I ignored their warnings.

Since I was a girl, my parents didn't think I needed a car. I was the oldest, and they didn't have the extra money, but my brother *did* get a car when he was in high school. Resentment grew into believing the lie that my parents didn't love me. I didn't see how hard they worked to provide and care for us. I became friends with an upperclassman who had a car and smoked like a fiend. She was worldly and a bit rebellious, and it was in her circle of friends I met my high school boyfriend. Soon our relationship was exclusive and intimate—definitely outside my parents' approval. My boyfriend escorted me to all the parties and proms, drove me to get my license, to school, and chauffeured me in his mom's Thunderbird convertible in the Christmas Parade. Bands from all over the state and float entries marched through downtown as I proudly sat on the back wearing the "Miss" title from my high school with a borrowed fur jacket and rhinestone tiara. We were voted best-looking seniors, and everyone thought we'd get married.

* * * * *

I took Dad's hard work and provision for granted. Finances were tight, and my parents didn't encourage me to go to college. It wasn't important for a woman. I believed that meant they didn't care, but Dad's sister insisted I give it a try. She and my uncle even helped me apply. Discouraged at my parents' favoritism toward the boys, I drifted further and further away from them. It didn't help that one of his sisters called Dad a male chauvinist.

However, Dad's opinion *was* important to me. His words, "Candy can do anything she sets her mind to do" stuck with me. I wanted his love and approval so much. And judging by his outward lack of affection and absence of any words of praise, I believed the lies in my head about his lack of love for me. I didn't realize that everything he was doing for me *was* how he loved. When I heard about honoring your parents,[1] it came with the threat of punishment.

Something inside me fought against Dad's authority—something critical and judgmental toward his grammar, his education, and his job. I wasn't outwardly disrespectful. That would have been disastrous. No one ever told me about being born with a rebellious

---

[1] See Exodus 20:12, Proverbs 1:8.

nature only God could change.[2] All those seeds of rebellion needed was the right environment.

* * * * *

The women's movement of the sixties was just beginning— the "second wave" as it would later be called (following the original women's suffrage movement). We now had choices women had never had. The thought of college, being a teacher, and living away from home stirred me to dream of more than marrying and staying home as a housewife and mother. Teaching would be a good career for me, I reasoned. I could support my husband's income and have summers off with the children, so I enrolled in a small teacher's college in the mountains of North Carolina. Having a career that would give me "freedom" from needing a man hadn't really occurred to me at this point. But that would come soon enough. Feminism promised to meet my deepest needs as a woman. It sounded so good.

Yet even as I followed through, as we drove onto the campus, my heart felt the tug of ties to my boyfriend. He remained in our hometown with no ambitions to go to college. Because I missed him, I found it hard to join in the social side of college life. I was led by emotions, and it wasn't long before I gave up my dream, quit college, returned home, and got an office job after the first quarter.

Soon I was going around with my old high school group, working in a boring job, and stuck in a routine that was killing my spirit. I shouldn't have been surprised that I soon broke up with him. It didn't take much. All I needed was a hint of infidelity when he dropped by an ex-girlfriend's house for a supposedly innocent chat. I never looked back. I returned to college. But just before I went back, a bomb fell.

---

[2] See Romans 8:6–7, Psalm 51:5.

3

Reap What You Sow

When I heard my mother's voice on the phone, I sensed that something was terribly wrong.

"Candy, can you come and get me? I need to come home." Almost breaking into sobs, she struggled to get the words out, "Mrs. Kelly called me here at work…she said Dad is going to leave me for her. Come now and get me, honey. I can't stay here."

My breath stopped. *What?* I was speechless except to say, "I'll be right there, Mom."

When I picked up Mom, she was shaking. "I can't believe it. And she called me at work. I just want to go home. I can't stay here."

She looked as if she would crumble into a sobbing bundle of pain and fear. Her voice was so pitiful that it wounded me too. I wished I could say something to her to console her. It was incomprehensible that this woman would call my mom and tell her that stuff.

I was the angriest I had ever been, but I couldn't say it. I couldn't tell Dad how angry I was and why. I didn't want to see him or confront him. I couldn't tell him how I felt, how I was hurt, and everything I believed about him was shaken. I never saw the hypocrisy of my reaction, holding Dad to a higher standard than any other human being or myself, for that matter. This wasn't Dad's nature—he wasn't a womanizer or whoremonger.

Dad was a Christian and loved Mom, but he'd committed a terrible wrong and hurt her deeply, along with the rest of us. He had

25

succumbed to the temptations of a seductress to be caught in a terrible situation. Disbelief and shame came upon us all. All the relatives knew, but no one said a thing. I couldn't imagine how he must have felt. Mom had always been the love of his life. Dad never said he was sorry for hurting us. Not once. I guess the only positive thing was that it was over, and he had not left Mom.

* * * * *

Anger has a way of coming out. Mine did, and Dad was an easy target. In rebellion, I openly drank and partied, even daring to come home afterward. Sometimes when we try to punish others, we hurt ourselves much more. And we can't even see that we're doing so. I started steering my whole life downhill. Thinking I was in control of the direction I was going, I gave in to temptations without any recognition of my need for God. *I want to experience all God has for me*, I thought, unaware I was giving myself over to the devil. I rejected the idea of being under my dad's authority—*and protection.* I was ignorant of the truth that my father's authority wasn't based on whether I thought he deserved it or not. I scowled when Dad quoted scripture, "Honor your mother and father that your days may be long on this earth."[3]

Back in college, I threw off former restraints and joined the social scene of the liberated college woman. It was 1963, and the women's movement became mainstream with Betty Friedan's book, *The Feminine Mystique*, and writings of other well-known feminists. This movement provided a receptive channel for all the anger I was experiencing, and I bought into the rhetoric. Along with the sexual revolution and all of the talk about women being "liberated" from their traditional roles, I was an easy recruit.

I used both that and my dad's fall to fuel my rebellious behavior and sought out approval and love in the wrong places. If I had to describe the college girl I became, it would be from the book of

---

[3] See Deuteronomy 5:16, Exodus 20:12.

Proverbs description of a beautiful woman without discretion: a pig with a gold ring in its snout.[4]

To prove my budding liberation, I smoked and drank and partied as much as I could in the mountains of North Carolina and still pass the courses. I was a dark-eyed, dark-haired beauty who even stooped to play a stripper in the college play, *Gypsy.* It was suggestive but not too revealing, and I made sure to invite my parents as well as my aunt and uncle to watch my debut.

I still got As in most of my science classes, but I lived on the edge. Instead of saving my body for that one man I hoped to marry someday, I was deceived in thinking that I would find love through sex. Nowhere had I heard about the negative effects that having sex without commitment would have on a woman's heart and spirit. If I had, I was ignoring every warning. Trying to be some kind of free spirit led to anything but freedom.

I turned my back on my parents and pretty much on all my relatives. I was the smart one. When I did come home, I was distant and argumentative when it came to disputing my parents', mostly Dad's, beliefs. But only to a point. Dad wouldn't tolerate disrespect, but he no longer deserved any. I felt justified in my anger and in my self-righteousness. They were the problem, not me. I had no qualms about receiving the clothes they sent and asking for money for cigarettes.

* * * * *

After two years, I transferred to the University of North Carolina in Chapel Hill, which carried more prestige and was more challenging. It also included more partying and guys, and more liberalism and feminism.

The ratio of men to women at UNC was ten to one. Was I here for a career or to get a husband? Prior to the sixties, college women were mostly looking for husband material. With the women's move-

---

[4] See Proverbs 11:12.

ment, that was changing. I was pulled between two cultures from two different worlds.

Feminists tended to label most men "male chauvinists," and I put Dad in that category. After all, look how hard Mom slaved at home to fix his dinner and iron his clothes. I didn't realize that she did it out of love and didn't complain, because she did everything out of love for all of us. I never seemed to see Dad's hard labor on the railroad to put food on the table all my life. How did I miss the dirty clothes hung in the closet after coming in from his tractor when he continued his work late into the day to supplement his salary? He never grumbled or complained about his hard labor; it was his way of showing love to his family. The feminist subculture taught me to see only perceived inequities.

I was completely ignorant of the godly makeup of men to want to provide and protect. The typical man of the fifties and sixties was a strong male figure who was expected to be masculine and couldn't be found cooking dinner or changing diapers. I'm not saying that was all good, but the women's movement of the sixties criticized men at the core of their very nature. It pitted women against men, as if we were all in some kind of competitive arena.

The academic world belittled the idea of a good woman staying at home for her children or supporting a successful man. And it rejected the idea of couples working together as one with different roles important to accomplish a purpose. In fact, Betty Friedan's *The Feminine Mystique* even compared the American housewife to a slave in a Nazi concentration camp. Everything was for self, and selfishness was essentially glorified. It didn't matter to us that Friedan, who was representing the noble cause of "liberating" women, was a card-carrying atheist communist.

* * * * *

It was a confusing time for me, because they were attacking the very foundation of our beliefs of a godly order in the family, where men were to love their wives and women were to honor their husbands. We were encouraged to do the opposite. The educated elite knew best. Women were no longer to be helpmates to their husbands, who were head of the family in leadership, protection, and provision. "I don't need a man to take care of me," I defiantly declared.

I was determined not to be thought of as "beautiful but dumb," the way my mother had portrayed herself. I enjoyed being in beauty contests, but I prided myself in my academic ability and my bright mind. I made all As in my biology classes at Western Carolina, but classes were tougher at UNC. When the women's movement came out protesting the emphasis on women's physical appearance, I leaped onto that bandwagon and declared that I wanted to be thought of as more than just a body. However, that didn't stop me from wanting the latest women's fashions, makeups, and hairstyles. I certainly didn't want to be a man.

My dad's words, "You'll reap what you sow," entered one ear and exited the other. And what about him? He was lucky Mom forgave him. I hated when he used the Bible to correct me. God was already fear-inducing and condemning to me, and I didn't want to hear more. I also rejected anything religious, because I thought it wasn't the intelligent, educated answer for my life. After all, my parents only had a high school education. I was the enlightened one. I challenged him only so far, because I still had enough fear not to disrespect him. Yet my heart was critical and judgmental.

* * * * *

To me, God was not personal and close, not someone I prayed to other than at church, meals, and bedtime—and I even gave up those prayers. God was just a punisher of those who do wrong. I had gone up to the altar years ago but had failed in every way to meet the standard I thought I had to reach, so why try? God was the problem, not me.

I made fun of the students who hung around the Baptist Student Union, and I joined the doubters in my philosophy class asking accusatory questions like, "Why does God let all these little innocent children die and these bad things happen?"

Lost in the whirl of my bad behavior was still the woman who wanted to be loved, cherished, cared for, and desirable for marriage. But I pushed the decent men away, shocked them with my irreverent behavior. I smoked and drank openly with the other liberated women and chastised men for opening doors for me.

* * * * *

"You'll reap what you sow."[5] I hated to hear that from my dad. Some of the reaping of what I had sown came while I was in summer school between my junior and senior years. After a raucous spring break in Nassau, Bahamas, I settled down as a serious science student in summer school. I met a student I really cared about, someone who was serious about school, from a nice family, and liked me a lot. We played lots of tennis, saw each other exclusively, and got physically involved as well. I visited his home and met his parents. It was a hot summer with no air-conditioning in classrooms or in the organic chemistry lab. The heat was especially hard to endure. Somehow I didn't realize that I'd missed two monthly periods.

One weekend as I lay in bed in my dorm, unusually severe pain that seemed like menstrual pain, but much worse, started and wouldn't let up. I lay in bed for hours, groaning with the most severe cramps I had ever experienced.

"I have some pain pills," one of my roommates said. I took them, but the pain didn't stop. After more than three hours, I felt the urge to go to the bathroom.

I walked down the hall to the common bathroom. No one else was there.

When I sat down on the toilet, I didn't realize what was happening until I looked into bottom of the bowl and distinctly saw what looked like the specimens I had seen in the science laboratory. But it wasn't a specimen. It was a very small baby.

My breath stopped.

---

5 See Galatians 6:7–8.

LIBERATED BY LOVE

Shock and fear overcame me. Anything I might have yelled or cried out got caught deep inside me.

Should I take it out? What if someone finds out?

Without thinking, I grabbed the handle and flushed the toilet.

The baby swirled so easily, so quickly, into oblivion.

I can't believe what I just did. It's gone. My baby! What will I do now? What will happen? I need medical help.

I silently went back to the room and cried out to my roommate what had happened. It was a silent cry that shook my whole being in agony and terror, but the nightmare had just begun.

The trips to the infirmary and later to the hospital were demeaning. Without giving anesthesia or a painkiller, they roughly pulled out what they said were remaining parts. The attendant said, "There were parts left behind. How did you do this?"

She's accusing me of aborting my baby! Indignant that someone would think I was capable of that, I emphatically denied her accusation. "I didn't do that. I would never do that!"

She, however, saw me as someone who would definitely do that. "You're a science major, so you knew how to do this."

I'm not the person they're thinking I must be.

Shame, a load of tortured emotions, and fear of my parents and others finding out ran through my mind. I was alone except for the one close friend who'd taken me to the infirmary. Questions continued to swirl in my mind as I was given a dilation and curettage procedure at the hospital. I was awake without any pain medication, frightened, and clueless about the effects of a miscarriage. No one told me much of anything. All the organs and systems would have been formed. It was not just a blob.

I wondered if it was a boy or a girl but didn't let myself dwell on those thoughts.

During recovery, I finally had a courteous visit from the young man whom we both assumed was the father. He made a curt offer of condolences and helped pay for expenses. The relationship ended after break when he came back to school and announced that he'd gone back with a former girlfriend. I was devastated. To him, I had just been a fling that he regretted, an entanglement he no longer wanted, a superficial relationship that had no serious potential.

My heart and mind seemed to collide with each other into a heap. How could I have been so stupid? Beside the loss of a baby, I lost what I had dreamed might be a husband. But our relationship and everything about it was no more than a fling.

* * * * *

After the trauma of that summer nonromance and tiny death, I had no one to turn to except my two roommates. We didn't talk about what had happened, but they didn't desert me. *What if I can never have children? Am I healed, or is there some permanent effect?* I couldn't cry or share my feelings. I couldn't go to my parents. Aloneness and rejection were my deepest companions. Waves of sadness swept over me, and I realized that I was dealing with emotions I couldn't understand. As usual, I tried to figure things out by myself without God, parents, or friends. I felt worthless, worse than I had ever felt about myself.

The sexual revolution that was supposed to free women to have sex without guilt or consequences never warned about the emotional and psychological effects, the depression and anger of feeling used, and of broken hearts and dreams. Instead it just encouraged us to just do what felt good.

I was left with confusion and denial of the pain and rejection. And this led me into still deeper deception. Searching for answers, I tried to understand what had happened to my baby and where it had gone. Reading Edgar Cayce, a mystic psychic who delved into all kinds of spiritualism, just added to more deception. Others who believed in reincarnation seemed to give a plausible explanation for the life that was gone. *Everybody has a spirit that lives forever*, I reasoned. *Would God put that spirit into another body? My baby couldn't be gone forever.* Rather than turning around, or getting my life straight—or repenting as the Christians would say—I continued on a downward spiral.

4

You've Made Your Bed

"Candy, do you want to go to the Ratskeller with me?" my roommate pleaded, trying to pull me out of my self-imposed isolation. "I'm meeting a friend—it's not a date. Come on and go with me."

Several weeks after my miscarriage, my feelings still raged all over the place. I was scared that people would find out. But the terrible feelings of emptiness and loss were the worst. I felt worthless. My life and future seemed over.

The last thing I want to do is meet someone. I don't even want to talk to a guy, I thought as I got up and dressed, knowing she was trying to be helpful

The guy was ordering his second beer when we walked in and acknowledged us matter-of-factly between deep draws on his cigarette, hardly cracking a smile, but pleasant enough. Barb introduced us as we sat down. "Don, this is Candy. She's my roommate this summer."

I didn't want to make the effort to get to know him, but after a beer, I felt more relaxed. By the second beer, I found myself engaged in an intellectual discussion about an idea I had from my philosophy of religion class.

"If Jesus came to save us here on earth, what would that mean if life were found on another planet? Would He be their Savior too?" I paused. "Or would there be another savior for that planet?" On and on we went about all kinds of subjects. That was the only time I would have mentioned the name of Jesus to anyone.

The buzz from the alcohol and the conversation felt good and helped me forget the sadness. I didn't mind that he was cynical and rather brooding; in fact, I liked his antiestablishment attitude. I could go tit for tat with cynicism. It gave me an outlet to vent the emotions I was denying. Deep down I carried a heavy load of anger—anger at being let down by men, at the guy who had rejected me just weeks before, at Dad, and at God.

* * * * *

Don and I commiserated in our rebellion and soon became soul mates in protesting the war and in our mutual distance from God and parents. He may have been intelligent, but he was just as mixed up as I was. He degraded his parents, especially his mother. He didn't respect me either. In a drunken stupor at a football game, he pushed me down as I walked away from him in embarrassment. Red flags everywhere. I ignored them all.

I actually thought that marriage would keep me from being rejected again and be the answer to my problems. And Don was willing to marry me. It didn't matter that neither he nor his parents weren't Christian. They footed the bill for his drinking, never missing a cocktail hour at home. It didn't matter that he was a heavy drinker, easily angered, with a violent streak. He was not the man my parents would have chosen for me. But he was a neatly dressed, rising senior with sandy blonde hair and nice features with a moribund sense of humor and wit, and that was unfortunately enough for me.

During our 1966 Thanksgiving break, I married Don in front of a judge, and I didn't even let my parents know. It was a relief to be away from campus and out of the dating scene. I thought I could care about Don and believed that I could make it work. I never wanted to go through the rejection and shame I had experienced the previous summer. Deep down, I wanted someone to love me, but I didn't feel loveable. Instead I was a very angry woman.

We moved into the second-floor apartment of a farmhouse outside of town and finished our last year. At times, we were like rebellious college roommates acting out a love-hate relationship that had nothing to do with covenant marriage. He was just happy to have enough cigarettes and beer.

I wanted a loving husband who adored me, but I didn't even love myself. Maybe he wanted a wife who would respect him. Neither of us got what we wanted. Pretending we were some romantic unconventional characters out of a movie or a novel only lasted while we had a buzz. Reality always followed as disappointment came in a hundred ways. *What have I done? Why?* Questions I never allowed myself to consider.

* * * * *

Don's parents were nice to me, but his mother was highly critical of his dad, who reacted with lots of anger—anger that carried into our marriage through his son. Don could never say anything sincerely positive to me or about me but rather made me the brunt of putdowns. Sometimes, I returned the disrespect back to him. I certainly hadn't been honoring my dad, and now I had no idea how to honor a man. For my birthday, he bought me a plastic flower and thought it was funny. But deep down, I didn't think I deserved much more.

Still hurting from the loss I had so recently experienced, and hoping for some sympathy, I decided to tell Don, "When I was dating that guy last summer, I had a miscarriage in the dorm. It was horrible. I didn't even know I was pregnant." It backfired. All I got from him was more disrespect. With his utter lack of feelings and my inability to express feelings, I was left alone in my pain.

Lashing out at him, pushing him away, I was sorry I had said anything. My anger found its outlet in criticizing him, which caused an even worse reaction. I felt worthless and hated myself even more. I felt I deserved the words he called me, words that I had never heard in my parents' home.

My parents and family did the best they could to accept my new husband, but they were shocked and had to have been hurt. Mom gave me a wedding shower after-the-fact, showing me much more love and forgiveness than I ever deserved.

After graduating from college, we moved to Atlanta, Georgia, where I taught school and he worked for HUD. Now came my biggest self-delusion of all: that this man would suddenly become a responsible, loving husband who valued me, and we could have a happy marriage. But we continued a lifestyle not much different than college students in a rented apartment, living from paycheck to paycheck.

* * * * *

After six months in Atlanta, Don joined the air force to avoid the draft that would probably have taken him to Vietnam, and I stayed to finish out the school year. After he left for basic training in San Antonio, Texas, I found out I was pregnant. I was happy and excited with a vision of family and being a mother. He seemed to be too. I never thought of the baby I lost. I just looked forward to the future, faithfully saved my salary, and made plans with no thoughts of career.

When school was out, I returned to my parents' home for the seven months Don would be in basic. With the past seemingly behind and no longer the college rebel, I was welcomed at my parents, but Dad and I were still distant and had little to say to each other. After falling so low myself, my attitude toward him had changed. Mom was just excited at the prospect of being a grandmother.

I didn't get any money from Don and spent very little on myself—only on bare essentials from what I had saved. I taught myself to knit, determined to make a Christmas present for my husband. After hours of practice, tearing out mistakes and persevering, I finally finished a wool fisherman's sweater with intricate cables. "Look what I made Don for Christmas!" I said as I held up my labor of love. I was also proud of quilted pillows with intricate stitchwork I made for all the family and the baby sweaters and hats I crocheted.

All my thoughts went to being a mother to this baby we were having and the life I was going to have in my marriage, very unfeminist.

* * * * *

It was 1968, and the women's movement had been in full force for over five years, but I was having my first baby and not thinking about a career. I dismissed a chilling dream about my baby dying, unaware of the effect the miscarriage was having. On December 13, after five long hours in hard labor, I gave birth to an eight-pound, seven-ounce baby boy, Mark, and he was amazing! All of my family was excited about the first grandchild in our family—and the first great-grandchild in Dad's family.

I could hardly wait two weeks when Don would come home from basic and see his son. I tried to imagine him in the role of father. Oh, how I wanted him to be as happy and excited about this beautiful son I was so proud of. On his arrival, he couldn't express much more than a kidding remark that Mark looked like Winston Churchill. Later he seemed genuinely happy to be around him and hold him.

When I proudly gave Don the sweater I had knitted as a Christmas gift, he handed me a camera he had bought for himself and used while he was in basic, saying this secondhand afterthought was my gift. He had nothing for his son. This was not the equality and respect I had hoped for. Instead, I felt used and disrespected.

I was embarrassed and hurt. My parents said nothing. The silence said it all. A slap back to reality. *He isn't even thinking about me or our baby. He spent his money on himself and partied while I was here thinking about him and planning for our baby.* I acted as if I didn't care and it was no big deal. The hurt ran deep, but denial was a safer place to go.

I couldn't go to the God of my childhood or my parents. He was still the condemning, unloving God who would punish me. I never prayed or sought God about anything I had done, but back at my parents' home, I saw what I had been missing. The peace, the love, and the respect they had for each other was evident that they had overcome the difficulties of the past and they had made a life together with plans and a future—a home, furniture, flowers, a yard—everything I had taken for granted.

I naively tried to believe my husband would straighten up, and that somehow, all of a sudden, he would become responsible and loving and caring. Telling him what he needed to do didn't help. It just pushed us farther apart. Something was missing from our marriage, but I didn't know what. I remembered hearing my parents' muted discussions before they fell asleep as they shared their day and concerns. I longed for that kind of relationship.

Leaving for Colorado in a Volkswagen bug with my husband and a new baby should have been an exciting adventure, but I fought back the tears as we drove away, not knowing when we would see our family again. Dad's words, "You've made your bed, and now you'll have to lie in it" weren't hateful, but they offered no encouragement for me to improve my situation. He must have felt bad for me, seeing my marriage had no true love and how Don treated me. They would never have suggested I leave him. Staying and making the best of it was the only option. I never talked to them about my situation. I didn't have to.

* * * * *

In the air force in Colorado, our lives continued to be an extension of college life: partying on weekends with no responsibility. This wasn't my idea of what a marriage should be as feminism had portrayed in its revised version. I had scoffed at the portrait of the domineering macho husband whose wife ran around serving him like a slave. What that picture omitted was the truth about a husband's God-given desire to provide and care for his wife as he would his own body[6]—something I could not admit I deeply wanted and needed but didn't deserve. My life had no semblance of the peace, respect, or love I had experienced in my parents' home as a child. The mantra, "I

---

[6] See Ephesians 5:28.

can take care of myself. I don't need a man to take care of me" came back to haunt me.

After Colorado, we were assigned to Anchorage, Alaska, for the remaining three years of his service. With our sixteen-month-old son in the backseat, we drove our Volkswagen beetle up to Vancouver, Canada, and caught the inland ferry to Alaska. I had mixed feelings about going with my husband so far away. I had felt safe and loved with my parents, but not with this man. Nevertheless, my adventuresome spirit was moved to anticipate the majesty of the awesome wilderness before us.

* * * * *

Our cruise along the inland waterway to Alaska took us past the magnificent scenery of the inland waterway of the coast of Canada. What should have brought us closer together only made me feel more isolated and apprehensive. When our bickering led to words, without a warning, I felt the pain of his hard kick to my shin that almost caused me to fall. I grabbed our son and went below to our cabin in embarrassment, anger, and hurt where I burst into sobs.

Where can I go? Who can help me? I was alone with no place to run. The painful knot on my leg incited me with all kinds of visions of revenge. *How could he?* I thought. *If only I had kept my mouth shut and did not say anything.*

He never apologized and asked my forgiveness. Not wanting Mark to witness the fighting, I thought, *I have to make this work*, all the while fuming inside.

With our young son in the backseat, we drove 750 miles on gravel through snowbank-lined wilderness on the Alcan Highway to Anchorage and Elmendorf Air Force Base. The hurt kept coming back. *He never says he is sorry for anything*, I thought, stuffing my feelings as I always did, afraid of starting another fight. The large bruise on my shin had started to turn shades of green. I seethed inside going back and forth between feeling like a victim and wanting revenge. I tried to forget Don's criticism and threats. But they pierced too deeply and continued to beat me down as my mind replayed every scene. It was a long time before I could even speak to him with civility. My main concern was our little boy snuggled in the backseat.

* * * * *

So far away from my home again, without friends, relatives, or God, I was pulled by all kinds of things. The antiestablishment rebellion, the women's movement, the sexual revolution, and the hippie movement that were in full force. Women were burning their bras and refusing to shave their underarms, and marijuana became the drug of choice. I gave limited assent by embroidering peace signs on my jeans and wearing pantsuits to work, but my heart wasn't in it. We took pictures of happy smiles by seasides and mountains, told stories of adventure, and sent them to our parents. My life was a lie to everyone.

Although I wanted to be equal and liberated, I was resentful of Don's refusal to take the lead and the responsibility of father and husband. Feminists were critical of the man who would take charge in a marriage, but I wanted this one to take *some* responsibility. It seemed I was the only mature, responsible one. I resented it and criticized him, seeing myself as morally superior, a feminist delusion that had begun to pervade society. I didn't understand how I was killing any possibility of love that might have grown out of a flawed beginning.

Even with all of the difficulties in my marriage, I was somehow able to present a competent, capable image to the principal who hired me to teach science in the junior high school. Staying home wasn't an option. I wasn't thinking about having a career. My salary was a necessity if we were to afford an apartment at my husband's insistence. Standing before my class, I sweated profusely, trying to hide my insecurity. *If they really knew me and my situation*, I thought. I felt like a victim, but it was the anger that gave me control.

* * * * *

With my husband's affinity for the hippie drug culture and its music, it was only a matter of time before Don got hooked on marijuana. It was illegal, but that didn't deter him—and I joined him, trying to keep the peace, finally giving in after protesting. Afraid everyone would find out, I made no friends at school or anywhere. I was isolated except for a few of his air force buddies who dropped by to smoke with him.

While I tried to maintain a professional image at school, my life at home was an extension of college life: partying on weekends, no responsibility, with parents—now me—paying the bills. His check went for a stereo, music, Volkswagen camper van, beer, cigarettes, and other toys. Without purpose or love, I was angry and felt used, more like a mother. This certainly wasn't the picture of equality and shared responsibility I envisioned in my feminist idealism.

Not even our trips into the Alaska wilderness, skiing, and camping out in our Volkswagen camper brought us closer. Our son, Mark, was a smart and delightful bright spot in our lives—the one thing we agreed on. No one knew my situation. I had no friends. And divorce wasn't an option for a mother and wife in 1970—at least not for me. I felt like a victim with no choice about my lifestyle or friends. The bed I had made was very painful, but I had made it and would have to lie in it.

5

Clashes of Death and Life

We never talked about having more children, but I felt excitement when I missed a period and began having other symptoms. I knew I was pregnant. Mark was three and a half years old. For a brief moment, I felt warm expectation for what I hoped was a little girl. As quickly as they came, those good feelings left. *We are not the normal, loving parents who would happily receive this report. Instead, I have a husband who cares more about dope than his family, someone who wants his wife to take care of him.* I dreaded what was to come.

When I told Don, he got angry, and in the fight that followed, he lashed out and kicked me in the stomach but didn't hit me square as intended. I lashed back but dissolved into the sobs of hopelessness. *How could he do this to his pregnant wife? Why didn't I leave?* were questions I didn't allow myself to answer. Trapped and alone, there was no avenue for discussion or reconciliation. I had nothing but contempt for him.

I hid my situation from everyone and put on a good front to the teachers at school, the neighbors, and a few acquaintances from the air force. The consequences of baring all seemed too devastating, so I remained silent with my broken heart. I told no one I was pregnant, not even my parents.

* * * * *

Abortion wasn't part of the feminist movement when it began with the suffragettes in the early twentieth century seeking voting rights for women. However, it became part of the feminist movement in the early seventies in America along with the sexual revolution and was legal in Alaska in 1970.

When one of the air force couples came over to smoke grass and shared about having an abortion, I was surprised. *They are married!* I thought. *Why have an abortion?* Passing the pipe, the husband proceeded to tell about his wife's recent abortion at Elmendorf air force hospital.

Breathing out a puff of smoke, Ed said, "Yes, we decided we weren't ready for a baby."

I couldn't believe what I was hearing. He was so nonchalant, as if he were talking about choosing not to buy a car.

I looked for his wife's reaction. With a dreamy smile and glassy eyes, she said, "Yes, it didn't take very long, and I didn't have any problems afterward, just a little bleeding."

I tried to remain calm. *She must have felt forced. How could she agree to that!* I didn't say anything.

Even though I had spouted a lot of feminist rhetoric, I never voiced support for abortion. I had never even thought much about it, and yet suddenly in this crisis of my marriage, the option for abortion came to the forefront. I couldn't get over how matter-of-fact and happy they seemed with the choice. I knew my husband was in agreement with their decision and felt pressure to also consider abortion. I said nothing.

* * * * *

In the week that followed, nothing changed. My situation seemed intolerable. I was not thinking of the life within me when I agreed to let Don take me to Elmendorf hospital to see a doctor about an abortion. I was thinking only of my own situation, believing I had no choice. My husband did not want this baby. All the pain I felt from the reality of my situation had turned to numbness. I could hardly believe that it had come to this: *my husband is taking me to get an abortion.* I sat silently as he drove to the hospital. It all seemed like a surreal nightmare. I didn't think about what was going to happen.

I never thought to call my parents, nor did I give any thought about what the Bible said or about the life of the baby. And I did not think or imagine how it would affect me. I was all wrapped up in rejection, pain, and hurt. *My husband doesn't love me. I don't have a choice. What will I do?* I thought. Deception was the avenue, and I didn't see a way out. It seemed as though everything was stacked against me.

My parents would have been horrified. They would have helped me, but I didn't even think about them. I was too afraid to face the consequences of saying no, of being left—alone. Fear and pride was actually the problem, but I was blinded to the truth.

At the air force hospital, even the doctor encouraged me to reconsider. He wasn't for abortion, but neither did he tell me of the possible effects it could have on me. I learned nothing about the emotions I would feel afterward, the effects abortion can have on future pregnancies, its long-lasting psychological effects, and effects on my marriage—even my sanity.

Yet something in me resisted and gave me courage when the doctor asked if I wanted to reconsider. *I don't have to do this. No, I can't be doing this. This isn't really happening.*

"Take me home," I insisted, hoping to call off this terrible plan. When we got home, we had another yelling fight. Isolated from relatives who cared about me and from sensible coworkers, or anyone who would have said, "Don't do this, whatever you have to do, don't," I didn't have the strength to go through with the pregnancy and go against my husband. Leaving and getting away with my son wasn't a remote possibility.

Fear of being left was greater than fear of killing the life inside me. Emotionally beaten down and emptied of resolve, I got into the car resigned to go through with it. I don't know what I was thinking at the time. But I had to turn myself cold and shut off the feelings I had for my unborn baby.

As they prepared to put me to sleep for the abortion, a simple D&C procedure, I kept quiet and didn't protest. I awoke in a room with a lot of women lying in other beds. I didn't know if they'd also had abortions. I didn't ask, didn't want to know. I didn't talk to anyone. Instead of a simple little procedure, I had lost a part of me that I couldn't get back. I felt a vast and empty deadness inside me.

* * * * *

Life went on as usual, but for me, it would never be the same. The little girl I had wanted so badly was gone, and I was left to try to make sense of what I had done. I stared at the hollow look of my eyes as I dressed to return to school the following week. How would I get through the day? There was no joy in my life except for our son. I couldn't smile. I kept working to help pay the bills and buy all the things I thought we needed or wanted. I didn't think my marriage could get any worse, but it did.

My parents even flew to Alaska to visit us once. While they were with us, we maintained civility and had a wonderful time touring together. But afterward, the fighting got so bad, repeatedly disturbing the family next door, the landlord asked us to leave. We found another place off base.

During one fight, he hit me on the forehead, and I hauled off and hit him, giving him a black eye. That was the only time I hit him. The large bruise on my forehead caught the attention of the school counselor.

She asked me into her office, "What happened to your head?"

I lied, "I was in a car accident yesterday and hit my head on the steering wheel." I let no one in. My public life was a pretense, and my private life was a secret.

To keep my sanity, I looked to whatever explanation I could find to explain my abortion and my life in general. I read a book on reincarnation to try to find an explanation. The life I had ended wasn't gone, anything to keep from facing the truth.

* * * * *

After the abortion, I started seeing a psychiatrist on base to find out what was wrong with me. Why was I so angry? Why so unhappy? Naturally, I blamed my husband. Don wouldn't go with me. Where was the independent-thinking feminist who would "take care of herself"? I attended a National Organization of Women meeting once but resisted the temptation to join and move into a more radical feminism with what I thought were mostly lesbians and man-haters. That wasn't for me.

After all the sessions with the psychiatrist, nothing changed. And it didn't seem to help that my husband worked in the psychiatric ward. These were his coworkers. I didn't talk about the abortion. I was too ashamed. I was in denial about it. I needed answers.

Don and I didn't even acknowledge the death of our own child. No grieving, not even a mention about what had happened. But anger came out in countless little ways, and our relationship grew worse, our fighting more frequent and intense.

* * * * *

Before he was discharged in 1972, I got pregnant again without any thought of contraception. Replacing my lost child wasn't a conscious decision, but years later, I heard an explanation about women who have had abortions getting pregnant again right away. This time, I had no pretense that my husband would be supportive.

My situation hadn't improved. If anything, it was worse. He assumed I would have another abortion. With no change in my husband or marriage, I felt I had no choice but to get another abortion before leaving Alaska. In my hopelessness, I didn't fight. But why again? After the horrible experience the first time? Years later, I realized once you cross that line, like any other crime or sin, it becomes easier. And I had not repented. Instead, I was a lost sinner who was still depending on myself rather than God.

This time, he took me to a private physician and sat in the waiting room of the Anchorage hospital with our four-year-old son while I was put under for the early term D&C abortion. Again, nothing was said of any emotional, psychological, relational, or spiritual effects I could possibly experience.

Abortion was still experimental and not even legal in most of the United States. However, it was touted as a right for women, that they should not be forced to have an unwanted child. I didn't know at the time, but I was in the majority of women who have abortions who feel pressured and would choose differently if someone would have encouraged them to keep their baby. But there was no one. I told no one what I was doing. Instead, I chose to please my husband over the life of my child. If ever I could have attacked him, it was then. Yet I said nothing. I was stone-cold.

My second abortion wasn't as difficult. But I was horrified at myself. I actually felt relief. *No! I don't want to feel this way!* I was shocked at my simply going through the motions. Numbed feelings got me through the day. I was becoming someone I hated. I tried to fix myself by reading books on spiritualism, metaphysics, and reincarnation. Everything but turn to God or my parents in this time of need. To agree to abortion, I had to deny what I knew as a woman, as a mother, to be true: I had ended the lives of two of my babies. At times, I felt I was losing it. The psychiatrist didn't help me.

I became more distraught and angry than ever. I stopped smoking pot with my husband, and the fighting got worse. One acquaintance observed that if we didn't get help, we would end up killing each other. I resented everything Don did, especially when he grew and sold marijuana, which was illegal in Alaska at the time.

The women's movement would soon have the court case they'd been chomping at the bit for—*Roe vs. Wade*. As with everything else having to do with abortion, this case was based on lies and deception, and I had two of the earliest legal abortions, both done safely in hospitals by doctors. I was asleep and experienced no pain, and I never had horror stories from abortion clinics. For me, the horror came later in thousands of ways.

* * * * *

We left Alaska in June 1972 in our VW camper with our son and returned to the lower forty-eight with a few beat-up pieces of furniture, no savings, and lots of pain. Even the good times were hard to talk about.

While we relocated, we stayed with my parents. Back around people who cared for me, I tried to have hope for our marriage. Out of the air force, finally away from the military atmosphere, I hoped things would change. I wanted to have love for him, unaware of the effect the abortions were having on my feelings and on every part of me.

I never let myself think about the babies I had lost. I never grieved. I was in complete denial, but my whole outlook was affected. I wanted to believe he would get a new job, and we would start a new life. One minute, I was hopeful, and the next, I was in the pit of despair. My future happiness was so dependent on my husband; I didn't even know who I was.

* * * * *

While staying at my parents, it became more obvious that family wasn't important to Don, nor was getting a job. At that time, I didn't realize the effect marijuana was having on his motivation to take care of a family, have work, and have a plan for our future.

Shortly after moving in with my parents, I found out I was pregnant—again. This time, I announced it right away. *I'm going to have this baby! No abortion!* Although not planned, I was so happy and so was my family. Don and I had no discussion about abortion. Even though miscarriage is more common after abortion, I never feared that anything would happen. *I want a daughter, even if he doesn't! This is going to be the girl I have always wanted!*

"Why is Don going down in the woods?" Mom asked.

"Guess he likes to get away alone." I pretended I didn't know he was smoking marijuana when he should have been looking for a job. Later Dad had to fix the lawn mower he broke.

Mom let me know, "Don was too rough on it. He acted mad that he was mowing the lawn."

Oh no. I felt the anger rise in me, then the embarrassment. *Can't he appreciate their hospitality? We're never going to fit in. He hasn't changed. Nothing has changed.*

My family was happy for another grandchild. I pretended that Don and I were together, but I was alone in my excitement. We never shared our feelings about it, never even argued about the coming baby, but we had plenty of other things to disagree about.

Finally, he got a job with the State of North Carolina in public administration. Everyone was relieved. *Maybe now we'll settle down and live a normal life,* I thought, still wanting to think my husband could change himself if he wanted to.

We moved to the town of Lumberton, North Carolina, into a rented house and began civilian life. The coming baby didn't bring us closer, but our home was more peaceful as I made plans for our new addition. He made friends at work I never met, friends who drank and smoked pot with him. I painted the nursery, made curtains, and bought used furniture—alone. And I read the natural childbirth books—alone, convinced he didn't want this child. I was shut off from him most of the time, going through the motions.

After living with my parents, I wanted to return to the God-and-church life I had known as a child, so I took Mark to church. Finding a back pew, I shushed my very active five-year-old, waiting for the service to start. The organist began playing at the front, and before I could grab Mark, he jumped to his feet, making a loud commotion on the wooden seat with his clunky dress shoes. I cringed when he said in a loud voice during what was a quiet time of meditation, "When's God coming on?" That was our last visit.

* * * * *

On May 13, 1974, with huge magnolia trees in bloom outside the hospital, Don drove me to the hospital in labor. I gave birth to a beautiful eight-pound, fourteen-ounce baby girl. Crystal was my long-awaited blessing. I was euphoric. Even Don seemed to be happy and relieved seeing we had come through it so easily. *Maybe he does care,* was but a fleeting thought.

When we got home, I wrote a letter to Crystal telling her how much I loved her and had wanted her. What a blessing she was.

Our lives were more tranquil during this time, except when I protested his going out to drink and party with people from the office. "Why do you need to go out drinking? You have a family now." The arguing escalated. His temper flared, and he came at me—pushed me down while I was holding Crystal, only a few weeks old. My heart ripped apart. Nothing had changed. Why didn't I leave? I would later ask myself. I felt trapped like a victim *and* held on to a lie, a fantasy that my husband was going to change. That may have been possible if I had known the power of prayer and been trusting God for my husband. But I was a long way from God. I *did* care deeply about the effect this fighting was having on our son—and now on our daughter.

* * * * *

When Don found out he was getting transferred to Raleigh, I hoped this move would be our ticket into a normal middle-class suburban life. We rented a home in a middle-class neighborhood, and I chose to be a stay-at-home mom. I couldn't bear to leave our daughter with a sitter and wanted to be involved in Mark's first year at school. Since my brothers and I had been dedicated to the Lord when we were babies, I asked Don if we could do the same. The Sunday we joined my parents in their church for the dedication ceremony was an answer to my heart's desire, but I had little confidence Don would honor his part of the commitment. As we answered "I will" together, pledging to raise the children to know Jesus, I thought, *I will keep these vows even if he never does.*

I knew Don would have preferred I get a teaching job. Still nursing Crystal, I enjoyed the wooded backyard and watching her first steps, trying to make all this work. Somewhere in my decision was the deep-down determination that I never wanted to sacrifice my children for career or finances again or please my husband as I had done in Alaska when it came to the children—never.

When news came that our rent-to-own house was being put on the market to sell, I was devastated we couldn't buy it. It would have been a perfect starter home, but we didn't have the finances and qualification to buy it. Feeling the anger rise toward my husband, I blamed him for our financial situation because of his smoking and drinking habits. We also didn't have my check to factor in. I didn't care.

I had made the best choice for the children, and I couldn't leave them, especially Crystal, to teach school. I had tried to make it work, skimping and doing without furniture, except for two foam chairs, a small dinette table and chairs, two beds, chests, and a baby crib. After nine years of marriage, that's all we had materially.

We moved into an apartment by the freeway. If that were any indication of the condition of our relationship, it couldn't get any worse.

But it did.

6

Losing Control

My world became smaller in every way as I turned inward to try to understand the unhappiness I felt and to figure out the reason for my discontent. Nowhere to go, no one to turn to. *I can make this work*, I told myself. Instead of being critical of my husband and starting fights, I tried to keep the peace for the children's sake. Unable to face the real problem I was having after the loss of two children, I endlessly asked, *What is wrong with me? Why don't I have any feelings for my husband? I don't want to be angry all the time.* My inability to feel love or respond sexually, as well as control my anger troubled me. It didn't help that every day he was around another woman who probably thought he was amazing and witty. Finding out that they smoked marijuana at lunch together with another employee only added to my torment.

My outlook was so dismal, I had to force myself to get up and take care of my children and carry on a normal life. Mark was a bright first grader, and Crystal was an active toddler who needed a lot of attention. I didn't realize that I had become so dependent on my husband, even for my happiness and my future. I had become exactly what the feminist hated. Whether dependent or independent, I hadn't found love, peace, or happiness in my life.

Desperate to find answers and gain control of my life, I turned to psychology and to my own reasoning. I could figure this out. After all, we were told that abortion was no big deal. It was just a simple procedure, so something else must be causing my feelings of anxiety, anger, and depression. I didn't drink or take pills like many women do to kill the pain. No more alcohol and marijuana for me.

If I could figure out the problem, I could change myself. My mind endlessly reviewed my situation. As I analyzed myself, psychology told me that my problems must be coming from my childhood and the things that happened to me, things my parents said or did that caused me to go down this path, so I dug into my past.

Up came all the things that must have destroyed me. "She looked like a boy," my mom had often said as she described my boisterous behavior. Dad had been too domineering, because Mom didn't think she was worth much, saying she was beautiful but dumb.

I also thought that some terrible thing must have happened to me that I didn't remember, something down in my subconscious to make me so angry and unhappy. And it was easy to put the blame on my dad for his moral fall.

But contrary to all this, almost fifteen years had given me a different perspective, especially when I compared my husband to my dad. Now I wanted a man like Dad, despite his faults, who would lead his family and want to provide. My mind went from one answer to another, never finding the truth. Instead of finding any permanent answers, I found confusion.

* * * * *

What I failed to ask was the obvious. Why was I staying with a man who was so abusive and had taken me to get two abortions? Why couldn't I tell anyone about my secret—our secret? Trapped in a tormenting dilemma, I was unable to expose my perpetrator—to tell what was happening to me. Then I would have to face what I had been a part of—the horrible secret I could not face. Instead, I tried to deal with all the effects without ever facing the truth. I lived a lie. I couldn't see anything positive in my life except my children.

I fell out of touch with practically everyone from the past, even my relatives. What would people think if they knew the truth about me? Analyzing my situation only led to deeper hopelessness

54

and sadness. Common social graces escaped me. The kid's behavior was undisciplined. I neglected the training they needed with endless distractions. Preoccupation with things that hadn't happened—negative things—dominated my mind and seemed to be insightful truths about my problems. Everything except packing up and taking the children as far away as I could go.

Comparing myself to others didn't help. The women who married each of my two brothers had husbands with successful careers, who cared about their children and loved them. They had nice homes, cars, and clothes. When I was with them, I was in a world I could never imagine for myself—a home with a loving husband, nice yards, dinners together, eating out, a vacation at the beach, plans, and a future—love.

Instead of being able to praise anything that Don may have done well or show him respect regardless of his failures, I could only think of the negatives. The concept that I was to give Don unconditional respect just because he was my husband was alien to me. He certainly didn't deserve it and hadn't earned it. On and on I could go. "You don't care about us at all. All you do when you come home is smoke grass and get stoned. You even smoke at lunch with Marsha. I can't believe it. That's all you care about. I thought you were going to be responsible," I spewed when I could hold it in no longer. Most of the time, he escaped with marijuana, glued to his headphones and music—unless I pushed harder. After the crying and the yelling, I felt guilty and hated myself.

He reacted with threats that sometimes ended in physical intimidation. On some level, I thought I deserved his treatment. He never threatened to kill me, but I felt like dying more than once. I often felt dead inside and only went through the motions of living.

* * * * *

Isolated from everyone, I taught myself to sew and made outfits for Crystal. I only went out to the grocery store or to take the children to the apartment pool, where Mark swam like a duck. But I had drifted far from the popular beauty queen I was my senior year in high school. I had no friends, not even acquaintances, and I was ashamed to talk to anyone in the apartment complex. They had to have heard the fighting. On rare visits to my parents, I pretended everything was all right, just as I always had.

Crystal was practically my whole life, my sole contact for most of the day before Mark came home from first grade. Unaware that my overprotectiveness was a reaction from losing two babies, I spent my day giving her all my attention, still nursing her in the evenings. I played with her, and we walked to the playground. For that time, I was a happy mother with a beautiful daughter.

In one of Don's fits of rage, he threw a radio out the second-story window of our bedroom onto the concrete walk. He didn't seem to care what the children saw or heard when he reached the point of exploding in what I saw as an immature acting out. I never saw my goading him being a problem and had no understanding of the gut reaction those flight-or-fight male hormones and adrenalin were having on his male makeup when he was attacked. But he knew how to intimidate me, control me with his anger. To get away from me, he would smoke grass in the bathtub with his headphones on. I disliked everything he liked: his music, his marijuana, his habits, and his friends. Then the guilt would drive me to try to make peace, to apologize, and to want to start over. It was a terrible cycle.

How odd I had once been the little performer in elementary school and the church plays, the brave explorer on my pony, the girl who wasn't afraid of the devil himself. Now fear was my companion.

* * * * *

Determined to make a change in my life, I started seeing a psychiatrist to find out what was wrong with me. *If only we could go together.* I asked him, but he wouldn't go. I wanted answers, and surely this doctor could help. So once a week, I drove alone to my appointment.

I didn't dream or remember dreams very often, but one I clearly remembered I told to my psychiatrist. In it I lived in a beautiful home with a husband who loved me. I was proud of him and happy.

Friends came for coffee; we talked about our children. Part of that dream was going to church. And on another visit, I blurted out to the psychiatrist, "What I need is a Savior," speaking of Jesus. I didn't know that psychology does not recognize that we are spiritual beings made in God's image; we're more like animals with high-level thinking abilities able to make ourselves better. What a lie.

I wanted our children to be raised in the church. We had dedicated both our children in my parents' church, and I wanted to keep the promise to raise them in the faith. But we never made it together to another church. I blamed Don for not leading our family, even though he was not a Christian and his parents had never taken him to church. I felt separated from God, guilty and unworthy, not knowing how to get back to God, caught up in a never-ending circle of anger, numbness, and depression with little feelings of love or happiness.

Seeing the psychiatrist didn't seem to be helping, but I never opened up about what was really going on. I didn't know how. I read self-help psychology books, and each week, I would drive the sixty-mile roundtrip, desperate to get answers, believing a revelation would come from this educated man who must have all the answers. Here was a man who had a great life and was the kind of man I should have married. I compared him to my husband who was a failure in my eyes. Don never went with me.

My psychiatrist was a behavioral modification specialist. During my hour sessions, I talked about whatever came to mind, never feeling any better. He didn't give me advice, just sat and listened. Looking back, I presume that I was supposed to figure out what was wrong with me, not realizing how futile that was. How could someone whose mind was so screwed up ever fix herself? Many years later, I came across a scripture that settled it for me: Jeremiah 17:9 said, "The heart is deceitful above all things, and desperately wicked: who can know it?" (KJV). I became more confused the deeper I tried to delve into understanding myself. The help the psychiatrist offered could not change my heart, only attempt to change my outward behavior, my thoughts, and my emotions—not heal me. I deceived myself, so I could deceive him too.

Psychiatry deals with feelings, but I couldn't explain my feelings. I didn't know what I was feeling or what I should feel. My feelings were always changing. I told him I had abortions, but that was all. Nothing seemed to mean anything to him. Abortion, in his profession, wasn't anything traumatic. After all, it was legal. It was for the best, so I couldn't be having any problems from abortion. And he apparently thought the same way. I didn't know I was still in denial, and this guy didn't help me get to the true root of my problems.

Confused and alone, desperate and hopeless, as I drove the familiar road to my appointment one morning, I was frightened by the thought that I should turn my car into an oncoming truck. Gripping the steering wheel tightly, I fought the temptation to end it all. "No! I love myself. I love my children! I love myself, I love my children!" I shouted over and over.

* * * * *

"Come on and get the kids. We're going for a ride," Don instructed me as though he had some mission in mind. It was Saturday morning, and he was angry at me. That's when I saw he had strapped on his hunting knife. Fear turned me numb. A few evenings earlier, I had been frightened by a scene on a TV program when a woman had been stabbed with a knife and lay dead in a pool of blood. *She looks like me*, I thought. "That looks like me," I spoke loudly. *That* is *me*, I thought. *A premonition?* Then fear.

This can't turn into another hate-spewing yelling match, I thought. Afraid of what might happen, I said nothing. Trying not to appear alarmed, I walked to the VW van in the apartment parking lot, carrying Crystal, who was just past a year, followed by Mark, our six-year-old. Climbing in the van with the children, I sat in the back holding Crystal, feeling a need to protect the children and staying as far away from my husband as possible. He began driving without a word. I had no fight-or-flight instinct left in me, just numbness. I wondered, *Where is he going? What is he going to do?* I stared out the window watching the leaves flickering in the breeze. Seeing the bright sunny day caused a calmness to come over me.

58

The van slowed down and pulled to the side of the road. Bracing myself for what might happen, I was relieved when Don turned around and said in a stern voice, "That's where you are going to end up if you don't pull yourself together."

I stared at the large facility before us—the state mental hospital in Raleigh, North Carolina. Something rose up in me. "No, I'm not," I rebuffed him. *He's trying to scare me. With our children, how can he do this and threaten to put me in this place?*

I hugged Crystal tightly as he drove away, relieved for the moment. We rode back without a word. He had never threatened me with a knife, but for the first time, I was afraid he might kill me. *What a coward. He is nothing.* In my mind, I envisioned how I would defend myself, what I would do to him. It wasn't a pretty picture. The children were thankfully unaware of the situation.

This gave me another reason to reject my fantasies in favor of believing I was in an impossible situation that could not be fixed. My world, except for my children, had become more and more hopeless. The anger gave me a feeling of being in control, and that's what I felt I was losing.

* * * * *

After all my visits to the psychiatrist, I became more confused and isolated. And though Don never exhibited the knife again, I began to fear he would kill me. Without telling me anything, my husband called my psychiatrist and arranged for me to be admitted to the psychiatric ward. I went along without an argument. I gave up fighting, gave up the anger and whatever control I thought I had over my life.

When will I be home again? Am I losing my mind? Who will take care of the children?

He ripped me away from my children without a word. I said nothing. I hadn't even weaned Crystal completely. My heart agonized. *What are they thinking? Do they feel deserted?* Fearful thoughts bombarded my mind. *I don't trust Don with the children. He's impulsive and might hit Mark in a fit of temper. And I am certain that he's resent-ful of the attention I give Crystal. He might hurt her.* I said nothing.

The attendant showed me to a small room with two single beds. A young woman sat on one bed, not acknowledging me at all.

"Don't try to talk to her," the nurse cautioned. "She needs to rest and has just taken her medication."

Both her wrists were bandaged. *She tried to kill herself.* I talked anyway. No response.

They gave me some medication.

I had no one to talk to and had no access to a phone. By this time, I was certain that some trauma in my childhood, repressed and hidden in my subconscious, was the cause of my problems, and if I could just figure that out, I would be healed. When an attendant came in to write down my information, I fabricated a story I had come to believe and even made up things as I went along.

Greater than my fear for the children was my fear that I might never get out of here. On top of that grew the fear that I really was going crazy and would completely lose my mind. The medication relieved the anxiety, and my mind went into neutral.

My husband didn't come to see me. I talked to him once. "What about the children?" His mother had come and stayed with the children, but she became so frustrated that she left, so he called my mother for help. She never spoke to me about it.

I talked to no one. I saw women like the anorexic girl starving herself, the OCD woman who continually washed her hands, and the one who wore a football helmet out of fear she would fall. No one talked to me. I saw my regular psychiatrist a couple of times, but mostly I just took their pills, sat around, and waited to get out.

One day my doctor came with some large cards with inkblots. Ah, the Rorschach test I'd read about. Fear gnawed at my insides as I looked at the gray inkblot. It was creepy. I searched for something to say. "A bat." I lied. It looked like a demon or something evil.

The images on the second card gave me a jolt.

The gray and red splotches were clearly evident to me. Without hesitation, pointing to the larger gray areas, my science training saw a familiar shape, "The gray part is a pelvic bone. That's a pelvis. And those"—pointing to the red areas—"are blood."

What would they find was wrong with me? Am I crazy?

Another card that was similar drew the same response. Again, the red splotches were blood. *Abortion*, I would not allow my mind to think. I felt nothing. Whether by habit or by inability to feel, I didn't know. After that I was put in a different place with more serious-looking cases. A few days later, I was back in the first section wondering if I would ever get out.

* * * * *

Finally, after two weeks, I was discharged. I found it strange that the psychiatrist said I shouldn't have to disclose my hospitalization if I applied to teach again. Maybe I wasn't crazy. That was good news, but I was certain teaching wasn't in my future.

Two weeks had seemed like an eternity. I was numb when I saw my husband, whether from the drugs or from still-dead emotions. I wondered if I would ever feel anything again. The children were in the car. As I smiled and greeted them, trying to act normal, I reached for Crystal. She seemed distant, almost as if she didn't recognize me. Sadness gripped me. *Will things ever be the same?* There was a pit even deeper than the one I had been living in, and I didn't want to go there. I was scared, shaky, and numb, but I was out.

We stopped by the grocery store on the way home. *I'm supposed to be able to buy groceries? I can hardly think.* Trying to focus, not knowing what we needed, I went up and down the aisles making the effort. Would I even be able to take care of my children? My mind, which had once been so bright, seemed to have failed me.

Many years later, I would come to understand that a short psychotic break is one of the many effects women can have from abortion. The list of effects is a very long one, and unknown to me at that time, I experienced most of them. Not one person, professional or otherwise, ever warned me of any of these effects.

61

7

Surviving the Aftermath

It happened yet again. A few weeks after being discharged from the hospital, I found I was pregnant. *Oh, no. How could I be?* I couldn't tell my parents or Don's. Somehow I had managed to keep things together—barely. I told only him and the psychiatrist, and I hoped this psych guy would give me input, but as usual, he only sat and listened. They both assumed I'd have another abortion. My third. Besides all our issues, situations made it obvious that Don was involved with his secretary. Hope looked impossibly lost.

"I would also like to have my tubes tied while I'm having the abortion," I said to the doctor's assistant without any emotion, determined I would never have another pregnancy. I wasn't prepared for the feelings of sadness. *Another loss*, I thought, *to add to everything else.*

Why did I keep getting pregnant? was a question I didn't ask. I heard years later that women who have had abortions often get pregnant right away with the desire subconsciously to replace the lost child. I didn't think about my baby at all. Was it to save my marriage? I couldn't see a way out. I walked in like a prisoner going to the executioner. Resigned. Hopeless. I was completely sedated. My husband waited. Everything was sterile, painless, and smooth—*but not for my baby.* This time, something was different: I dreamed I was going through what I thought were the flames of hell. It was very real, and the thought of dying and being eternally punished and away from my children was horrifying.

Afterward, thankful to be awake and see my children again, I shook off the fear. Yet my mother's heart knew that abortion was wrong. Thirty-two and I would never have another baby. My tubes were cauterized. No offer from my husband. More emotions denied, more sorrow and pain unexpressed—stuffed down again.

I couldn't call my parents and tell them what I'd done. I didn't have a friend to talk to nor did I have anyone else to confide in. I had told my parents I was having my tubes tied, to which my dad objected, "You're still young enough to have other children if you get married again." *They think I'm going to get a divorce.* Maybe they were just hoping. *At least I will never go through the horror of abortion again.*

* * * * *

In the months that followed, things deteriorated to even more irreparable depths. In July of 1976, we made a disastrous trip to Pennsylvania to visit his relatives. It was obvious that he was done with me and our marriage and made no pretense with even small considerations. Hostile and angry, his temper flared when Crystal was crying. He slapped her on the thigh hard, leaving a large red mark. I seethed to the point my anger felt scary. We hardly talked the entire trip. He was directing his anger toward the children—our two-year-old daughter.

It wasn't long after our disastrous trip that an argument escalated to physical danger. With little provocation, he chased me out of the apartment. For the first time I ran. I ran, knocking on doors for help. "Is anybody home? Please let me in! Call the police!" No one opened a door. He gave up, and I returned to the apartment after the police had come. That was the end.

Divorce brought relief from an oppressive man as my feminist side had learned well, but not from the effects. It brought fear that kept me from feeling I was free—finally. I struggled with feelings of remorse and chastised myself for it. How could I feel bad about his leaving? I should be glad? But we were married for ten years. A part of me—the part I hated—was gone. Now, who was I? What I had feared and dreaded for so long had happened. I was alone.

No time or money for a psychiatrist, I had to work. Miraculously, with only a few weeks before school started, I was hired to teach high school science and math. How I was going to manage, I didn't know. Driven by fear and the need to provide, I had overcome the biggest hurdle and would be back in the classroom in the fall. *How will I manage? How can I do this? Teaching and the children?*

My family thought this divorce was for the good. Unbelievably, no matter how bad things had been, I suffered a loss. Rejection and betrayal were worse than death.

I felt totally alone except for two very needy children. The only salvation was that my parents hadn't rejected us. As undisciplined and hurting as my kids were, and with my own history of rebellion and disrespect, Mom and Dad still opened their arms to us and never stuck their fingers in my face with an "I told you so." We had a place to go on weekends and holidays—a place to get away and rest, a place to be loved.

* * * * *

Walking into first period high school physical science class that first morning, I tried to smile confidently. Going through the motions, I counted every minute 'til the bell rang. Thankfully the other physical science teacher was helpful and encouraging. I relied on my outgoing personality and natural teaching ability to get me through, but I was maxed out on the stress scale.

My family was about 160 miles away, but even the three-hour trip in my VW bug was a huge ordeal. Pulling the car over, I screamed, "Mark! Stop teasing your sister! Crystal, stop paying attention to him, and both of you stop fighting. I'm going to have a wreck." Wherever I took them, I was always fearful of how they would behave. I felt so helpless and guilty. *What a failure I am as a parent*, I thought. *How does he get to just walk away?*

It wasn't hard to see that Mark was angry from our situation. When the children were with their dad, all kinds of thoughts tormented me about their safety and exposure to drugs and to another woman. Even with all the anger I was experiencing, I didn't want to keep them from seeing him.

* * * * *

Not surprisingly, the stress started affecting my health. I began having serious abdominal and intestinal pain, weakness, and nausea. I would wake up in the middle of the night, writhing in pain. X-rays of the large intestine and upper digestive revealed no reason for the pain. Doctors thought it was an irritable bowel attributed to the stress in my life and didn't prescribe any medication. Eating caused a lot of pain and discomfort. Sometimes just water would send me writhing.

Too tired to cook, I stopped at a McDonald's on the way home from school with the children. My intestines had been hurting, and I hadn't eaten much all day. I ordered a chocolate milkshake, hoping to keep up my weight and energy. I took a few fast sips, then felt the familiar cramping and sharp pain with nausea. I heaved the milkshake and whatever down to bitter yellow bile. This scene repeated itself more than I cared to admit.

What is wrong with me? I have never experienced abdominal pain from stress, even during the most difficult times in my marriage. I have always had good health. I calculated the factors on the stress charts that applied to me: divorce, new job, finances, and both children in school and daycare. I was off the charts! And those were just the outward things.

* * * * *

"Ms. Walker, this is your son's school. I'm calling to let you know that Mark had an episode in the classroom and ran out of the building into the woods." I was speechless.

"I can't leave my classroom," I said with panic in my voice. "Is there no one who can go look for him?"

After the teacher found him, I had a conference with the principal. They put Mark in a classroom for emotionally disturbed children. He would even be taken to school in a taxi. I could do nothing but agree and accept their decision, but I couldn't accept this as something permanent.

Mark's teacher told me, "He is a leader and will influence others to follow him in whichever way he goes, good or bad."

Mark had watched his dad lose control, throw things at me, and threaten me. He had also witnessed his mother disrespect and demean his father, something I regretted later. Irony of ironies, at home I was dealing with the same kind of problems as at school: out-of-control children and ineffective or divorced parents.

Giving my son the love, discipline, and guidance he needed to grow into a man was beyond my capabilities. I couldn't be both mother and father. Being a good mother was even beyond my reach. I was so wounded—so was he. Reaching his heart to assure and love him in our situation wasn't possible when it took every ounce of energy to go through a day that brought challenges pulling me in every direction. Sharing my burden wasn't possible—I was alone with no help from their dad.

* * * * *

When Mark angrily jumped out of the car at a busy intersection on a four-lane highway, I frantically followed him, trying to coax him into the car. He was out of control. I enrolled him in baseball and the YMCA for swimming classes. Nothing lasted very long. My heart ached for my son, but I had no answers. His behavior was also an issue at school.

His teacher suggested I take him to a child psychiatrist. Hoping for some help, I agreed. The first appointment, the psychiatrist asked him to draw something from that day at school. He carefully drew a pizza he'd had for lunch. Mark was gifted in art as well as reading and other subjects. He played a little basketball with the psychiatrist and was asked to wait outside while he and his staff went into their office.

Wanting to hear what they were saying, Mark crouched outside the door.

When we started home, he was very angry and told me he had overheard them laughing hysterically and saying, "He drew a pizza! He drew a pizza!" He refused to go back, and I didn't have the energy or will to continue. Another failed attempt.

My brother, who was married with three children, called and offered to take Mark. Sadness gripped my heart. *There's no way I can give up on my son.* I knew he needed a dad or at least a man in his life—a good man. He wasn't listening or obeying me. But I stubbornly held out, overcoming the sickening, sinking feeling in my stomach.

"No, I can't do that, but thank you for being willing." At this point, I even wondered if a bad dad is better than no dad at all. That thought didn't get much traction!

* * * * *

The stress also was affecting me. Unable to sleep, I tossed in bed with abdominal pain that wouldn't go away. It was tormenting. I picked up a book by Norman Vincent Peale, *The Power of Positive Thinking*, which had some quasi-religious precepts in it. The book mentioned God, and I was seeking help in any way I could.

As I fell asleep, I felt a distinct tug. I was suddenly in a beautiful green pasture and felt peace and the most wonderful feeling of love, love for others I had never felt before. It seemed so real. I had never felt that kind of love before, neither for or from anyone else. But I wanted to go back to my children so they could be with me too. The green pasture and the feelings that went along with it did not seem like a dream. I rarely dreamed.

When I left that beautiful place, the darkness and pain came back over me, but the impression remained. I tried to make sense of it. *Perhaps this was some kind of vision God gave to encourage me.*

It seemed so real. Could I have left my body? What did it mean? Was I dying?

* * * * *

My second year teaching I transferred to a junior high closer to my apartment. Once again, I was blessed with a team teacher who covered for me and shared in planning lessons. She even kept my children for me to go on a cruise with my family to the Bahamas. I swam, dined, and danced like a princess—a life I could not otherwise dream of. I felt like Cinderella, knowing the life I would go back to.

I was thinner than I had ever been and always carried the underlying feeling of weakness, with a slight fever at times and soreness in my right lower abdomen. *Can this be from anxiety or nervousness?* I thought, remembering Mom's family tendencies. Nothing made sense.

After three years, the children's dad moved to Pennsylvania with his new wife, his former secretary. She had divorced her husband, and she and Don were gone—out of our lives. No doubt, the child support would probably stop. I wanted the children to keep their relationship with their dad, but every time they were with him, I agonized 'til they returned.

My intestinal problems, abdominal pain, and attacks grew worse. I thought, *If I had some support from my family, maybe the stress would be less and this problem would get better.* After three years, I handed in my resignation, and we moved in with my parents 'til I got a job.

* * * * *

Instead of the pain improving after moving in with my parents, it got worse. So did the vomiting. I was unable to do anything but go from bed to couch. My parents were more than alarmed. I couldn't feed my children, help Mom clean, or anything. Nothing I ate would stay down, so I avoided food altogether. Getting out of bed and getting dressed was about all I could do. Even standing up was difficult

69

without nausea and vomiting. My weight dropped to 104 pounds, and my large frame protruded like a concentration camp victim.

How am I going to find an apartment and get a job before school starts? I thought, feeling weak and helpless.

I made a doctor's appointment to have more tests. The results of a follow-through X-ray were shocking, yet a relief.

Pointing to a small white line on the X-ray through a six-to-eight-inch section of intestine called the ilium, the doctor gave me the news: "The walls of your intestine are so inflamed that the opening is only as wide as a small string. That is indicative of Crohn's disease."

Never heard of it.

"There is no cure. But we can treat it with prednisone, which will relieve the symptoms."

No cure? I went numb. *Incurable.* I couldn't cry for myself even though I wanted to.

"Will I have a normal life?"

"There is no reason why you can't when we get these symptoms under control."

I like that much.

"You'll have to take the medication for the rest of your life."

Kill me now.

At least I had a name for the suffering I had endured for so long. All kinds of thoughts raced through my head on the way home. *Would I die from this? Would I see my children grow up? Do I have a future? What is my life going to be like?*

As I walked into my parents' kitchen with the news and sat down at the table, I was looking for some sympathy. They were relieved—it was treatable. *I just heard I have an incurable disease, and they're happy.* No one in my family had ever had Crohn's disease or even heard of it. *Why me?* I thought. Reading about perforations and fistulas in the *Merck Doctors' Manual*, I confirmed the diagnosis: *Crohn's disease is incurable. People die with this. No, that's not me!* I threw the book into the trash.

* * * * *

Resisting the temptation to feel sorry for myself, I turned in my application to the city-county school system the following week. Getting dressed for my first interview, I was shocked at my face in the mirror. *How thin and small*, I thought. The drive across town was a major effort.

The principal who interviewed me offered me a piece of candy on his desk, making some comment about my thin appearance. Every bit of strength I could muster went into presenting a favorable impression. The next week, he offered me a seventh grade position teaching science.

My parents were so happy, but I was skeptical. Working full time, managing an apartment, and taking care of two children seemed huge and overwhelming—impossible. I never spoke what I was feeling. That would mean giving up. I had to keep going and hope things would get better.

I had literally risen from my death bed for that interview. It was years before I saw how God helped me through this time. Before school started, I had moved out of my parents' home, rented an apartment, and enrolled the children in school. Thankfully, the prednisone gave me more energy as the days went by.

* * * * *

I didn't dwell on the disease or talk about it. Maybe it was denial like everything else that was unpleasant in my life. Each day was a challenge with numerous possibilities of a crisis at any given time. Somehow I made it through each class, home with dinner and bedtime each day.

Crohn's disease was an autoimmune disease said to be exacerbated by stress, and I had plenty of that. I knew there was no known cause for this terrible disease nor was there a known cure. For now, prednisone was the only answer. It helped alleviate the symptoms of a much deeper problem.

It never occurred to me that I was part of the fallout, a victim of the women's movement instead of the liberated woman I had envisioned so many years ago. I hadn't spoke of feminism or expounded its virtues for many years. I was too busy trying to survive the aftermath of the lies I had believed to make sense of what had happened. In the meantime, I carried the pain and grief of the past with no awareness of what was causing my intestines to literally rot inside me.

8

Dad Hits the Nail Right on the Head

Putting my past behind me and my deepest secrets beyond any conscious memory, I managed a shaky start for a new life, glad to be back near my parents and thankful to be working.

Walking into my seventh grade science classroom that first day, I worried about a possible Crohn's attack. *What will I do if I can't make it to the restroom down the hall?* Putting a bucket in the stock room for an emergency, I wouldn't let myself go to the worse scenario—would I have the energy to teach a full year? A month? Or even a day?

Adjusting to managing my apartment, the children, and a full-time teaching job was gradual. Prednisone gave me relief from the severe inflammation, but most afternoons, I plopped down on the couch after a dinner of fast food, unable do anything but rest. A summer of inactivity had left me weak, but the demands of single parenting didn't let up. *At least I'm near my parents now*, I thought.

* * * * *

"Ms. Walker, Mark threw a desk across the room when he got upset today. I've had to put him out of the classroom into in-school suspension," came the call I dreaded. *Not again.* And not knowing what to do would again bring a surge of panic and helplessness. He was ten—three years without a father—and carried a lot of anger.

73

"We don't want the kids to dislike us," Dad told me when I expressed my desperation, hinting for them to help with the discipline. I felt so alone and inadequate to help my son.

On the positive side, Mark was a natural athlete. He loved playing tennis with the adults, but basketball was his passion. He amazed the family with his "globetrotter" tricks, getting lot of praise and positive attention. I was thankful for the respite on Sundays at the family farm. More often than not, we went to church with my parents and stayed Sunday afternoons for tennis. They were my lifeline to normalcy, to anything loving and good. I breathed it in deeply in our brief respites, only to return to the hard realities of being a single mother on Monday morning.

After two years, I enrolled Mark in my school to keep an eye on him, but that didn't take care of the effects of divorce and the absence of a father in our home. Shortly after he began seventh grade, he was put into in-school suspension for fighting with an African American student, almost causing a race riot. I constantly ran interference for his behavior issues and academic work, even doing his homework. When Mark made the JV basketball team, I was proud and hopeful it would be a positive outlet for him. There were no lasting answers for my situation.

Thankfully, Crystal adjusted to our new life easier than Mark, but she still had issues. She soon found out if she felt sick at school, Grandma would come get her. After several times, we put a stop to it. Mom was her new buddy who loved to spoil her. Crystal was my pet too. I didn't realize why for many years. I protested when Mom had a table full of tempting treats that greeted us each visit—to no avail.

* * * * *

Being in my hometown had its advantages, but I compared myself to friends from high school and family. They had lasting marriages, homes, children in little league, friends, and roots in the community. I had no friends and had a past that they could never have imagined. How I longed for that "normal" life that everyone else seemed to have. At thirty-six, objectively looking at my situation was

hard: I had failed at marriage, failed at motherhood, failed econom-
ically, socially, and spiritually. I lived in a small apartment, the sole
provider for my two children, with a few sparse pieces of furniture,
living paycheck to paycheck. For all I had been through, I was still an
attractive woman—thin but not sickly looking.

Taking care of myself and two children at the poverty level
wasn't easy. I joined the growing number of single-mother families
without a father. The early eighties brought in the largest divorce rate
that had ever been recorded—mostly due to women seeking equality and liberation promised by the feminist movement of the sixties
and seventies. Abortion was supposed to free women to reach their
potential, to be that CEO or doctor. I was anything but free.

My lack of confidence and self-worth was evident in many ways,
mostly with the hurt and rejection I felt when my family left me out
of something or when I couldn't afford vacations, a home, or even
eating out. No one knew what I had come through, and I didn't tell
them. Any critical comment from Dad or my brothers caused me to
ache inside, and the tears would flow. Where it showed up most was
my intestines. Spasms and pain would hit, leaving me breathless, and
my stomach would heave long after everything had been vomited up.

* * * * *

I hadn't forgiven their dad either. I didn't want to vent to the
children and make them hate their dad, but it was hard to keep from
showing my anger. It popped up when I couldn't afford the things
they needed. He was getting off too easy! I tried to make my paycheck
stretch to the end of the month. Asking for help was humiliating.

"What has happened to you?" my cousin asked when I showed
no anger toward my ex. "You used to be a fighter and wouldn't have
let him get away with how he's treating you."

*If only she knew. My outgoing personality, adventuresome spirit—
where is it?* Fear had taken its place. I worked hard and never missed
a day of school because of sickness. I *had* to work.

It was hard not to be bitter. With my teacher's salary, I was
barely able to support the children. For the most part, I made it on

my own, paying rent, utilities, and a car payment, as well as food and clothing—all without using credit cards. But this didn't give me the great sense of value and personal worth that feminism had promised in the independence I was supposed to be enjoying!

I sold some things to my parents for extra money for the kids one Christmas and finally threw out the royal blue foam chairs when I was able to replace them with two cheap love seats. *At least they look better.* Trying to ignore that I was in a roach-infested apartment on the east side of town only worked part of the time. Crystal was a latchkey kid who was not allowed to go outside after school, especially after a little girl disappeared and was later found dead in the apartments beside us.

When a teacher at school asked how I stayed so skinny, I said, "You wouldn't want to have what I have to be skinny." At times I felt almost normal, but the painful episodes in the bathroom reminded me I was anything but normal. Surprisingly, I missed very little school. Prednisone was my friend.

* * * * *

For the first time in many years, I had other people in my life. I had acquaintances at work, but no one really knew me—no real friends. I took the children to the beach with our family and even attended a summer oceanography field trip for teachers. For the first time, my children were getting to know their cousins, aunts, and uncles. I even ventured out to date through a video-dating group. The couple who started the business liked me and offered me a free membership if I would be in a TV commercial advertising the group. The commercial was fun, but the dating was disappointing. I hated trying to impress them and sell myself. Years later, I would thankfully acknowledge that I had been protected from a worse fate than being single.

After two years in my apartment on the east side of town, I allowed myself to think about a future that seemed pure fantasy. Truthfully, I wanted to get married again. I yearned to experience the love I had never known. I wanted to know what real love was like, a husband's love. In my dream world, I believed that was still possible. I wasn't confused about my sexuality, but sex had been associated with sin or with abuse and hadn't been experienced like God intended.

This time, I wanted a Christian husband but didn't know how to meet one. I was attractive and friendly, but the diagnosis of Crohn's disease and the issues with my children brought me back to hard reality. My few attempts to date left me discouraged about the possibility of ever finding anyone. More than anything, I didn't want to make the same mistake. I reasoned that with the right man, I could be a good, loving wife.

I also wanted to get back to God—and to church. *Church would definitely be the best place to find a good guy*, I thought. So I dressed the kids in new Sunday outfits, and we visited a nearby church. Sitting in the pews with two antsy children, I felt completely awkward and out of place, acutely aware of how we didn't fit in the congregation. The middle-class couples and families were in a different world from us. *What man would want us?* I went back to our little apartment like Cinderella going back to the hearth in ashes and rags. I put up a good front, but beneath was a broken, beaten down woman who was dragging around a past that was too much to bear. I didn't know that God took my tentative, fearful hope of being loved, of having a family with a Christian husband and a dad for my children seriously and was about to answer that unspoken prayer in a very unexpected way.

* * * * *

One afternoon in the late fall of my sixth year of teaching, a phone call jolted me out of my lethargy. "Your dad met this nice man at work and wondered if it would be all right to give him your phone number." Mom's voice was excited. She added that he was nice looking and neatly dressed. Mom must have been praying, because she acted like this man was the one.

"He's heads above anyone else she's dated," Dad had told Mom.

Up to this point, I haven't done a very good job picking out men, so why not? What do I have to lose? I thought.

"Sure, he can call me." I tried to keep collected and cool about it, overcoming the negative thoughts.

I could hardly contain my excitement after hanging up, but I quickly checked myself. *Be careful*, I thought. *Still, for Dad to introduce someone to me is amazing. He must be someone really nice if Dad likes him.* Our relationship wasn't close, but it was much better than when I left to go to college.

* * * * *

Dad was the number one salesman for a major heating and air-conditioning company and had customers in Lincolnton, North Carolina, and all over the western part of the state. At sixty-two, he was a handsome, outgoing man with a genuine smile and warm handshake. That day, he had called on a Lincolnton propane plant where a guy named Vernon Thompson, who was division manager for eleven propane plants in North Carolina, also happened to be. As I found out later, they sat and talked for a while, and the subject of schools came up. Dad mentioned that he had a daughter who was a schoolteacher and that she was having a hard time making it with two children while on a teacher's salary. Vernon left with a favorable impression of this handsome, friendly man.

Vernon said he thought, *If she's anything like her dad, I want to meet her. If I meet Lawrence again, how will I bring up the subject of his daughter?*

Their second unlikely encounter happened about a month later. Getting up the nerve, Vernon spit it out, "You said you had a daughter who was a schoolteacher?"

"I have a picture of her in my wallet." Dad pulled out a picture of me, Mark, and Crystal.

Vernon blurted out, "I'd like to meet her."

"I'll ask her if I may give you her phone number, but after that, you're on your own, because she's never listened to me before."

Dad didn't know it, but after all these years, I was ready to listen.

And according to Vernon, nothing could deter him.

And nothing did.

78

Then Vernon called, said he'd be in my area on December first. "Would you like to go out for coffee or dinner?" he asked.

I didn't want to decide, but I was definitely interested. Since he came highly recommended, I boldly said, "I'd like to go out for dinner," all the while thinking, *It's my birthday, and I don't have anything planned. Why not make an evening of it?* December first was a school night and my thirty-eighth birthday. I carefully did not tell him it was my birthday, and I had no plans. *Don't get any unrealistic hopes about this,* I thought, carefully guarding my feelings.

* * * * *

This was the first time my dad had ever fixed me up with a blind date. Actually that hadn't been his intention at all as I found out later. No one I had met so far had come anywhere near being a candidate for marriage. Fortunately, I hadn't let my feelings and my vulnerability send me down the wrong path. Later I realized how much God protected me for more than five years and how little I had to do with meeting Vernon.

When he rang the doorbell, I was more than excited. Quickly straightening the living room and putting the cat in the bathroom, I checked my makeup and hair in the mirror.

I won't let him know I have Crohn's disease. Not on a first date.

My face belied its usual thinness, looking almost normal rather than puffy from the prednisone. In the last six months, I had let my dark hair grow out and hang to my shoulders with its natural curl. This was the first time my hair had been long in many years, maybe ever. I was fashionably thin in pants and a jacket, the only positive benefit of Crohn's.

Trying to keep calm, I pushed away my biggest fear: *Would I be able to eat without having to run to the bathroom to throw up?*

* * * * *

A well-dressed man in a business suit with a nice smile and friendly manner greeted me when I opened the door. His face was strong, tanned, and confident. Looking very distinguished with neatly combed salt and pepper hair and a moustache, his smile and mannerisms put me at ease. I could tell he was pleased to take me out. I already felt special because of our introduction, yet I cautioned myself. I did not want to be hurt.

At dinner, he started talking about his idea of what a wife should be. I heard, "The glue that holds a family together…to be taken care of and treasured…"

This all sounds too good to be true. Is he talking about marriage? He didn't know he was talking to a former women's libber who years earlier, and without hesitation, would have challenged him and put him in his place. After six years of struggles, alone without a husband, and main support for the three of us, I kept quiet and listened.

He also didn't know that I had a hard time trusting he was for real. It sounded like a line, but he was talking to a woman desperate to believe that happiness and love were possible and that it wasn't too late for her. I didn't want to turn him off with some stupid remark when he was pouring out his heart. *Is he for real? He doesn't really know me or know my situation.*

As the evening drew to an end, he invited me to his company Christmas party. Then I asked him to my faculty party. He was planning a trip to Oklahoma to visit his parents and his children from a former marriage that had ended seven years earlier. I couldn't believe what was happening, but I didn't want it to stop. *This is too easy. It can't be for real.* But I wanted to be the woman he was describing, someone who could fit into his life.

I was impressed with his obvious respect for his mother, his work ethic, career, and Christian background. Besides, my dad liked him and had introduced us.

After it did stop, I called Mom. "How was he? Did you like him?" Mom asked, excited to hear about the evening.

I gave up trying to play it cool. "Tell Dad that he hit the nail on the head." I wanted that to be true more than anything.

Of course that just fueled the idea Mom had from the beginning that this was going to be "Mr. Right" for me. I wasn't certain of anything except that I was eager to see Vernon again.

As I drove to pick up the children and later slipped into bed, I thought about what had happened. *Has God brought Vernon into my life?* Chances of finding the right man for me *and* the children seemed so small. *Is he the one? He seems to like me and wants to see me again—and at each other's Christmas parties!* This was all too good to be true. More amazing than anything, I didn't have to sell myself. He liked me without my having to do anything but just show up. Cautions dampened my feelings. I quickly pushed down feelings of excitement, unable to let myself hope or dream. *If he really knew me...? But maybe he really is my Prince Charming*, I thought, drifting off to sleep, unaware that my life would never be the same again.

9

I, Vernon, Take Thee Candy

Among the things I did not know about Vernon Thompson was that he was working in North Carolina because of circumstances we would later see as God's intervention. He had believed at the last minute something led him to ask for his assignment to be changed from Missouri to North Carolina. Meeting my dad hadn't been by chance, he later told me, because it was highly unlikely that the two of them would have met twice in a month at the same place.

He told me the story of their first meeting, how he was impressed with Dad the first time they met in the company break room. When Dad mentioned he had a daughter, Vernon immediately became interested. "Your Dad was what I would call a 'gentleman's gentleman,'" Vernon said, praising Dad.

I found it noteworthy that Dad didn't know Vernon was single. And Dad wasn't trying to fix me up. I couldn't believe it was just a coincidence. *It must be God*, I thought. I wanted it to be God. And through my Dad. It had to be God. But how? For me?

Two weeks after our first date, I walked into his company party with him, and I quickly realized that I was the object of everyone's attention. Vernon obviously liked being with me. I felt special. Very special. We danced and danced to the Everly Brothers and other oldies 'til I had holes in my stockings.

That night, I spent the night at his place, not telling him about my reservations. Maybe I was too desperate to tell him how I felt. Was this going to end up as another really bad decision? I hadn't wanted this relationship to start out this way. I chastised myself. I knew he liked me a lot, and I enjoyed our time together. Regret was what I felt more than anything.

The following weekend, I introduced him to the teachers at my faculty party, still unsure of where this was going. One thing I did know for certain was that I had no desire to challenge or put down this man in any way. The five and a half years without a husband and father for my children had tempered what vestiges of feminism remained. I felt vulnerable, afraid, and excited all at once. Was he really serious?

* * * * *

The third weekend, I knew I had to tell him about Crohn's disease. Tentatively, I began, "There's something that you have to know. I was diagnosed with Crohn's disease almost three years ago." I took a deep breath. "I will have to take prednisone the rest of my life." After hearing all the medical facts, he didn't seem disturbed at all. *He doesn't realize how serious this is. Incurable.*

How could he not be troubled? He was supposed to be troubled. Before I could express more doubt about my future and give more details of my condition, he asserted, "You're going to be healed."

I thought, *You aren't the one hurting. You don't know what I've been dealing with.* Yet on second thought, his response astonished me.

No one else had ever said that to me. I hadn't heard it in my parents' church. Or anywhere else. And in spite of all my doubts, I wanted to believe that! I had never known anyone who had been healed of an incurable disease.

He acted as if it were no big deal. *Well, that didn't run him off.* Relieved, I hugged him, wanting to believe everything was going to work out for our future. *What would he do if he really knew me?* was a question I didn't ask.

Whatever he knew about healing was more than my ignorance, especially anything the Scriptures may have said about healing. My announcement hadn't phased him or deterred him. But I was a long way from believing in healing. I thought he was just being optimistic. At that time, I was oblivious of any encouragement from God but later realized those were words of faith and prophecy, something I knew nothing about.

I also ventured to tell him some of the problems in my first marriage. He was in disbelief and dismay that anyone could treat a wife and children that way. But I kept the abortions and some other things from him, afraid he would reject me. I hadn't thought about the four children I had lost. I had never told anyone.

Can this attractive, successful man really be serious about me? I thought. I wanted him to like me so much. I still look back with amazement how God brought us together when I had nothing to do with it except say *yes* and show up.

* * * * *

When Vernon left for Oklahoma for Christmas to see his children and family, he put my picture on the dashboard of his car, calling me every chance he got along the way. I felt more and more assured of his sincerity but still struggled with thoughts that I was in the middle of an amazing dream too good to be true.

Then, the dream I had dared not let myself dream came true.

He returned with an engagement ring.

It was the first diamond I had ever had—a beautiful one-carat solitaire marquise diamond "Will you marry me?" were words that I had only dreamed of hearing.

All my thoughts slipped into the bliss of the moment as I answered without hesitation, "Yes, I will." Somehow I managed to push the ring on my finger even though it was a size too small! We chose Saturday, June 19—six months from our engagement—to be our wedding date. Six short months! I didn't know how I was supposed to feel. He said he loved me, and he wanted to marry me and to be a dad to Mark and Crystal. That was enough, more than enough.

* * * * *

Looking back, I'm amazed that I didn't have more hesitation after such a terrible first marriage. Everything had happened so smoothly. It seemed meant to be. He told me about his divorce seven years earlier. He admitted he was the one who had left her. I struggled with thinking about his children without a dad but was glad it hadn't been for another woman.

His oldest daughter was married and expecting her first child. He spoke highly of his parents, especially his mother. That had to be a good sign in any man and was the opposite of what I heard from my children's dad. He also spoke affectionately about his son and three daughters. The youngest would have been a couple years old when they divorced, a year older than Crystal. He proudly displayed pictures of the girls in gymnastics and cheerleading.

Vernon also confessed he had thought there weren't any decent single women left. He said he had prayed to God that if he were to stay single for the rest of his life, he could accept that. Then he met me. I didn't see myself as that decent woman he had finally found— but I wanted to be.

My family's approval, his profession as a Christian, and his willingness to take the three of us as a family was all I needed. My feelings didn't enter the picture. I went forward hoping everything else would work out. On one level, I didn't want to believe anything negative. I believed this was a God thing—with Dad's approval, it had to be. Underneath was apprehension I never acknowledged: what he would think if he really knew everything about me?

* * * * *

After our engagement, my life was full of expectation and change. As we celebrated New Year's Eve together, I wondered what the coming year of 1982 would bring in my life. With so little time to plan, I spent almost every day after school and weekends working on the details with a limited budget. My new fiancé continued to work in Raleigh while I finished out my school year. I proudly showed off my engagement ring every day, counting each one until I would be Mrs. Vernon Thompson. Not very feminist of me.

We saw each other almost every weekend, all of us adjusting to this new dynamics—a family of four. After watching us together, Mom had commented to Dad, "Vernon really loves her. I can tell by how he looks at her so lovingly." Their confidence and support meant so much. Vernon was nothing like the man I married back in 1966. He took his role as provider and leader and head of the family seriously. I didn't think about my former life.

I was a lot different too. At least I wanted to be. I wanted to be a wife—no great aspirations for a career. Secretly I envisioned staying at home. How dare I? No feminist demands from this woman.

The closest thing to a prayer was the thought, "Please don't let me repeat the same mistake." I was going to have a church wedding! A Christian marriage!

* * * * *

In my feminist years, I would have classified Vernon as a male chauvinist, as I had my dad. Now I wanted a man to take care of me. Shocking. I loved that he wanted to take care of me. At the same time, I was scared—scared to trust, to believe, to love.

My biggest concern was my children. What about discipline? Before the wedding, we sat down with them for a serious discussion. Vernon's voice was businesslike as he addressed Crystal and Mark, "Your mother and I are getting married, and I want you to know that I love her and won't tolerate your treating her with disrespect. I will treat you like my own children."

It was strange hearing a man speak to my children with those words. Both children accepted the "new dad" speech rather well. Treating them like his own meant more than just providing and taking care of them. It also meant disciplining, as we would soon find out.

I determined to trust Vernon to say and do the right thing. It was scary giving up my single-parent mentality. Vernon was salt of the earth, an Oklahoma farm boy, with very definite ideas about child-rearing. He didn't have any drinking or smoking habits and was a hard worker with ambitions—a businessman. I liked the idea of being the wife of a businessman who was climbing the corporate ladder. Most of all, he professed to be a Christian.

* * * * *

We met with the pastor who was marrying us. Agreeing that divorce was wrong and a sin, we prayed with him, repenting, asking God's blessings on our marriage. I didn't let myself think about the past or about the abortions. I was leaving all that behind. Everything was going to be different. We confessed our faith in Jesus as our Savior and declared we wanted to raise the children to know God. I was oblivious of what really needed to change and how that was going to happen. But this time, I wanted God in my life. It never occurred to me to confess the abortions. It didn't occur to me I was being dishonest not to tell Vernon.

Valentine's Day 1982 came with a surprise box of candy, heart-shaped with lace. I proudly shared it with the children. Later in the month, the four of us were going to Mom and Dad's fortieth wedding anniversary party where all of my relatives would meet Vernon.

As we walked through the mall, my new fiancé insisted on buying me a new dress and shoes for my parents' anniversary. I felt like a queen in the new fashionable blue pinstriped dress with white sandals. As we stood in the anniversary party's receiving line, I was so proud to introduce him to everyone. We seemed like a family that day. *The next family gathering in this church will be our wedding*, I thought. It still didn't seem possible.

* * * * *

Later, while packing some things for our move, I found out what Vernon meant when he told the kids he wouldn't tolerate their treating me with disrespect. Vernon asked Crystal to help fold a large blanket in the living room, carefully showing her how. After several attempts, she had a little tantrum and poor attitude, not wanting to do it. Vernon took off his belt and calmly gave her a spanking. I was shocked. Mark ran upstairs. And this was before the wedding!

Not knowing what to say, I blurted out, "You can give him one too." He didn't. I knew I had to support Vernon, so I didn't rush to her. He hadn't been abusive or angry—calm discipline without rage. *Don't say anything. Don't interfere.* Somehow I kept quiet. At some level, I knew not interfering in front of the children was crucial, and again very unfeminist. Relieved when peace returned, I realized the truth: I had spoiled her. I was proud I hadn't caved and blown it by giving her the sympathy she wanted, proud I had supported the man who wanted to protect me and love me. A victory had been won—over myself—for myself and my children. I had to believe everything would work out, but I didn't know how. We went forward with our plans.

* * * * *

One Sunday while Vernon was in town, the four of us attended church with Mom and Dad. The sermon struck a deep cord in my heart, revealing a small part of the magnitude of what God was doing in my life and a glimpse into the wretchedness of the past I hadn't faced. I went to the altar and wept at the end of the service, knowing this was a turning point in my life, the start of something I could not have imagined. I was overwhelmed with what God was doing. My husband-to-be came up behind me and put his arm around me. If only he knew.

At last our day arrived! Just one day after the school year ended, after my last grade was turned in, a beautiful clear, sunny day smiled on us that afternoon in June. My husband-to-be fit in with the handsome Keaver men in their tuxes. Someone commented that he and Dad looked like they were related. They were alike in a lot of ways. Dad was Vernon's best man.

Crystal was sweet in her peach Victorian dress and little nosegay of peach roses as my maid of honor. Mark ushered guests to their seats like a perfect gentleman. Later on we had a big laugh when he told us he had stuffed the pants of his tux with towels, trying to make his legs look larger. Thirteen and not yet a man, he did well ushering guests to their seats.

Waiting to enter with the traditional wedding march, I heard the clear baritone voice of Dale Jarrett singing "The Wedding Song (There is Love)" by Paul Stookey. *Yes, Jesus. You are here. You are blessing our marriage*, I thought.

I walked down the aisle alone, with children and a smiling handsome groom and an entire family watching. My long hair was swirled up behind with small peach roses matching my nosegay bouquet. The simple off-white Victorian dress size 6 hid my frail torso with lace covering my protruding backbones. It was a simple and sweet ceremony but worth the whole world to have a wedding, a ring, and a man who loved me.

"I, Vernon, take thee Candy..." was a commitment to much more than the woman standing before him. Even though neither one of us fully understood, it was a commitment to become one with all that I had been, was now, and will ever become in this life.

"For better, for worse; for richer, for poorer; in sickness and in health; to love and to cherish, 'til death do us part," we each declared before our family, friends, and God. We had no way of knowing how life would call us to fulfill those promises to each other in the years to come.

Later, when we looked at our wedding video, we saw three distinct flashes of light. They coincided with each of us saying "I do" and when the pastor pronounced us man and wife. [7]

We were amazed. No lights, not a single flash bulb went off during the entire service. Was it God showing His blessing on us? A confirmation?

* * * * *

---

[7] See Mark 10:6–8.

My parents and brothers were so thankful my children and I would be taken care of and had a man who loved us. Knowing I had not been in control, I had no other explanation except it was God, not understanding His love and grace, who brought us together. I had only said *yes* and steadfastly refused to let the negatives drown out what I believed was God's will for me. I felt unable to make anything work—so inadequate, so unsure of my health, my emotions, and my heart. Our love would have to be greater than all of that. God brought to me the familiar scripture from Corinthians quoted in so many marriages:

> Love is patient, love is kind. It does not envy, it does not boast, it is not proud. It does not dishonor others, it is not self-seeking, it is not easily angered, it keeps no record of wrongs. Love does not delight in evil but rejoices with the truth. It always protects, always trusts, always hopes, always perseveres. Love never fails. (1 Corinthians 13:4–8a, NIV)

The love passage sounded good, but I had no concept of how that would be manifest in my life. I also didn't know Jesus's faithfulness and His promises that went along with my newfound faith and commitment to Him and my husband. "Would he still love me if he really knew me?" was a question I dared not think.

I believed that Jesus was there, ordaining and blessing our marriage. We had the blessings of my family, the church, and relatives in the covenant we made. I didn't understand all the implications of this covenant. I felt weak and inadequate with past failures to keep my promises on that day. Fearfulness had tried to discourage me at every turn. I didn't know that covenant wasn't about feelings, and nothing was too difficult for God, not even the broken life I brought to Him and to Vernon that day.

Mr. and Mrs. Vernon Thompson

A church wedding

Our Colorado Home

View from balcony

Four plaques and an alder wood box

Joseph's alder wood box

Starting the farm house

Finished house

Home for 18 months

Room for gatherings

Kitchen in farmhouse

Liberated by love

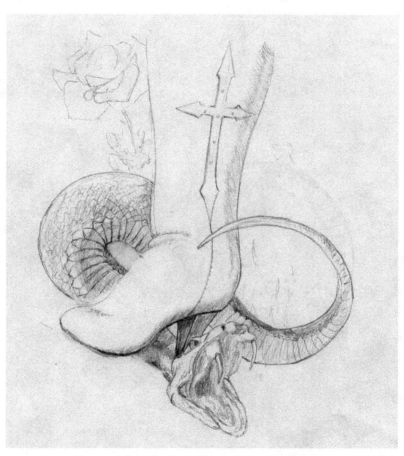

Overcoming the lies of Satan through Christ:
Under my Feet, Deceived no more

10

We Become a Family

After our honeymoon to Hilton Head, South Carolina, we joined my family and the children at Myrtle Beach, South Carolina. My parents and brothers were happy for me, but mostly relieved. My brother Stan joked that they would have paid Vernon to marry me. I had a husband now—one who loved me and my children and wanted to provide for us. All in only six months. After a very long and hard six years, it hadn't sunk in what had happened. In a short six months, my life had completely changed. Sometimes I still felt I was in a dream that could end at any time.

Moving to Raleigh was different from the first time in 1975. I watched my husband in amazement as he stacked my old worn-out furniture on the back of a pickup. *That's my husband*, I thought, seeing the "farm boy" come out as he tied everything down securely, Beverly-Hillbilly style. I liked his "self-assurance and take charge" attitude, as if there were nothing he couldn't do.

"I can do a lot of things," he had said before we were married.

He sounded a bit arrogant to me, but I had thought, *That's like my dad*.

Vernon commented, "I can't believe you have nothing to show for those ten years of marriage."

"I have Mark and Crystal. They are the only good things that came out of all the bad."

"That's right," he agreed.

Everything from the past was behind, where I wanted to leave it. As we drove by the old apartments on the freeway, I pushed away any thoughts about my life there and felt nothing.

I have a new life, I thought, *a new husband, someone who loves me, and a nice place for us to live. I have a husband who has a good job and wants to provide for me and my children.*

* * * * *

Focusing on the external changes in my life, I was ignorant of how keeping all of the hurt and pain from the past would affect my marriage. I was also ignorant of God's plan for me—a plan that would meet my deepest needs and heal the hurts I was determined to keep hidden.[8] I didn't know God wasn't through with me nor about the long journey ahead that was going to take me to places both spiritually and naturally that I couldn't imagine—places He had prepared for me before I was born.[9]

My new husband was full of plans and dreams for the four of us. The children and I moved into the duplex he had been renting filled with antiques he had collected. Vernon didn't spend money on frivolous things, like entertainment or expensive restaurants. As a hobby, he had collected antique furniture for the pragmatic reason that the stuff would hold its value. I admired the beautiful pieces that were now also mine—hard to believe! It all came with the "Mrs." title that I had scorned years before. No more.

This former feminist wanted to be at home, cooking and cleaning for her family and her new husband—like Ozzie and Harriet—the perfect little wife. I tried my best to be the opposite of that once-rebellious woman thinking that I could change myself by just having the desire, oblivious of what that would entail. Naïve and ignorant of God's Word on the subject of marriage, I forged ahead depending on my feelings and limited knowledge of how to honor

---

8 See Psalm 147:3.
9 See Jeremiah 1:5.

and respect a husband. He was easy to please, and with my desire and God's help, we had an easy adjustment overall.

However, there was one thing that escaped me in my perfect life. Wanting so badly to fall into the arms of my new husband, enraptured with passion, I was disappointed when that didn't happen in our sex life. It wasn't him; it was me. Lack of passion was understandable with my first husband and in relationships that were just using me with no commitment. But this was with my wonderful, loving, considerate, committed husband. I was discouraged. I expected myself to just suddenly change. What was wrong with me? I didn't let him know. He certainly had no problem. *It will happen*, I thought, not understanding the role of trust in our marriage. Yet I felt alone and separated in this very important part of our marriage. *But sex isn't the most important thing*, I reasoned. *Love is.* In the meantime, I pretended, like everything else I was keeping from him. *How can I trust him with all of that?*

"God, help me love Vernon as I should love a man, to feel love as I've never been able to feel for a man" was my silent prayer, concerned more about feelings than about the God-kind of love from the Bible verses from our wedding. I had a lot to learn.

* * * * *

In the fall, we moved to a rented home in a middle-class neighborhood. At the edge of the woods behind the house was a stream lined by Carolina hardwoods beginning to get their fall colors. The scene drew me, invited me to walk in the cool, dark soil along the stream with bare feet and spread a blanket on the grass in the warm sunlight to watch squirrels and listen to birds. I dared myself to be happy, remembering my childhood adventures and love of the outdoors.

I loved making homemade pies and biscuits and having meals in our dining room. *Does all of this really belong to me now?* I thought as I carefully arranged the placemats and tableware, admiring the hand-carved English oak sideboard with matching server, table, and six chairs. I felt like a princess as I paused to gaze at everything.

The children each had their own bedroom. We had a family room, a living room, and a full basement! It seemed like a mansion compared to the apartments. Everything was different. Meals were no exception. No fast food for us!

Vernon said, "And when you cook, you're not going to be preparing three different things. We're all going to eat the same meal." Right there he put a stop to my being the kid's short-order cook and told them they were going to eat what I fixed with no complaining.

I knew he was right and let him be the head of our family, but it wasn't easy, especially at first. I was smart enough to know that this was very important if we were to have peace and respect in our home, something that had been missing for a long time.

We hooked up our antique wood cookstove in the basement for extra heat, and I cooked a big pot of beans on it for one of Vernon's favorite meals: ham, pinto beans, cornbread, and cabbage with homemade fruit pie and ice cream. That was second only to country-style steak and gravy and homemade biscuits.

"I've gained ten pounds," Vernon announced in unbelief. "I've weighed the same since high school." My southern cooking was anything but fat-free, but he never complained. Bojangles' Famous Chicken 'n Biscuits and McDonald's had lost some good customers! I loved my new life.

The children were happy too. They didn't complain about the change of diet or the rules. There was no arguing or fighting. It didn't bother me that I was breaking all the rules of feminism by submitting to my husband and letting him be the head.

Crohn's disease didn't give me severe problems as long as I took the prednisone, but nausea and pain reminded me of this chronic companion. Letting go of the total responsibility of discipline and provision for two children didn't come automatically. I could always find something to worry about. Having a husband as the head certainly relieved some of the stress. Another stress reliever—no teaching! I was no longer the breadwinner for the family. After so many problems with Mark, my instinct was not *if* but *when* that dreaded call would come. I tried to be the perfect wife with perfect children.

Relishing the thought of my ex-husband knowing I had married a man who wanted to take care of me and love me was easy. I was glad he knew we were doing better than he did for us. I have a man who loved me—finally! Someone who thought I was beautiful. And the children now have a good life—a nice home.

There may have been just a twinge of compassion for his being so lost and hopeless as I savored my new situation—but not much. I tried not to gloat too much, knowing it wasn't the Christian thing to do. But I still did a little. My life *had* changed, and I didn't want to have resentment and anger toward Don. I thought that was gone, but evidently not. So I just put him out of my mind. What I couldn't put out of my life was the secret we shared that I had denied for so long.

* * * * *

It wasn't long until my Cinderella life was disturbed by the dreaded call. "Hi, this is Mark's principal. This morning on the way to school, Mark threatened a school crossing guard with a knife." My heart sank.

"That's terrible. I didn't know he had a knife. My husband will be down there as soon as I call him at the office. Thank you for calling."

On the verge of panic, I did as Vernon had asked me and called him at work. In 1982, a small pocketknife wasn't the contraband it is now, but still. A short time later, in came the two of them, and down to the basement, they went. I closed my ears. *I hope Vernon doesn't get mad and lose it. What if Mark fights back? Or challenges Vernon?* I didn't hear anything. When they came upstairs, Vernon looked at me calmly. "I'm taking him back to school now." It was over. I breathed and sat down to relax.

Vernon told me later he calmly reminded Mark, "I told you what would happen if I got a call from school, and I'm a man of my word, so bend over." Mark got licks with the belt, took his punishment, and was returned to school after missing only one class. I felt good about my part, which was to say nothing and support my husband. I found it remarkable that Mark wasn't angry or defiant afterward and behaved better at school.

Proverbs says if you don't discipline your children, you hate them,[10] and Vernon didn't think that meant "time-out." That was it. It was over quickly with no after nagging and threats of even worse consequences as I was prone to do. Restarting discipline at thirteen was not easy on any of us, but we had faith it would work out.

We bought Mark a dirt bike that was an outlet for all of that pent-up emotion. Soon he was doing tricks, turns, and amazing stunts on it. He was extremely athletic, and we loved watching his showing off at the bike park—always the daredevil on the edge of disaster.

Crystal had her own room with a white bedroom set and seemed to adjust well to our new life. She did well in school, which was just a short walk behind the house. Overall, she was a sweet, well-behaved third-grader who didn't need very strong discipline. At least not after the blanket incident.

Vernon also warned Mark that if he brought home failing grades, he would get the belt. I thought that was extreme but didn't say anything, because I saw that extreme measures were needed when things had gotten so far out of hand.

The previous year, I even did his homework at times after continually reminding him to do it. I had been at the end of answers. What a relief when Vernon told Mark I would no longer be doing his homework. When he never opened a book the first semester of eighth grade, keeping quiet was one of the hardest things I've ever done. When the report card came home, it was worse than anticipated—mostly Fs—the worst ever. Another trip to the basement, and Mark began to believe Vernon was a man of his word.

Mark turned fourteen in December. For most fourteen-year-olds, it would have been too late to start with this kind of discipline,

---

[10] See Proverbs 13:24.

especially from a stepdad. Yet to my surprise, Mark neither challenged Vernon nor showed disrespect.

* * * * *

There was finally a father in the home. The children responded to Vernon's fair treatment and to what I would understand better in years to come—the authority that is God-given to fathers in an order God set up in the family. He was kind to the children and didn't threaten nor belittle them. I could never have been both mother and father to my children. I felt more secure with my husband's protection and love, but trust was a process. I never ridiculed Vernon nor did we argue in front of the kids. After the past sixteen years, I was a very fast learner when it came to being a supportive wife.

Vernon didn't ridicule or bring up Mark's past mistakes but gave him a fresh start. Somehow, Mark responded to this kind of discipline. He seemed to want boundaries from his new dad. Our home was a place of order—Godly order—and Vernon was the head. He wasn't perfect; no one is. But even a bad father can sometimes be better than no father at all.

Years later, I read the Bible verses about a father's discipline saying the child the father disciplines is a true son.[11] It came natural for Vernon. It was how he was raised—something the kids' biological dad never had. Yet this kind of parenting is still a consistent choice.

Shortly before our first Christmas, I got an unexpected shock. All my expectations of spending time with my family, vacationing together at Myrtle Beach, the grandchildren growing up together, my husband spending time with Dad and my brothers—all were suddenly changed when Vernon dropped the news, "I was asked to take over a propane division in southern California. I have to report in January." We had no choice, not if he wanted to advance with the company. I dreaded telling my parents.

* * * * *

---

[11] See Hebrews 12:8.

Our first Christmas was truly a joyful one spent with my family, but it also brought bittersweet good-byes in light of our recent news. The predictable and possibly boring life I had known so well, with its comforts and familiarities, would be no more. The idea that I would refuse to move or try to convince my husband to stay never occurred to this former feminist. He was the head, and I agreed with the decision. We all adjusted to the idea and began to make plans.

With the company paying movers to pack, I didn't worry as much, hoping all my new treasures would make it unscathed. Even though I was sad, I didn't dread this move—and Vernon helped relieve my fears. Mom and Dad were tearful yet relieved. I imagined they were thinking, *Candy has a man who loves her. They are a family, and she is happy now.*

God is the One who brought us together, I thought, holding on to that certainty more than anything. *And my husband loves me.*

"We're off to the land of fruits and nuts," we said, laughing about our move and all we had heard about California. At this point in my new Christian life, I didn't know that the plan God had for me was more than I could ever have dreamed or imagined and was going to be anything but boring. My part was to say *yes* and support my husband. For once, not being in control was okay.

11

Confessions of a Zealot

G oing across the country with two kids and our cat, Rufus, we didn't have a lot of time for sightseeing. The mountains and rock formations were all so different from the green-forested Smoky Mountains of North Carolina. Each horizon brought new wonders we had seen only in pictures. I imagined how California would look, never having been there.

As we settled into the long trip, we talked about a lot of things with the children, about our future together and our hopes. Vernon talked about the Bible, starting with Revelation and the idea of a *rapture*. This was new to the rest of us, and scary for Crystal. I was a bit uncomfortable but kept quiet, because I knew very little about the Bible and didn't want to oppose my husband. The Presbyterians and Methodists never mentioned getting suddenly zapped up out of here. Finding a church was first on my list once we found a house.

* * * * *

We stopped in Oklahoma for a short visit with his parents and his four children. As we drove down the dirt lane and over the rickety bridge to his parents' farm, I could feel the apprehension, hoping they would like me. The farmhouse was older than I imagined, with little room for company, packed with collections of ceramics, whatnots, and other things his mother deemed valuable. I had expected something different—something that matched the carefully groomed meticulous man I had married. Instead, I found they lived very simply as they had for the past thirty or more years in the same little farmhouse with kitchen and bedroom add-ons, treasures packed in every nook and cranny. They were sweet, pleasant, simple people with little pretense. They welcomed the children and me, but I sensed the divorce had been hard for everyone.

The next day, we took Vernon's son and his two younger daughters out to eat with Mark and Crystal. It was awkward and uncomfortable for me. *How must they feel seeing their dad with another family?* I tried to keep my mind on the meal and be as nonthreatening as possible, guarding every word I said.

I didn't cause the divorce and had nothing to do with their past relationship with their dad, I reasoned, but I represented a lot of unknowns and possible threats to their relationship. My feelings were torn between compassion for their situation and anticipation I had for my new life and marriage.

We also visited Vernon's oldest daughter, who had just had his first grandchild. The next morning, we said our good-byes to his parents, not knowing when we would see them again. I felt relief, yet some sadness, when we pulled out of the drive on our way again.

Confident in my husband's love, I hoped to have his children out to visit and have a good relationship. So did he.

* * * * *

Headed toward Amarillo, we found out Vernon liked to tease. He kept us in suspense about our leased home, pointing to a desolate-looking community out on the wilderness with no trees, saying that was what our town was like. No fighting in the backseat this trip.

After a harrowing drive down a foggy Cajon Pass at night, we finally arrived in Upland, California, and checked into a motel. Eager for daylight to get a look at this foreign land, the kids woke us with shouts of "Look at the trees and all the flowers!" And in January!

We ate breakfast at a bright and colorful Swiss chalet restaurant called Griswold's. Everything seemed like a fairytale, with me as the princess and my Prince Charming beside me. Birds of Paradise were in bloom with blue lilies of the Nile in flower beds around businesses and homes along all the streets, far from the dead, gray winter we left behind.

Soon we settled in a rented home in a nice neighborhood in Upland with the kids enrolled in school. Green grass and fuchsia bougainvillea colored our backyard. I still couldn't believe it was winter.

By summer, we bought a house in Alta Loma, California. Walking through the spacious two-story stucco home full of antiques, I had to pinch myself. We even did a video of our home to send back to my parents—Jackie Kennedy–style. The antiques Vernon had collected were the perfect accent to our Spanish-style home with arches throughout. I really did feel like Cinderella! Located at the top of Sapphire Street, where orange groves had once flourished, we could see all the way to Ontario airport from the second floor sunporch outside our bedroom on a clear day.

* * * * *

What was most amazing was I actually had a husband who wanted to work and had a good income. Even though I didn't have to worry about providing as I had for so many years, I could not completely feel secure, knowing nothing of God's promises to provide.

We didn't waste any time finding a church to fulfill our commitment to raise the children to know Him, choosing the same denomination my parents attended where we were married. Sitting in church with my two children beside me and my husband's arm around my shoulder, I felt cherished, valued, and loved. In the peace of familiar old songs and the fellowship of other Christians, I let go of any anxieties.

The smell of his aftershave mixed with cologne reminded me of that distinctive masculine presence from my childhood. *Vernon is so much like my dad. Has it been only a year? It has to have been God the way we met. Is this really happening? My children sitting beside us in church hearing God's Word.* I hugged them just to make sure all this was real. Crystal still had her soft, fair baby skin and loved to cuddle. When it came to her, my affection was easy and natural. Mark looked like a young gentleman in a tie and neat shirt and pants. I wanted to believe this was the beginning of a miraculous change for him. For all of us.

* * * * *

I took on my new roles without any hesitation, the most important one being wife and mother. I had no problem cleaning, keeping an orderly home, and cooking for our family dinners. My concerns about all of the added responsibility on my health were unfounded. The kids were well-behaved in our home. Rarely did Vernon have to step in with discipline. When Crystal complained that the kids in her fifth grade class were teasing her about her front teeth, calling her "Bucky," Vernon told her to haul off and hit them next time. That would stop them, he was certain. I was horrified. Surprisingly it worked.

The dream I had while seeing the psychiatrist in Raleigh—having a loving husband in a nice neighborhood with our own home, caring friends, and family with my kids involved in wholesome activities—had finally come true. My children now had lives I only dreamed possible when I was a single mom. They came home from school to two parents. We ate meals together. We never missed a church service. With all of this, there remained a place in my heart that yearned for something I couldn't identity.

The "Mrs." in front of my name gave me position, wealth, and relationships that I hadn't earned or ever experienced. I gladly gave up my independence and the Ms. title to conform to my husband's life. As wife of a division manager of a nationwide propane company, I liked meeting new people, and my husband seemed proud to introduce me to his employees. Vernon oversaw more than one hundred employees in fifteen locations in Southern California. Dropping by his office one day, I listened as he enthusiastically explained the remodeling and improvements he was making and the training meetings he initiated. I was impressed by my new husband's confidence, especially when he so effortlessly quoted numbers and figured out his division's performance. I was proud of him, but praising him profusely didn't come naturally.

Vernon wore suits to the office, drove a company car, and was always neatly groomed. I smiled and kissed him good-bye as he left each morning. He had come up through management without actually having been on the trucks with experience delivering propane, but he knew how to make a profit. He made goals and exceeded all expectations. However, all of this failed to give me the true confidence and security I needed.

* * * * *

My year of staying at home came to an end when we moved into our new home on Sapphire Street in Alta Loma overlooking the valley. It was a fixer-upper, my first ever house—a Spanish-style stucco two-story home with a red tile roof. We needed my salary if we were to do the needed upgrades and have income for decorating, as well as provide the lifestyle we wanted.

Remembering past teaching experiences, I applied to teach in the California school system with a great deal of apprehension. Crohn's disease and prednisone were still a very real part of my life. *Why can't I just keep on being a housewife?* I thought as I signed up to take the California State Teacher's Competency Test. It didn't help to know that 30 percent of applicants failed. Thinking about it gave me the jitters. The fact I had graduated from a top-rated university and taught school for six years under difficult circumstances didn't help—as if Californians were a higher species than this southern belle. My hands were sweating as I began.

One part of the test was math, and the other two were grammar and writing. I erased the essays four or five times until finally satisfied I had done my best. Finally, I turned in my completed test, along with a prayer for favor.

When the results came, I was surprised and elated. Proudly I showed Vernon the results—one wrong answer on the English, none on the math, with no deductions on the two essays! Writing with compassion and transparency about my recent marriage and the love that had come to me and my children hadn't been easy. I had struggled with the mechanics of writing, but my heart had come through. My confidence soared!

With determination and confidence, I began teaching seventh grade science. This time, I taught with a different spirit—God's Spirit. Truthfully, I became a zealot. With my newfound Christian religion, I thought all the California teachers in my school needed Jesus, and I was the one to bring the truth to them.

* * * * *

My commitment to Christ was more about going to church and *doing* things for God than having a personal relationship and growing in God's Word. Our home was the perfect place for entertaining, and I was excited at the possibility of using it for God. However, as I became more involved in a fellowship of believers, my conscience began to bother me about the past, specifically the abortions. I began having a lot of anxiety and thought it must be about my past.

It had to come out. I was more concerned about telling Vernon the truth than I was about choosing the right words or how it would affect him.

If God had brought us together, then God would work this out between us, I reasoned. I knew at some level I needed to be healed, and I hoped this confession would help. *I can't keep this any longer. I have to tell him.*

The kids are out of the house. I'll tell him as soon as he comes home from work, I thought one afternoon. The urgency seemed to be paramount. Patience had never been a virtue of mine. Neither was tact. My insides were churning, but I managed to keep calm. It couldn't wait.

As soon as he walked in and sat down, I sat down across from him, and in a serious voice with little emotion, I slowly began.

"Honey, there's something that's been bothering me that I need to tell you."

His expression turned serious, "Sure, okay, what is it?"

I just blurted it out—the words seemed almost unattached, words never before uttered. "I had three abortions in my first marriage."

His face showed the shock. He didn't say anything.

I looked at him, hoping for some compassionate reaction, an arm around my shoulder or a comment that he loved me and a word of comfort.

"What's wrong?"

"I don't think I love you anymore," he said in disbelief, looking sad and hurt.

All of my fears were confirmed in an instant. *He doesn't love me!* Instead of being my comforter, he had become my accuser. That was the worst thing he could have said. I had just shared my deepest secret, one that I had told no one. *What a mistake! Why did I think this was what I should do?*

Then he started asking questions—or accusations. At least that's how they felt to me.

"I don't understand why you didn't leave or just refuse to have the abortions. Why did you keep getting pregnant?"

I didn't have answers. I was surprised at the intensity and the feelings that threatened to come out like an erupting volcano. I was afraid I was going to lose control—lose my husband, my mind, everything. I attempted to defend myself again, stifling my sobs.

My throat tightened and burned as I continued. "I was four thousand miles away from anyone. He kicked me in the stomach," I said between the heaves that shook my body. Nothing was going as I hoped. My reasons sounded lame. I didn't feel forgiven—not from my husband, not from God. *How can he ask these questions? It's like I'm on trial.*

I was feeling so much condemnation from my husband. What did I expect?

Gathering my composure, I said, "At that time, I thought I had no choice. I was trying to make my marriage work and had no friends or family near me, and I was away from God."

My ears heard myself saying these words for the first time aloud to another human being. I had been in denial for almost ten years.

Vernon was shocked, hurt, and as I later learned, also afraid. He had just had a bombshell drop. The woman he married couldn't be the woman before him who was confessing unfathomable deeds. He had put me on a pedestal. He had thought there may be more things even worse to come, he told me many years later when we were able to talk about all of this.

But I felt terrible—worse than before I said anything. Instead of escalating the argument, I focused on my husband's feelings and pain. Instead of attacking him, I humbled myself. How I had changed.

I didn't fully understand what Christ had done for me when he hung on the cross. He had taken my sin on Himself as well as the shame and pain I was still carrying. The fear of rejection was so strong I couldn't admit who I had been—or what. It was years before I knew God's Word well enough to comprehend God's full plan of redemption and reject the condemnation I was feeling.[12]

"Honey, I'm sorry that I didn't tell you. I guess I feared you wouldn't marry me if I had. I was afraid to tell you. Please forgive me. I felt I had to tell you now." Back all those feeling went, back into that place of protection and up went the walls. The numbness returned.

I just wanted things to be back like they were before. In the end, he wasn't angry. I don't know how we moved on without help after such a major event in our marriage, but we did. The door wasn't open for a deeper discussion of my abortions at this time. But the door *had* been cracked for a measure of light to come in. Our lives continued as they had before with no more discussion.

Maybe he hoped that would be the end of it, and it had been taken care of. Perhaps we both did. However, it was only the beginning. God wanted me free, if I could just trust Him and let Him lead and guide me instead of taking things into my own hands. I didn't know how to do that—not at this time in my infantile steps as a Christian.

My confession to Vernon did embolden me to step out in defense of the unborn. Even though I thought I had botched telling

---

[12] See Romans 8:1.

my husband, God began to turn it for good. Neither of us was ready for me to shout about my abortions from the rooftops, but at least he knew. He agreed to go with me to a protest against abortion, and Crystal joined us with our handmade signs and many others from various churches and pregnancy centers. She didn't yet know the miracle of her birth and how God had saved her. Someday she would understand.

* * * * *

With the renewed awareness of my Christian faith, I saw alarming things in the school curriculum, in the teachers' union, and in the philosophy of the schools. And I wasn't always quiet about it. Wherever possible, I stood up for truth. I didn't want to get fired, but I also didn't want to compromise.

God gave me the desire to develop an abstinence program for my sex education class. I was shocked by what two male teachers were teaching. They had the boys and girls together and were showing photographs on slides of male and female genitalia with syphilis sores.

As I sat in the darkened classroom, looking at one of the slides of a male sex organ, one girl near me innocently asked, "Is that a finger?" This wouldn't have upset me before my repentance and commitment to God. But now it did. *Oh my gosh.* Yes, some things are definitely taught at too young a child's age. As a parent, I would have objected to my own daughter's being in this course, and I did not want to be accountable for this to God or to the parents.

There was no way I was going to use the curriculum in a way that I felt would break down the natural modesty of the seventh grade students. The principal even agreed to my request to separate the boys and girls during one presentation. God was giving me favor!

* * * * *

Refusing to join the teacher's union that supported candidates who were for abortion didn't win me any friends. I found ways to legally put God into the curriculum, even putting up a patriotic bulletin board with a coin in the middle that had "in God we trust" on it. The principal let it stay up but called me in when I posted a page against abortion from a newspaper—a full page ad that showed a three-month unborn baby sucking its thumb in bright color with the caption, "I can suck my thumb, I can hiccup and feel pain...and my life can be ended legally." It didn't fly even though I was teaching the development of the unborn in science.

Undeterred, I bought small plastic replicas of unborn babies at the three-month stage to pass around to the children in the class. The line I walked was a narrow one as I tried to expose the truth about abortion. Only my husband knew why I was so passionate about this, and even he didn't know it all, no one did. Only God. My anger about abortion was a righteous anger, I reasoned. But it separated me. I felt like an outsider.

The zealot that had been unleashed was on a mission. The old Candy had taught sex ed as a how-to course with little qualms about how I influenced the children. The new Candy fearlessly tried to stand for the truth. The new Candy may not have won a lot of friends, but the image of a little three-month-old unborn baby was burned into the hearts of those seventh graders, and the fruit of that only God knows. All the while, there remained a place in my own heart where no one was allowed—the secrets that kept my love bound up with the pain, guilt, and shame of the past.

12

The Shaking Begins

Eager to get involved in church, I agreed to teach Sunday school to the youth, even though I knew very little past John 3:16. Trouble came when I answered a student's inquiry about her Jewish friend: "Yes, you have to believe in Jesus to go to heaven." Our new pastor did a lot of explaining to her upset parents but wouldn't deny the truth. His stand on the Word of God resulted in much criticism.

The denomination had gone liberal, even disputing the most basic of beliefs of Christianity. After years away from church, I was shocked at what had happened to a denomination that started out so fervently in the truth. Even though there were many God-loving people in our local church, we became disenchanted with the liberal California hierarchy. Locally our feminist associate pastor was a thorn in the pastor's side and opposed him theologically. And I, the repentant feminist, could not agree with the way the denomination supported her in what I recognized as undermining the male authority.

* * * * *

We supported our pastor and his wife in their difficult trial. God used them greatly in our lives. My eyes had been opened to things of the Spirit when the pastor's wife, Reba, took me to a Women's Aglow meeting. I saw women excited about God as I'd never seen before. They were talking in strange tongues and giving messages from God. That was also where I first heard Christian praise songs outside a hymnal. I had lots of questions. Reba helped me understand the scriptures to back up what was happening. I wanted what they had, determined to overcome my initial fear.

Through their ministry, God brought a young man into our lives who was a talented singer and needed a place to live. We were blessed by what God did in his life during that time, bringing his future wife to him and putting a call on his life to become a pastor. My heart was to bless others through our hospitality and warm home.

I wanted more of what God had revealed through our pastor and his wife. But I only got more of the other stuff. The new pastor was very liberal, and when asked the basic question, "Do you believe in the virgin birth?" said, "Well, we don't know how that could have happened." That was when my husband made his final decision to leave, and I agreed.

* * * * *

The first few years in California, as I grew spiritually, we also prospered materially with our two incomes. I assumed that my blessings were partly a result of becoming a Christian, as well as my husband's and my hard work. We could now afford to fix up the house and buy luxury items I had never dreamed of owning.

All of my fears that Crohn's disease would limit my life drastically were unfounded; although, the soreness and cramping were evidence that I wasn't healed. I was amazed that I had the energy to take care of my family and a large home as well as work a full-time job. I never had to use a bucket in the stockroom but still took a daily dose of prednisone.

Our second Christmas in our dream home, Vernon surprised me with a beautiful pearl-and-diamond necklace and earrings. I had never had a diamond before the engagement ring he gave me. It was the most beautiful set I had ever seen: a double strand of real pearls with a large diamond and gold clasp. I wore the set to school almost every day until the end of the year, just to show off what my husband had given me. We went to auctions and bought jewelry and art pieces and more antique furniture for our big house. Among my collection of jewelry was an emerald bracelet valued at more than $10,000. We paid for Crystal to have piano lessons after purchasing an antique parlor grand made of burl walnut and original ivory keys, made in Dresden, Germany, in the mid-1800s. Although I couldn't admit it, material things were more important than my spiritual growth.

We sold my Honda Civic and bought a used BMW that drove like a dream. California was the place of fancy cars, and we had joined the club. Later Vernon bought a used Mercedes to give us full luxury status.

* * * * *

Both Mark and Crystal adjusted to California, losing their southern accents within the first weeks of school and making friends easily. Unfortunately, Mark's weren't the ones we would have chosen. He wasn't as open about his friends as Crystal was about hers and kept us on our knees when some of his friends met with disaster that he narrowly escaped. He still had his ups and downs and showed interest in art and tennis. I was thrilled when he made the tennis team and amazed at his taking sewing classes and making his own jacket for a prom. He gave his life to Christ at a church camp, but it seemed not to last when troubles came.

We flew out Vernon's three youngest children for Christmas, wanting to make it a special time for them. California had so many attractions, so of course, we went to Disneyland. With both incomes, we could afford the splurge, as well as Christmas gifts for everyone and sent gifts on birthdays throughout the year.

It still was hard, knowing their standard of living was a lot lower. I knew—I had been there. His son had suffered with epilepsy since he was twelve after having an accident on a small motorcycle on the farm. Vernon's relationship to him was different from the girls—nonsympathetic toward his condition. He said there had been no medical evidence for the seizures and seemed to imply that Brad should be able to control the seizures and didn't have to have them. I felt the tension and stayed out of the conversation.

My conscience also bothered me because we spent so much and never tithed to the church. I had a bad habit of bringing up things at the wrong time and in the wrong way, so my feelings on this weren't received very well when I made a critical comment about our low giving when we walked into church. I wanted to obey God and be in His will now that I was a Christian. We were less involved in the second church after our first experience. Also, we were busy fixing up our home and accumulating more stuff.

* * * * *

The eighties were a prosperous time, with California real estate increasing by leaps and bounds. Vernon explained that our home had gained a lot of equity from the growing economy. He showed me the numbers on our assets and explained that we were worth far above what we owed, even with the financing of cars and spending our paychecks to fix up the house. It sounded good to me, but we had no savings. I tried not to let that bother me and trust what he was doing. Our lives appeared to be headed only upward.

My fears were confirmed when we went out to dinner with his boss and another executive from Tulsa. I tried to shake off the feeling that things weren't going so great, but I distinctly felt uncomfortable, because they were distant and unfriendly. There had been hints of criticism with Vernon's work, but nothing prepared me for what happened, of all times, when my parents were visiting us from North Carolina.

Early the next day, I was surprised to see the company car drive up. Vernon stepped out carrying an armful of papers, and the car drove away.

What is going on?

He came directly upstairs and walked in with a troubled look. "They fired me. Bill Good just walked in without any warning and told me I was fired without any reason. They brought me home with the contents of my desk." He was shaken.

My head was racing. Nothing made sense. He had improved the division in profits, discovered theft by a manager, who served time after being convicted, and also saved the company lots of money in other ways. But one of his area vice presidents had been disgruntled toward Vernon about remodeling the office, yet Vernon was commended on the productivity of the division. He always maxed out his bonuses and had more than doubled the division's earnings. He had also fired a manager who had been stealing.

There wasn't time to process all the questions and talk about what had happened. We went downstairs and attempted to smooth over what my parents obviously suspected. Somehow we got through that visit as graciously as could be expected. I put on a calm exterior, but inside I was rattled as never before in our marriage. Over half of our income was gone! My teaching salary wouldn't pay the bills, and we had lots of them. Fear about losing everything hit me as I tried to keep from accusing my husband. *What did he do to get fired? They didn't fire him for nothing. What will we do?*

The corporate world was difficult to understand. Vernon had replaced a popular manager who had been demoted. He thought it was jealousy and politics. He explained that even though he had saved the company thousands of dollars on a job, the man he had contracted for it didn't have workman's comp—a technicality. I had been oblivious of what was going on. As promised, he hadn't brought home problems from the office. Now they were right in my face!

My unspoken expectation that my life as a Christian was supposed to be smooth sailing was blown apart, and I had no theology to explain what was happening. My trust had been in my strong, self-assured husband, and I had no answers for what we were going through.

* * * * *

Not one to sit around and feel bad about the situation, Vernon immediately started exploring other opportunities. It was the most stressful period in our marriage. After three years of teaching, I had two more years before my credential had to be renewed. Fear and uncertainty attacked me as never before in our marriage. The familiar pain and cramping became more frequent and sent me to the bathroom with heaves of bitter yellow bile.

Vernon's propane connections opened the door to a partnership two hundred miles north in San Luis Obispo. He accepted a position that required a roundtrip of ten hours and took him away from us four to five days a week. We sacrificed with the expectation of moving north to a promising future. He was optimistic and took me up there to see the area and a beautiful home he had already eyed.

Looking for a way to produce more income, we also invested in a flower shop in Pasadena as equity partners with a couple who would be operating the business. They were a Christian couple Vernon had met through his propane connections. All of this didn't give me a feeling of great security, but I didn't object.

We got an SBA loan and went into more debt, with our home being the main source of equity. I nervously watched as they discussed the arrangement in a nice comfortable restaurant. It all sounded so good on paper. None of us had ever worked in the flower business, but I kept my reservations to myself. Located in an upscale section of Pasadena, Vernon felt it had a lot of potential. It felt scary to me, but I let him make the final decision, submitting to my husband's leadership. I wouldn't be working in it anyway—I thought.

* * * * *

The next two years were difficult with my teaching and raising the children while Vernon commuted. His regular salary was replaced with one that was dependent on his performance. On the weekends, we would plan our lives around the new business he was building up north.

Mark's life had been up and down in high school with dubious friends we never met. He didn't graduate with his class but earned his GED with no plans for college. The hardest time with our son was when he crossed the line with Vernon. He challenged Vernon by talking back and threatening to go to his dad's in Pennsylvania to live. Vernon responded by putting him on a plane that very day and sending him to live with his dad with a one-way ticket.

My heart was fearful for my son, knowing the temptation that would be there. This incident almost moved me beyond my resolve to support my husband's decisions. *How could he?* I thought. I said nothing. Every day I prayed and found the strength to support my husband in his decision and believe for my son's return.

Then, surprise! After three months, he wrote how he appreciated us and wanted to come back. He had been treated very badly and saw the difference. We were so happy and thankful and welcomed him back and gave him back his car. He decided to go into the navy, and we sent him off to San Diego with new hopes for his success and a good future. We proudly attended his graduation as a medic following in Dad's footsteps.

While Vernon was trying to get a partnership started, Crystal had two serious surgeries. She was diagnosed with severe scoliosis, and surgery was scheduled after everything else failed. I sat with a friend in the waiting room with Vernon miles away, feeling alone and fearful during the seven-hour surgery. *My beautiful daughter—with a rod down her back! How will her life be normal—marriage and children?*

Before entering high school, she underwent another seven-hour surgery on her jaws to correct lousy orthodontics. It seemed that I was fighting this all alone with Vernon 250 miles away, trying to get something started in the propane business. Fearing she would carry the effects throughout her life, I struggled and felt her rejection and pain as she tried to adjust to a body brace in high school and seven years of orthodontics. I struggled to trust God as things seemed to be out of control, wanting to believe in healing and a good outcome. Wishing my husband were with me, I was thankful for a friend who sat with me until Crystal came out and in recovery.

* * * * *

Rather than renewing my teaching contract, I resigned so I could work full time in the flower shop until we moved up to San Luis Obispo with visions of being a stay-at-home wife once again. All that ended three months later, in November, when the propane partnership in San Luis Obispo dissolved. My world crumbled when shortly afterward the couple managing our shop bowed out without warning, leaving the two of us with a couple of employees to try to make it work. I was shaken.

Suddenly, our income was reduced to what we could eke out of our floral business. Fearful thoughts raced through my mind, *How will we ever pay our mortgage and expenses? What if we lose everything?* The anxiety and uncertainty were overwhelming. I learned how it feels when a door slams shut on a dream. The stress of all this went straight to my intestines.

When the pain began, I ran to the bathroom holding my side. This time, it was different. The spasms didn't let up. Neither did the vomiting. I panicked when I realized I was throwing up the contents of my intestines. *I need to go to the hospital. I can't drive myself.*

Vernon's in Pasadena at the shop, too far away to get here. I was scared. *Crystal. She's at our neighbor's.*

"Crystal. Is Cindy's mother there? Would you ask her if she could take me to the hospital? I'm throwing up. I need to get there quick," I said, trying not to sound frightened.

Prednisone had kept the Crohn's manageable, except for one brief hospitalization—but no longer.

In emergency room, the doctor took X-rays. We waited. When the X-rays showed possible perforations, Vernon was at least an hour away. Crystal was scared. I reassured her I would be all right, but I wasn't sure myself. Vernon finally made it to my side. We realized I would be going through a life-saving surgery. I was facing what I had believed would never happen: fistulas and possible perforations—the next worst outcome for Crohn's disease.

My faith was weak. I was even unsure of what God's will was for me. I lay at the mercy of the doctors. I didn't know how to pray for healing nor that I had an enemy who wanted to kill me.

The night before surgery, I felt extremely sick and alone. Sitting up on the side of the hospital bed, I thought, *Am I going to die? I can't lay down.* My body was bloated with massive doses of prednisone, as if someone had pumped me up to the point of popping, like a rubber toy. I didn't know that at that very moment, a huge abscess was form-ing outside my small intestine and filling with poison.

* * * * *

The surgery the next morning lasted five hours. I realized the seriousness of my condition when Vernon recapped the doctor's report. "You had a two-foot section of your intestine cut out that had an abscess the size of a grapefruit. And it had somehow remained in a membrane and had not burst." It was clear that I had been spared a much worse, and probably fatal, outcome.

I learned how much a person could be traumatized and thank-ful at the same time. Then I told Vernon what happened in the oper-ating room, "Before the surgery was over, I woke up on the operating table." He looked concerned. "I tried to speak but couldn't, and I had a terrible, searing, white-hot pain with a bright light all around me. Finally, someone realized what was going on and mercifully put me out again. The next thing I remember was going to ICU." Just the thought sent chills through my body.

Later that day, a little lady from our Sunday school class came into my room with a card and gift from our class. I read the Scripture aloud, "He sent His Word and healed them, and delivered them from their destructions" (Psalm 107:20, KJV). "Thank you for bringing this. I really appreciate your visit."

Her gift was a Precious Moments figure praying. So sweet. But the Bible verse made the greatest impact. I didn't understand the significance this promise would play in my life for many years. It was the first scripture on healing that I had ever received personally. This dear woman was definitely my angel that day.

I found out that God knows our address and has no problem reaching us when we're in a desperate situation. Even though I had rededicated my life and become active in church and even taught the youth, I knew very little of God's biblical promises for healing or for the provision we so desperately needed.

* * * * *

During the week in intensive care, the tubes and needles that had kept me alive were extracted, and I got a full view of the foot-long incision down my midsection, held together with staples and tension sutures. The pain that seemed to radiate out to my whole body was blessedly eased every four to five hours with welcomed shots of morphine. I couldn't stand or sit. As the pain gradually lessened, I was weaned off the morphine to pain pills. All the while, my husband was trying to keep a business going thirty-five miles away.

After two weeks, I was ready for my first solid meal—it was Thanksgiving. I fought off having a pity party as I looked at the hospital food and ate alone. Thanksgiving with our family in our beautiful home was one of my favorite times.

Mark showed up unexpectedly. AWOL wasn't what I wanted to hear. He had been doing so well in the navy. Fortunately, a doctor's verification of my emergency surgery kept him out of serious trouble. How long that would last, we didn't know. Peace seemed never to follow when it came to Mark.

What is going on with our lives? Why is all this happening? I wondered. There weren't any answers that were acceptable. Was it our fault? God's? My husband's? *Isn't everything supposed to go smoothly since we're Christians? Why was I having such a hard time trusting? What can I do?*

The most important part of my progress was the long-awaited bowel movement, which was the final test before I could be released from the hospital after two long weeks. Imagine, looking forward to pooping.

Finally, out of the hospital, Vernon drove me home down Euclid Avenue to Alta Loma on a wonderfully bright sunny day in November. Everything seemed to be in sharper focus as my senses took in the many varieties of trees and the landscaping and the mountains—as if I were seeing them for the first time. For some people, the greatest feeling is simply to be warm and thankful to be home.

13

Don't Think You're Healed

My Christmas gift was being at home with my family on the way to recovery. I didn't know God had another gift for me. While still recovering from surgery, Vernon and I went to hear Dr. Richard Eby, a well-known Christian TV guest with a testimony about dying and going to heaven. At the end of the service, Dr. Eby gave an invitation for prayer for those wanting to be baptized in the Holy Spirit.[13] *I want all God has for me. Here goes*, I thought, overcoming my fear as I walked up front.

When he prayed, I didn't speak out with those unknown sounds. *Did I not get it?* I thought.

That night I tried making noises in the bathtub. Good thing no one heard me because I probably sounded like a lunatic. This was all new territory in my walk of faith. Tongues was supposed to be the evidence that I had received the filling. Or so they said.

Questions came. *Is this real? Is this really from God? Can the devil fool me? Did I really receive the baptism?* I was baptized with water on my head as a baby in my parents' church, but I never heard there was another baptism, a baptism in the Spirit.[14]

---

[13] See Acts 2:4.
[14] See Acts 1:4–5.

I remained quiet and thoughtful about what had happened, hoping tongues would come later.

* * * * *

What didn't recover was church trouble. Our pastor in our second church was humiliated and dismissed with some alleged accusations. *Not again*, I thought. *I liked them. I don't believe all that about him.*

We didn't hesitate when we were invited to another church—nondenominational.

Vernon, Crystal, and I found a seat near the back our first Sunday. The pastor, his wife, and daughter walked to the front in a somber, humble manner.

The pastor spoke, "It is with heavy hearts that we come to you today and let you know we have just learned. Our daughter, Pam, is pregnant."

Oh my, how sad.

The pastor went on the explain how his daughter had been at one of the other youth's home and had been with the friend's older brother in a one-time encounter and how this young man would not be allowed to see her again. He then said that they were willing to step down from pastoring—whatever the church decided.

All over the room, people stood up and made their way to the front. They hugged and cried, giving assurances of their support and love. This was different from anything I had ever experienced in a church. This was where I wanted to be.

Still healing from surgery with an ugly scar from sternum to pubic, my faith felt weak. The reality was Crohn's was still there—I hadn't been healed, just given emergency surgery to save my life. The prognosis was still incurable. I was ignorant of the truth about faith being dependent on God's promise and not on what the facts were telling me.

Our financial situation hadn't changed either. We were still in a very difficult place. Though nothing had changed in our circumstances, things began changing inside me as we committed ourselves to this fellowship of Christians.

* * * * *

Finally, we were in a church where people were demonstrating what I had only heard about—the gifts of the Holy Spirit. And they were praying in that unknown language—tongues. These people weren't weirdos but sincere, loving Christians. I felt the love of God in that place. Also, they believed God still healed today. I began to *hear* the scriptures and wanted them to be for me. Leaders spoke out words from God—words of prophecy, exhortation, faith, and encouragement. *God brought us here. What a wonderful church*, I thought. Something had changed. I was more open to everything in church—the music, the preaching, the Bible.

The pastor was gifted, I found out, in what was called the gift of prophecy. I looked up to him as if he were almost a god. When strangers came in to church, he would sometimes lovingly ask them to stand while he gave them an amazing word from God. This was always received very well by the visitors. I thought he probably knew everything about me, so I kept my distance and took in everything he said. I wanted so bad to get something from God through this man who had such a direct connection.

The people were so friendly and happy. I wanted to be like them and to have what they had, not realizing I already had everything they had. I hung on to every sermon and loved the praise music. Raising my hands and clapping to the music, I thought, *Everyone is looking at me. What are they thinking?* "Give thanks with a grateful heart…give thanks because He's given Jesus Christ, His Son…"

When I heard about the woman who was healed by touching the hem of Jesus's garment,[15] I wanted to be that woman. "Please, God, heal me," I begged as I imagined I was touching His garment. The sore knot in my lower abdomen was still there after church. *What is wrong?* I thought. *I can't give up.*

---

[15] See Luke 8:43–48.

I questioned why all this bad stuff was happening to us. Wasn't everything supposed to go more smoothly now that I was a Christian? Hearing that God was good and the devil was bad had put things in the right perspective. Sometimes I still felt like a spectator rather than part of this group that seemed so spiritual, so far beyond me. I loved all I was hearing and seeing in church, especially how God had called the pastor to start the church and how much he was loved. I was relieved to know he couldn't be removed by a denomination vote and the whims of disgruntled parishioners.

* * * * *

After a minimal recovery of less than eight weeks, I was back with Vernon in our flower shop, traveling the freeways early mornings and late evenings. He was in a difficult situation with little help. Even though he didn't pressure me, I couldn't stay at home any longer. I didn't understand why things hadn't worked out for Vernon in the propane businesses, but now we were together trying to save our investment and everything we owned.

Every day was the same—six sometimes seven days a week. I put my favorite cassette tape in and propped my feet up on the dashboard and leaned back for the long drive down the 10 and 210 freeways to the shop.

"Give thanks with a grateful heart…" I sang with my favorite praise song. The words brought a smile, as I relaxed for the next twenty-five miles. I felt God's presence the most when I listened to Christian music.

However, once in the shop, I felt the stress of selling and taking orders. Thoughts of losing everything creeped in. The pressure weighed me down again and again.

How are we going to pay all the bills for both places this month? Can God bring us through? Is God punishing us? We were in survival mode.

Valentine's Day was extremely stressful. The biggest flower holiday of the year had been a flop as far as making a profit. Our partners had left, and we were learning the business as we went forward.

Easter hadn't been any better. We hoped to have a good Mother's Day to improve our sales.

The Sunday before Mother's Day, Vernon, Crystal, and I drove to the shop after a church potluck. I felt unusually tired. This made seven straight days, working long hours. My attitude wasn't the greatest.

Shortly after arriving, a gut-wrenching abdominal pain started that would not go away. *This can't be happening again.* I ran to the bathroom. "Vernon, I'm hurting really bad." I called out urgently.

Seeing the pain wasn't subsiding, Vernon said, "Pasadena General is the nearest hospital. I'm taking you there." I said nothing, holding my side and groaning as he helped me in the car.

I tried to fight the barrage of negative thoughts, *Am I going to die? Not another surgery! The stress—too much—no rest. What did I eat at the potluck? What about healing?*

After six hours in the emergency room, I was assigned a room, and a second surgery was scheduled for the next morning. Dread and fear washed over me thinking about the last surgery.

Before being wheeled into surgery, our new pastor came into my room to pray with us. My spirit lifted. I wanted a word of hope. He asked how I wanted him to pray. I wanted to say, "Heal me with no more Crohn's," but didn't have the courage or faith. Remembering my episode six months earlier, I said, "Just to wake up in the recovery room without any pain—not on the operating table."

Along with my request, he prayed exactly what I needed to hear.

"This sickness is not unto death, but for the glory of God," he prayed.

I'm going to make it through the surgery. I'm not going to die, I thought as peace came over me. I found out later these were Jesus's words as He reassured Lazarus's sister that her brother's sickness wasn't unto death but for the glory of God.[16] That scripture was like a direct Word from God.

As attendants rolled me into surgery, I was glued to my favorite praise song with earplugs attached to my cassette player.

---

[16] See John 11:4.

Instead of going into ICU after surgery, I awoke in the recovery room under a heated blanket. Smiling at me from the bed beside me was the sweetest face of a little girl. *She must also be recovering from surgery. My prayer has been answered*, I thought, closing my eyes. *I'm alive and in recovery.*

Thankfully, only six inches of abscessed section had actually been cut out, accounting for the two and a half feet total that was now gone from my small intestine. No colostomy! Also good news!

* * * * *

"Don't think you're healed," the gastroenterologist told us at my follow-up appointment. "You have abscesses all over your intestines, and we only took out what we had to."

I couldn't believe he said that.

"Jesus is going to heal me," I told him. I wouldn't have been able to say that after the first surgery six months earlier. As much as an expression of faith, I was trying to counteract my fear.

Now, more than ever, as we sat across the desk from the doctor, I wanted to believe Vernon's prophecy before we were married. I wanted to believe what I was hearing at church. I heard the diagnosis, but to myself I said, *No!*

The doctor dutifully gave my husband and me the medical facts so we wouldn't have any false hopes, while I thought, *He doesn't know it all!* The man told me I'd have to take medication the rest of my life, and it would only lessen the symptoms. No hope for healing. *I don't have to believe what he's saying! I want to be healed, and I want Jesus to heal me.* I was determined my faith would not ultimately be in doctors and medicine.

Vernon also believed with me. "You're still going to be healed," he told me as we left the doctor's office.

Doubts entered. *What if the abscesses keep reoccurring and necessitate surgery after surgery? I could be left with little or no intestine, and my only nutrition would be some liquid through a shunt into my subclavian vein.* Struggling to fight these thoughts, I tried pushing them out as quickly as they entered. I still did not know God's Word and the power of the Holy Spirit inside me to overcome these thoughts and fears.

* * * * *

Every Sunday at church, I heard about the goodness of God. "God is good, all the time. All the time, God is good," the whole congregation would shout aloud. What about our financial circumstances? Was God causing all of this for some reason? Since I didn't know the Word, that's all I had to go on, but I *wanted* to believe the good I was hearing.

The problems with the flower shop and our finances were still there when I returned. It was like an albatross around our necks. Nothing had changed. But I was alive. We were not quitting. There were moments when I yearned to be in the comfort of our lovely home, but I couldn't quit. Vernon was determined to hold out 'til he got a good offer for the shop. There was nothing to do but keep going.

We took note of every "facility" along the way on our early morning drives to the shop, never knowing when the need would arise with little notice. Diarrhea was an effect of having a shortened small intestine, and caffeine exacerbated the problem. At least I wasn't throwing up all the time.

I learned that taking out the ileum also removed the section that absorbed Vitamin B12, so I began taking shots to replenish the deficiency. Other than having to be near a bathroom, I wasn't on any special diet but was cautious about trying food again. Prednisone was still a daily regimen. My nutrition had been seriously diminished by vomiting everything, and the acid from my stomach affected my teeth, as evidenced much later when I began having a lot of dental work.

Regardless of what was going on, I still wanted to believe. I did what I knew to do. I had learned that the devil hated to hear praise, so he must have had a hard time in our van. When everything around us seemed to be falling apart, we worked 'til we were bone-tired, getting home late to get back up the next morning and do it all over again.

My husband had made choices that hadn't worked out, but he never gave up. Crohn's is exacerbated by stress, and I had plenty of that. I tried not to blame Vernon for all of our losses and our dismal economic situation; my Prince Charming was human after all. I was the submissive wife in every way I knew how and did my best to keep from complaining or voicing my fears.

He carried the financial burden while I learned how to arrange flowers and decorate windows. At least that was how it was supposed to be. I didn't know the details of our business, but I did my best to help him. Actually, I became very good at selling, decorating, and even arranging flowers. My natural creativity served us well in taking orders for funerals and weddings, learning pricing and buying flowers at the LA flower mart. We made a unique and beautiful spray of orchids for Crystal to carry to her senior prom and altered my own senior prom dress for her. My heart was thankful to see her having a fun-filled night as she and her best girlfriends drove off in a painted-up van to the LA Hilton.

* * * * *

We made the best of a difficult situation. Unfortunately, I hadn't developed much of a prayer life, and there wasn't time for Bible studies or other church activities. At least I didn't fall into the temptation to point out his mistakes and tear him down. The old Candy wouldn't have hesitated.

I grabbed onto every sermon as if each were just for me and joined in when I could, even dancing a little at a women's conference. I still had to fight off the feeling that I didn't belong and that everyone else was more spiritual than I was. Occasionally, I became aware of a lot of anger, anger toward my husband. *Why?* I thought. *Please help me, Jesus. I don't want to be angry. Forgive me.* At that time, I wouldn't admit that I was questioning his love. "If you really loved me, you wouldn't have let this happen," were words I never would have said. I doubted my husband's heart toward me and didn't see the effect my past was having on my marriage. The result was fear and confusion, neither from God.

* * * * *

I never told anyone at my church about the abortions. I just put on a good front and went on. Only in looking back years later did I clearly see God's hand in my life through these very difficult times. In the six months following the first surgery, God had taken us to the exact church where we needed to be and had given me hope for healing and for the goodness of God. He had saved my life in two surgeries. It was God who six years earlier had put it in Vernon's heart to tell me I was going to be healed and sent him to love me. At that time, I wasn't even in church or reading the Bible, but God put in my heart to want to know Him and to follow Him. But without God's Word, I didn't have answers for everything that happened to us. I know my parents were praying for me.

To me, God was still more a punishing God than a loving God, and I was still performing to be accepted. I wanted so much to be a part of this wonderful group of believers. I felt the love of God in this church like no other, but the financial blows, the surgeries, and all that had happened in our lives seemed to say I was a failure and didn't measure up.

When someone in church gave me the Scripture Romans 8:28, "And we know that all things work together for good to those who love God, to those who are called according to His purpose" (KJV), I took it to mean it was God who was doing this bad stuff for my good to teach me a lesson. At some level, I believed I deserved it. I kept all of the hurt and pain, the shame and the guilt from my abortions in a place dominated by fear, still in denial, still needing His healing and forgiveness.

14

Dad, You Didn't Make a Mistake

"Dad, you didn't make a mistake," I kiddingly assured him on the phone from the flower shop. "I'm all right. We're going to make it. The Crohn's disease is better. I'm going to be healed," I proclaimed with tears rolling down my cheeks. "Love you. 'Bye. Talk to you soon." I was thankful I could tell him I loved him.

"Your dad loves you," Vernon assured me again, just as he had when I voiced my doubts and hurt early in our marriage.

No doubt about our hard situation. I was determined not to speak negatively of my husband to my parents, nor would I let them know the details of what we were experiencing. Only weeks after recovering from this second surgery, and with next-to-no experience, I had gone in to help run the shop. I gained confidence as I learned how to operate the business and actually began to enjoy the creative part. Vernon had enough confidence for both of us. His mantra was "If someone else can figure out how to do something, then so can I."

Shortly after our business partners left, we had joined in a class action suit to get out of the franchise and started over completely on our own—new name and all.

"All right, you can name the shop," Vernon agreed when I asked him. After brainstorming together, I said, "What about 'Blossoms 'n Things?" It stuck. We changed the sign and were now sole owners.

141

Blossoms 'n Things had an upscale address with lots of potential, but we had no more money to invest. The settlement from the partnership dissolution in San Luis Obispo was quickly eaten up, and we were dependent solely on our floral and sales abilities to survive—both sorely lacking

* * * * *

Soon we were both working in the flower shop six and seven days a week, driving the southern California freeways, spending little time at home. Vernon didn't waste time trying to get another propane venture going, but in the meantime, he was our deliveryman.

Crystal helped on weekends and holidays. She was a natural with customers and with decorating the shop. *At least we are together*, I thought, feeling bad that she was giving up being with friends on weekends. The shop had now become home.

Showing me a list of our expenses, Vernon said, "We need to make $18,000 a month to break even. Our rent alone is $4,000, and the rest is payroll, utilities, yellow page ads, and the cost of our products."

There was no salary for owners on his list. Vernon told me to watch the costs going into each flower arrangement. In order to make a profit, we had to keep our cost in each bouquet to 18 percent.

"How am I supposed to do that?" I asked in disbelief. However, when I set that goal and developed a tracking sheet for each item that went into a bouquet—including the designer's time—we made it!

Everyone was expected to help, but we had no money for salaries. To my disappointment, I was unable to go back to North Carolina to my grandmother's funerals. We managed to go back to Oklahoma for his daughters' weddings, but Vernon didn't give them away. I felt his pain and watched him gracefully comply as their mother walked them down the aisle. With limited resources, keeping our relationships in the midst of surgeries and financial shortages wasn't easy.

Sometimes our next meal was from the cash collected that day. We exchanged flowers for pizza with the restaurant across the street and rarely got home before bedtime. Our creativity and ingenuity got us through each day—really it was God, but it felt like it was all up to us, or me.

I knew God was involved when we were able to foil attempts to scam us or pay with bad credit cards. To collect all of the profit, we made deliveries all over the LA basin rather than wiring out to other florists. Despite the stress of long hours and a hand-to-mouth existence, the Crohn's stayed under control. But diarrhea and frequent pain reminded me that I was not healed. I never had a salary. None of us did. On my birthday, he came in with an expensive Dooney Bourke handbag. He loved buying me expensive gifts. A brief getaway for our eighth anniversary to a bed-and-breakfast ended with disappointment because of a Crohn's attack. Planning anything was always iffy because of a possible flare-up, but at least there were no more surgeries. We were together, 24-7. And we still made it to church when we could.

* * * * *

While Mark was in the navy, Vernon's son, Brad, came to live with us and helped in the flower shop. We told him about scriptures for healing and took him to church, hoping he would be healed from the seizures. When he fell to the floor in the shop with a horrible seizure, I yelled, "In the name of Jesus, I command you to come out of him!"[17] Whatever it was remained and eluded our efforts. The seizures left Brad dazed and bruised. I had read the story in the Bible of the boy who had seizures, falling in the fire and water and how he had been delivered—definitely different from the science I learned.

This was all new to us, but we believed the Word of God and stood on God's promises for Brad's healing and deliverance out of that terrible affliction. Because of this hindrance in his life, he hadn't been able to complete much of anything he had tried as far as jobs and school. He had never had a driver's license or meaningful relationship with a woman.

---

[17] See Mark 16:17, Luke 10:17.

Vernon kept declaring that he would someday be healed and have a *normal* life with a job, a wife, and kids. We prayed for that. I believed I was going to be healed also. Just when, I didn't know. Despite not yet seeing results for either of us, I still chose to stand on what little Word I had heard and tried to share it with Brad.

* * * * *

Normally I wasn't afraid for my safety, but one experience left me shaken—and thankful. Shortly after closing time near Valentine's, while sitting in the back room waiting for Vernon to return from a delivery, the front bell rang. Wishing I had remembered to get the key from Vernon and lock up for the night, I walked to the front.

A large young man met me, holding some bills. He was not dressed as our typical customer, and he had a serious expression. I couldn't help thinking of a woman in a shop nearby who had been assaulted by some thug from Los Angeles. Shivers ran up my back, and my mind raced when he asked for a twenty-dollar bill for the small bills he had in his hand. That was the opposite of what most people would ask, so up went another red flag. The fact that he wasn't friendly and happened to be African American—though I told myself I wasn't prejudiced—also gave me alarm.

As I walked behind the counter to the cash register, I detected a nervous intensity in the man. Hitting the register key, I said, "I don't think we have much money in the register." Seeing his right hand come up from behind the counter, I almost swooned, fear gripped me so hard. Without thinking, I grabbed my chest and the counter and began to moan with my eyes closed. I kept up the act as if my life depended on it.

With irritation in his voice, he said, "What's going on?"

"I think I'm having a heart attack," I said, still not looking at him.

Then after moving around the end of the counter, I pointed to the door, still moaning, and said without looking, "Go, go get help." I kept insisting, almost falling to the floor.

He uttered some kind of curse and left, getting into a waiting car. My heart was beating so hard that I thought I might really have a heart attack. Just a few moments later, a lady walked in and asked if I was okay, saying she had seen the man leave. She thought he looked suspicious getting into the car out front. I called the police, who confirmed that he most likely intended to assault me, rob me, or worse. There wasn't anything they could do.

Still shaken, I turned off all the front lights and went into the back to wait for Vernon in the dark, too relieved to be angry. I knew God had protected me. We had no weapons or cell phones. We never forgot to take precautions again.

Glad to have a great testimony of how God had helped me foil a robber, or even worse, I told everyone at church and family back home. God knew just what would work with that man.

Sadly, we had no time to participate in most activities at our church. My relationship with Jesus was still mostly going to church on Sunday, listening to Christian radio, singing praise songs, and giving a testimony when we saw God involved in our lives.

* * * * *

I bought Christian tracts and gave them out with candy outside our store at Halloween, witnessed to our employees, and laid hands on them for their healing. There was little time to develop a personal relationship with Jesus—studying, praying, and reading the Bible take time.

Looking back, I'm amazed I stepped out in faith as much as I did. I just wanted so badly to believe what I was hearing at church. As my faith grew, my health improved with it, and prednisone kept the Crohn's under control.

Hardest of all was understanding this man I had married who was so different from my own dad. He didn't mind taking risks. His confidence in the face of seemingly impossible odds came from his childhood experiences. During those long hours riding back and forth on the freeways, we heard stories from his childhood. His dad wouldn't let them use the word "can't." "'Can't' died when he was a calf," Robert Thompson had told his young son.

Growing up on a farm in northeastern Oklahoma, the oldest of five children, he took on the responsibilities of an adult when he was twelve, baling hay and driving farm equipment.

"If the baler broke down, I had to figure out how to fix it," he told us. He said that I had been spoiled because all I did was ride my pony.

I half kiddingly told him that the treatment he got would be called abuse today. "It was survival," he quipped, then told how his dad walked eleven miles, carrying four-gallon cans of cream to sell so he could buy groceries for the family. We kidded him about walking to school for miles barefoot in the snow, which wasn't far from the truth.

Vernon didn't like my complaining about our situation, because he had seen much worse. No matter how bad things got, they could never be as hard as he remembered on the farm. Eyes in the backseat would roll as he began his familiar lecture. He reminded us he had been a respectful, obedient son, regardless of the hard times on the farm. These attitude training sessions were good for me too, I must admit.

* * * * *

To my relief, Vernon listed the shop for sale, but the economy continued to drop, and our hopes seemed to diminish for making any kind of profit on it. No offers.

"Maybe it's priced too high?" I tried to reason, to no avail. All I could see ahead was financial disaster. My faith was more dependent on us than on God. We worked as hard as we knew how and sacrificed in every way possible to keep going. I was determined I wasn't going to be a controlling wife—not after my disastrous first marriage. With little understanding of what a godly wife would do, I had a hard time reaching any kind of personal victory. My suggestions and opinions never seemed valid to my husband. "You don't understand the business world. You were a teacher with a regular salary coming in," he would tell me. Figuring out how submission worked was difficult. Letting him make the final decision and trusting God so I could have peace in this situation was foreign to me.

Nor did I know God's promises for providing our needs,[18] no matter what the situation. Without an understanding of God's promises and His truth, I was subject to every imagination the devil could throw at me. I was told to have more faith, to trust my husband's heart. *How do I do that?* I thought.

* * * * *

When the bottom fell out of the economy in the second half of 1989, a state sales tax man came into the shop without warning and stood by the register to collect the money we owed. Embarrassed, I hoped no one I knew would come in.

"Why didn't you tell me we were having a problem?" I asked Vernon, trying to stay composed. I acted as if nothing were wrong as I helped customers, but the knot in my throat held back the flood of anger. *How could he let this happen?*

We sold anything not attached to the building to pay our house payments, gas, and groceries and kept the shop going. We sold the Mercedes and gave my used BMW to Mark for finishing first in his deep-sea diving class after being discharged from the navy. He was off to the east coast on his new venture, and we were scrambling to save a shop and a home. Only the Oldsmobile was left—and it wasn't running well. And of course, the Ord, our van with the missing *F.*

Vernon did everything he knew to get something going in the propane industry. He was also selling propane wholesale in another business, whatever it took to bring in some income. Always the dreamer, he had a vision for a nationwide propane company. I didn't understand how that was going to happen when we had no money. People were always presenting him with outrageous opportunities that sounded good when he explained them to me. We traveled to Tulsa to look at a ten-story building in one deal and talked to Mickey Rooney about being the spokesman for a company he was working on.

---

[18] See Philippians 4:19.

"How can this happen? We don't have any money," I said—not what he wanted to hear. When he was determined, no amount of rationalizing would have any effect. "You don't know anything about business," he would retort when I objected.

When an opportunity came to supply balloons and flowers for an auction company on Sundays, Vernon didn't turn it down. Our work-week became seven days—church was out. Reluctantly, I supported his decision. At least we were together. The radio became our church.

* * * * *

Finally, in February 1993, the flower shop sold for about half of what it would have brought before the California real estate market plummet in 1987. But we were free. The daily grind on the freeways was over. The bad news was we had mortgaged our home. What had looked great on paper had suddenly vanished. We had no equity left. After paying all the bills for the shop and the SBA loan, there was no profit, or anything, left. *This is not supposed to be how our lives go— losing everything. Why?*

"At least we didn't have to declare bankruptcy," Vernon reminded me as I struggled to understand. All of the hard work and sacrifice. I was really down. Everything looked dismal. I couldn't cry or feel much of anything, but I did refrain from complaining and accusing him of failure like I was tempted.

Caught in the downturn of the economy with a house in need of repairs, Vernon got his real estate license to pay the bills, his fifth job in ten years. For a year, he worked refinancing people's mort-gages. He sent out over a hundred resumés to propane companies in other parts of the country. No offers. I began to substitute-teach, but my heart wasn't in it. I wanted to be optimistic, but it seemed as if everything was falling apart, and I couldn't stop it.

* * * * *

Desperately needed encouragement came from our church fam-ily. During a special service, a guest speaker who had a gift of prophecy spoke directly to us what was considered to be a word from the Lord: "God is welding the two of you together, as a blacksmith welds iron, so that one part cannot be distinguished from the other...and He's turning up the fire."

What does this mean? I thought. *It sounds scary instead of encouraging. How can things get any worse?*

Another visiting prophetic Christian speaker pointed to my husband during a service and gave him the Scripture from Job in the last chapter, verse 12, which said that the Lord blessed the latter end of Job's life more than the beginning and that he gave Job new children and restored all he had lost materially. That was really good to hear. *But I'm not Job's wife,* I thought. *I don't want to be Job's wife. She didn't support him but told him to forsake God and die.*

The most encouraging word for me was one from an elderly gentleman who was considered to be a prophet. He sat before our congregation, being too feeble to stand for long periods, and gave a word from God to each one who came before him. I wondered if there was anything good for me.

"A love letter," he began, when it was our time. "A love letter— and the Lord says that every morning He will go to the post office to collect." I felt as if I had heard it directly from the Lord. I wanted to be a love letter to Jesus more than anything, but I didn't *feel* like a love letter at the moment. I was sorry for my lack of faith. He told Vernon he would be a pillar in the church and would speak terror into the powers of darkness. *Wow, that is a great word. When will that happen? Doesn't seem like it will ever happen.*

All the doors to the propane business in Los Angeles shut on Vernon. The only one open was in the Rocky Mountains in an obscure town I had never heard of. Vernon said he had always wanted to live in Colorado, describing the beauty of those majestic mountains to me and how the West still presented opportunity for an entrepreneur based on how hard a person would work instead of bloodline and family ties. I wanted to believe we were on the right track so bad. Wrapping my mind and heart around his vision didn't come easy, but I could still say when we talked to my parents, "Dad, you didn't make a mistake."

15

A Celebration and a Tearful Goodbye

I n the midst of our losses and giving up on our dreams in California, God answered my prayer for my daughter—our daughter—and brought us a great blessing. After agonizing with her through an ugly duckling stage with surgeries, a back brace, and orthodontic braces, I had great joy for what God did for her and for us.

For years, Crystal secretly had a crush on a young man in our church we nicknamed "Tom," referring to his resemblance to Tom Cruise. They grew up together in our church and were friends. After church camp, Crystal had burned her secular music in the drive-way, declaring her love for Jesus and hanging on to her dream. She didn't date before sixteen, because Vernon had set definite boundaries. And when she did date, no one was to come to the house to pick her up without coming in and meeting us—no horn-blowing in the driveway.

After graduation, she worked for us in the shop. Then on a youth trip to Romania, her relationship to Ed—a.k.a. Tom—grew into something more than friendship. I prayed that she would get her wish. She was so smitten with this handsome young man of her dreams. At the time we sold the flower shop, Crystal's relationship with him was moving in the direction of marriage. They had the approval of parents and the pastors. They were so much in love and were doing this the right way—God's way. We had only six months to plan for a wedding

For the past five years, most of her teen years, our life as a family had been anything but traditional. We had practically lived on the freeways and at our flower shop. More than anything, I wanted to give her a beautiful wedding—a Christian wedding—using all our connections and skills in the floral business to make her dream come true.

* * * * *

Even though I loved the church and wanted to be a part of it, I still felt like an outsider, like I didn't belong. I let our work schedule prevent me from getting into the Bible except on Sundays. Even though I was water baptized with a group from church and had been prayed for to be filled with the Holy Spirit, I still looked up to these Christians as if I were less than they and could never be as spiritual. Never did it occur to me that my past was the problem. I never told anyone except Vernon about the abortions, not realizing 'til years later how my secret was an opening for Satan to lie to me in other areas of my life and mistrust my husband.

Our failures in business didn't help either, because I thought we must have been out of God's will to have ended up in this situation. I concluded we must have sinned a lot to be losing so much. I didn't understand how my past and everything I had kept hidden was being used to make me feel guilty—lies from the enemy that I wasn't as good a Christian as everyone else. Without a good foundation in God's Word, I was a target for the doubts and lies from the enemy— Satan. I struggled to believe differently, but I didn't fully understand what came with my new life with Christ. I saw other Christians as being a lot more holy than I was.

Although we had no money from the sale of our business and hadn't sold our home, my husband found a group in Colorado willing to give him "work-equity." *Not another partnership*, I thought, but it seemed our only choice. He would start up a propane division in a small mountain town in Colorado for an oil company out of Kansas, and we would be dependent on his making it go.

"Do you believe this is God's will for us?" I asked my husband, wanting assurance and peace.

"All I know to do is ask God to shut the door if it isn't," he answered. That was biblical. I had to accept his final decision. It was inevitable. The children wouldn't be going with us. He would go on ahead of me to get started. We would have an income and money to pay for the wedding—a blessing I underestimated at the time. After the wedding, I would join him. I couldn't think about what that would mean and how I would feel.

* * * * *

Without much thought or discussing it with Vernon, I decided to tell Crystal the circumstances that had surrounded her birth. I wanted both her and Ed to know how special she was and what God had done for her. It wasn't easy, because I wanted this to bless her not hurt her.

I carefully began, "I've wanted to tell you what I've kept from you all these years. That I had three abortions when I was married to your dad."

"I got pregnant with you while we were at Mom and Dad's, waiting for your dad to get a job after getting discharged from the air force. He was on marijuana and had been abusive. While we were in Alaska, when I got pregnant, he kicked me in the stomach and took me to get an abortion. I didn't want to, but I gave in. I had two abortions in Alaska, but I wanted a girl so badly. When I got pregnant, I told everyone, and they were so happy. God gave me the girl I wanted, and you were so beautiful. I was so blessed."

She was shocked.

I knew this was a lot to be telling her. It was so hard.

She hugged me, and I told her I loved her.

"I'm telling you, Crystal, because I wanted to tell you how much God loves you and how special you are."

"Mom, I'm so sorry that happened to you. It must have been terrible. I love you."

"I love you too. You were such a beautiful baby. Everyone was so happy when you were born."

"Thank you for standing up for her," Ed told me later, sincerely showing gratitude for my decision in that very difficult situation.

They seem to be at peace with all I shared. Hopefully.

* * * * *

Thinking about our discussion years later, I wished I had done things differently. There were so many questions unanswered. Ignorantly, and not realizing my own selfishness, I had hoped this would also help me. I wanted to be free and didn't know how. I thought about how the children had lost four siblings. I didn't know how that would affect them and their relationship with me. I was so afraid of their reaction.

Oh God, you're going to have to take care of this. With the upcoming wedding, there wasn't time to sit down together and talk about it. Maybe that was all we could do at the time. Looking back, I certainly wished I had waited for that revelation to my daughter who was planning her wedding. At that time, I was ignorant of God's love for all of us and His desire to see me whole and healed.

Even though I attended a postabortion class through a pregnancy center while we were still in the flower shop, I kept my secret from friends, relatives, church—even our pastors—nor did Vernon and I talk about it. I kept my feelings protected. And if I wondered how God had saved Crystal's life, I had no answer except that we were living with my parents who loved me and welcomed the news of another grandchild. I went against my husband and chose life. God helped me and her. She was a miracle child, no doubt. God had brought a father into her life who loved her and had raised her for the past eleven years. I wanted her to understand everything right now, but I couldn't say the rest.

Vernon planted three red crepe myrtle trees in the front yard— one for each child. I hadn't told him about the fourth—the miscarriage. The children didn't know the significance of the trees because I wasn't able to unlock any of my grief or pain with them or Vernon. But these symbols didn't give me the freedom and healing I so desperately needed. I was ignorant of the years this would take and what would have to happen in my life.

The lost children—their lost brothers and sisters—were real. But a full acknowledgment of their lives would have to wait. For now, I had to let it go and say no more. I wanted them to know what I had gone through—the rejection, the abuse, and the psychiatric ward. But I couldn't go there. Instead I pushed that part back into that place of protection where at times I felt nothing, not even warm feelings of love for my living children.

* * * * *

Love isn't just a feeling though—not the kind of love that gives your life to another. It's a sacrificial commitment. I loved Crystal so very much that way. I would do everything within our means to give her the wedding she wanted. And we did.

This was a time of celebration and praise for a wedding orchestrated by God. In our most difficult financial time of our eleven-year marriage, God provided everything we needed. He had given Crystal a sweet nature with a lot of compassion for others—always thinking of her brother and parents. It had been hard for her—for all of us— at the flower shop for the past five years. I can only remember once when we had a fight through all her teen years. She had been such a blessing. I couldn't imagine my life without her.

At the same time, God was also blessing us in Mark's life. We had been distant for many years, but Vernon's presence seemed to always pull us together as a family. He loved the children and had been a good dad in many ways. We were seeing more promise and light out of the darkness that had threatened to take Mark's life so many times.

Prayer had to be the answer. Vernon and I had called out to God in distress when there seemed nothing we could do. My mother and dad had believed the best for him, and now we were seeing promise and hope overcome what had seemed to be a bent for self-destruction. I had been harder on Mark than on Crystal—something I would come to understand years later and regret that I didn't know how to give my son the praise for his accomplishments he needed so much from his mother as a young boy.

But I believed Mark's creativity and intelligence, with all God had put in him, would not be wasted. He was serious about a young woman named Sherry and living with her and her little boy. My newfound Christianity would have preferred they get married, and I had mixed feelings about their relationship. Those concerns probably kept me from fully reaching out and accepting her. It was hard for me to separate what I knew to be sinful behavior from the person and show her warmth and love, but she seemed really nice. There was no doubt as to where we stood on this—Mark certainly knew. Still, things were looking up. She seemed to be a positive influence in his life, but we hadn't come to know her very well.

* * * * *

While I substituted in the surrounding schools, I was also the main planner for everything from flowers to the reception. Vernon sent the money to pay for everything from his new job in Colorado. I was thankful for his willingness to give her a beautiful wedding.

Our house was on the market, but our income for the past five years had not allowed upkeep and maintenance. We regretted our missed opportunity to sell it during the height of the housing boom.

The prospect of leaving friends, our first home, and our wonderful church deprived me of peace. I even had nightmares. My whole foundation seemed to be shaking. Was this really God's will for us? Over the past eleven years, the children had grown up into beautiful adults, but I wanted to be a part of their lives as much as ever. Mark was twenty-four, Crystal, nineteen. There was so much I would miss in their lives—grandchildren, birthdays, holidays. But again, my dream was not to be.

I tried not to think about leaving them so far away and leaving all that had become familiar to me—this time with more uncertainty than when we left North Carolina. Satan was having a heyday, showing me every possible negative scenario, and I was falling right into his plan to give me discouragement—feeling defenseless without a weapon to fight against the images in my mind.

My main comfort was that Crystal was closely tied to the church we had attended for the past five years, and the people in the church loved her and Ed. It was a time for celebrating God's blessings and not being sad for losing a daughter.

* * * * *

On January 1, 1994, the evening wedding went beautifully as planned—a celebration of our church and family with God's hand upon this couple who were so much in love. With candles and tulle draped down the long aisle, Crystal's evening wedding was formal and elegant. Vernon, handsome in his black tux and silver hair, and the only dad she had known, proudly walked her down the aisle.

I watched with delight as Crystal danced with her new husband at the reception. My parents from North Carolina shared this beautiful wedding day of the granddaughter everyone believed was Mom's favorite. Our church family brought the food for the reception dinner on tables I decorated with wintergreens. God provided everything else Crystal had wanted through Vernon's new job. His desire was he wanted her to have the wedding of her dreams and to bless me with being able to give her the best we could. I was so thankful we were able to give her the desires of her heart for the wedding, while God blessed her with the desires of her heart for a husband.

Our dream was a reality. I could relax and enjoy the occasion. What joy and blessing God was providing for our whole family, especially for our daughter. Jesus was still with me and had good plans for me, not to harm me! He hadn't left me.

* * * * *

Our plans were to leave for Colorado as soon as the wedding was over. Vernon was fifty-three, and I had just turned fifty in December.

There won't be another church like this one anywhere else, I was think-ing as we attended our last service. I was struggling with emotions and also with the beginning of menopause. Everything was hitting me at once.

I felt like a stranger to this driven man at times. *This can't be God's will for us.* In his absence for five months, I had become more isolated from everyone yet desperately wanted to hold on to some-thing. In our five years at the flower shop, I had made few friends at the church and had little knowledge of God's promises for me. My faith in my husband had been shaken after five business endeav-ors, the wholesale propane business and the real estate being the last two. I had almost died of Crohn's disease, and we were losing our health insurance. It was a disturbing time for me spiritually, and I was plagued by fear and uncertainty, even to the point of having tormenting dreams.

When he talked about what was happening in Colorado, I lis-tened with little enthusiasm. Thoughts came; I couldn't speak. *How can he love me? He doesn't even seem to care about what matters to me. I don't want to leave my children or my church.* I quickly shoved those thoughts down, refusing to allow them more access to my heart.

Vernon and I had seen each other three times in five months. I didn't feel a part of his new life in Colorado. He kept up his positive outlook, but there hadn't even been a bite on our home. With no alarm system, we were leaving everything, including our expensive antiques, unprotected. I was overwhelmed. It was all too much. *Stop it—let me off!*

Mark, Sherry with her little son Kory, Crystal, and Ed came to see us off. *We're leaving, and I don't know when we'll see them again.* We hugged with promises to stay in touch. As we drove out of the drive, I cried so hard that Vernon stopped the truck and said, "Do you want to go back?" Vernon's voice was stern.

"No," I said, gathering my composure. "I'm okay." But I wasn't. I had a hundred questions and no answers—questions I couldn't ask my husband.

On we went. No turning back. Where would I go? I had never imagined we would be leaving California, at least not like this. The

U-Haul truck was carrying two propane tanks, our clothes, and a few household items, pulling our Oldsmobile with 250,000 miles and a bad transmission. We were being shaken just as prophesied—all that could be shaken was indeed being shaken. The question was this: What would remain when the shaking was over?

16

In the Fire

Taking in everything as we headed down Sapphire Street, I said good-bye to our home of ten years, past the row of palm trees, the neighbors, the mountains, stores, and businesses. *The three crepe myrtles—the memorials for my babies*, I thought. *We're leaving. I won't be here to see them grow.* I strained to take in as much as possible. Gradually gaining my composure as we pulled on Interstate 15, I relaxed as we headed for the high desert and beyond. My feet went up on the dash with a sigh of resignation. My heart quieted.

I thought about our last consultation with our pastor. I had been relieved to hear God wanted Vernon to have a company of his own. *How is that going to happen with no money other than Vernon's salary and no investment money?* I wondered. *Maybe the house will sell soon—hopefully.* We had prayed for God to shut this door if we weren't supposed to go in this direction. The door hadn't shut. I recalled the saying when God shuts a door, He opens another. This was the only open door. *Shaky ground for a move*, I thought.

Refocusing on the positive helped allay my fears. *I have to trust God in a way I have never done before.* My mother's comment to Dad before we were married, "Vernon really loves her," had stuck in my mind. *He's not giving up. We have each other.* One verse I remembered, Jeremiah 29:11, came to mind. *God does have a good plan for my life—whatever is happening.*

I looked at Vernon and smiled. "I'll be all right." He needed to know I was with him. I touched his shoulder. "I love you."

I was unable to see him the way God wanted me to see him: a fifty-four-year-old husband struggling to make a new life for us who wouldn't give up and was willing to do whatever to take care of me. He loved me. I just couldn't see why everything had been so difficult, why things hadn't worked out for us. How could I trust this next venture was going to work out? Vernon's heart was already in Colorado. Mine was still in California.

* * * * *

We had lots of time to think and talk on the two-day trip. The wedding had been beautiful, and Vernon hadn't complained about paying for it. He brought me up-to-date on the Colorado business. Describing the Sangre de Cristo Range some fifty miles from where we would be living, he said, "The name means 'Blood of Christ., peaks above twelve thousand feet top the range that stretches from New Mexico to Salida. Beyond that is the Collegiate Range, another series of fourteen-thousand-foot-plus peaks that form the Continental Divide." Vernon was a wealth of information. I tried to imagine it all.

His good mood and optimism were comforting, so I put my fears to rest and studied the map from town to town. He always saw the possibilities, while I still tended to be negative with plenty of thoughts about the losses we had just experienced and the attacks on my body that had almost taken my life. The thought that no one, including God, cared about my heart's desires tempted me to go to despair—lies from the devil. Not recognizing the old feminist thinking, I particularly felt that my needs and desires weren't important to my husband. I was a long way from trusting my husband and seeing his determination and refusal to give up in despair as his love for me.

"I know the plans I have for you, plans to prosper you and not harm you,"[19] ran through my head, reminding me of what God had to say about this. The idea that I wasn't important to God was

---

[19] See Jeremiah 29:11.

a lie—that I was less important than my husband, a man, or treated unfairly. Much later, I would finally come to know how much God *was* thinking about me and the good plans that He had for me—plans I couldn't yet see. In the meantime, I struggled with few answers.

"I want all God has for me," I had declared after my second surgery. Was all this bad stuff from God? But God was good! My view of God was changing from the angry, punishing God to a God who wanted something good for me, but I had a long way to go.

My pastor had told me, "Don't be led by feelings." I took that to mean feelings couldn't always be trusted. Then neither could my thoughts, which were up and down, back and forth. I didn't know if God had allowed this to happen or if Satan had authored so many losses and difficulties, and we were on the wrong track. I needed peace and assurance.

While Vernon was getting started in Colorado, I had come across a little pamphlet that listed all the Scriptures that said who I was in Christ. I fell asleep repeating those over and over. "I am a child of God.[20] I am an overcomer.[21] I am called of God.[22] I am a chosen generation.[23] I am more than a conqueror.[24] I am an heir.[25] I am seated with Him in heavenly places.[26] I am chosen.[27] I am forgiven.[28] I am free through Christ Jesus."[29] *This is who God is saying I am.* I was encouraged, but grasping the significance of it and truly believing it would come later.

---

[20] See Romans 8:14, Galatians 4:7.
[21] See Revelation 12:11.
[22] See 2 Timothy 1:9.
[23] See 1 Peter 2:9.
[24] See Romans 8:37.
[25] See Romans 8:17.
[26] See Ephesians 2:6.
[27] See Ephesians 1:4.
[28] See Isaiah 43:25.
[29] See Romans 8:2, John 8:32.

I kept the little pamphlet and took it out to read as the miles piled up behind us. Somehow it helped. A feeling of peace came over me.

* * * * *

"I don't understand why you didn't ask for company insurance when you negotiated for your job?" I asked while riding along the second day. My health problem was still a very big issue in our lives. Our eighteen-month extension of health insurance that had covered my two surgeries had ended.

"They wouldn't go for it—insurance wasn't part of the agreement. I didn't have a choice."

To continue our old policy, premiums would be almost $800 a month because of my preexisting illness. It might as well have been eight million because we had no savings, no cushion, and not enough income. *Why hadn't he insisted on insurance before agreeing to come to Colorado?*

"You could have insisted and made it a condition," I continued, resisting the urge to say what I was thinking. *If he really loved me, that would have been most important!*

Rather than escalating into a full-blown argument, I let it go and set my mind on other things.

"You're going to be healed," Vernon said.

He still believes what he told me before we were married. I want to still believe too. I'm taking just a small dose of prednisone. I had hoped healing would instantly happen when I was prayed for several times, but the symptoms hadn't left.

A big sign on our church wall in California had read, "Victor Not Victim."[30] I thought about that. I had been a victim in my first marriage, and now I was fighting the feeling that I was a victim again. This situation was not the same, though it felt the same in ways

---

[30] See Deuteronomy 20:4.

that seemed I had no control. Feelings, more feelings. *God, you didn't make a mistake*, I reminded myself.

* * * * *

From the green grass and flowers of California, we drove into the small mountain town under a cold, gray Colorado winter sky. Although I had visited Vernon once at the apartments, it was still a shock to arrive permanently.

The apartment complex was the only one in town and stood directly across from Walmart. The rented furniture was cold and stark compared to the antiques we had left in California. Our apartment was no larger than a motel suite and a one star at that.

"Oh great," I said sounding disgruntled, "the cars' headlights are shinning right into our bedroom and living room windows here on the first floor. I wish our apartment were on the backside."

Since Vernon was sensitive to anything negative, I tried to be positive and keep my thoughts to myself. It had been more than twelve years since I'd lived in an apartment complex. As I unpacked our personal belongings, I stopped the temptation to let my emotions take over. *I can always teach school. This isn't permanent*, I assured myself as I tried to find room in the small kitchen for everything I needed.

Thinking we had possibly seen the worst after surviving the flower shop, I hoped this new opportunity, with Vernon on a regular salary, would bring us into the prosperity we had once enjoyed. However, I had no desire to jump in and help in the propane endeavor.

It wasn't long before I came to appreciate the beauty of the surrounding mountains, somewhat adjusting to the quiet, rural, small-town atmosphere. On clear days, the snow on the distant mountains and wide-open clear blue sky were breathtaking. Instead of the hazy smog we were accustomed to in California, we could see for miles across the valley. The sun even shone brighter. I enjoyed our trips out into higher elevations, where I could get lost in another world and forget about everything else.

* * * * *

Choosing a church from the yellow pages wasn't my idea of seeking God for this important decision. My only request was for a Spirit-filled church—no dead denomination. Our first Sunday, everything in me screamed, *No, this can't be where God is bringing us! This little old church couldn't be right.* But I had no alternative suggestions. The pastor was weary, and his wife worked hard in a job that required most of her energy, so she was unavailable for fellowship. It was hard to relate to the worship and the sermons. I had no interest in making friends with the people. *Everything* seemed bad here compared to the wonderful fellowship we had left in California.

I especially missed my children. Still I tried to be cooperative and supportive with my husband and look for positive things. It helped. I didn't realize the battle that was going on in my head or the source of the battle, but I knew that no matter what it looked like, I was not going to do what I had done in my first marriage.

Dealing with anger was the hardest thing. *I'm a Christian now, and I can't lash out at my husband,* I thought as I fought against the urge to complain. "Be angry but don't sin," was the reminder I had gotten in church in California. *How do you do that? Forgive me, God. Help me.* I didn't want to go back to that woman who always had a snide, critical remark—the one who could cut a man down with her tongue, reminding him of every failure and shortcoming. That wouldn't have gone over well with Vernon anyway. I couldn't do that to him. Sending a photo of us smiling with the beautiful Rockies in the background back home and to our children gave an impression of happiness that I only wished I had.

* * * * *

Nothing in our transition went smoothly. I applied for one of several full-time teaching openings. No offer. My heart wasn't in it, and perhaps they sensed that. Secretly, I was relieved because I just didn't have it in me after the flower shop. I signed up to substitute and took some courses at the University of Colorado to get my teaching credential while Vernon forged ahead to build a propane division. At least he got a salary. My Colorado teaching credential was delayed. When I asked about it at the State Office of Education, an employee rudely said, "Why don't you just leave and go back to California?" Since God hadn't shut the door, I decided this must be Satan trying to discourage us.

All this happened after I went into debt to take certification courses. Then when I finished all the testing and courses they required, I found out that the requirements had been changed. Oh joy. So none of that was even necessary. I had never before encountered these kinds of roadblocks when seeking a job.

After all that, a secretary in the main office in Kansas confidentially told Vernon that she was hearing talk about getting rid of him. *Not again.* That news was softened by our pastor's encouragement. Vernon had hired him to work part-time for the propane company. This godly man gave us some very encouraging words at this critical time "I was riding along and praying about your situation, Vernon, and I believe I heard the Lord say that you were to have your own company." Our pastor in California had told him the same thing.

God is in this, I thought when he told me, breathing a sigh of relief.

* * * * *

It wasn't long after that when the Kansas company offered us $20,000 to go back to California and not compete with them. We gave them a flat *no!* The partnership ended. Vernon would not take any money from them or sign any agreement. It was a very hard time. We had no money at all and had not sold our home in California, but going back and giving up was no longer an option for either of us.

But *another* bad deal? Unbelievable. Especially hard was the vindictive treatment afterward when we didn't take their offer. They spread rumors that our tanks were stolen. My thoughts started sliding down again. *Losing our finances is bad enough—now our reputation, our name.*

As we rode the winding road to Westcliffe to visit a couple we had come to know, Vernon's voice brought me back from somewhere I escaped to. "Candy, you aren't even hearing what I'm saying. Have you heard anything I've said to you?"

"I'm sorry." That's all I could say. I couldn't cry or yell. I was numb. Again. There seemed to be nothing I could hold on to for the courage and strength I needed so badly.

Our parents and relatives didn't have a clue. Dad couldn't understand why my husband wouldn't get a good sales job and be happy with that. Vernon's dad wanted us to return to Oklahoma and live near them. They couldn't understand what we were doing. Sometimes I didn't either.

"Vernon wants to start a nationwide propane company," I told Dad. "He has a vision for it from God." I knew it sounded grandiose, but I wanted to have faith in what Vernon wanted to do. Maybe it would happen if I believed enough. Mostly I thought that my husband would use this company for God's glory, for money for promoting the gospel. I tried to encourage my husband and be the support he needed, but I was afraid this was just another big dream.

My uncle wrote a letter advising me to be careful and not use the equity in our home for the business endeavor, saying that a startup would take at least $200,000. They knew it was the only home I had ever had and didn't want to see me end up without a home. They didn't know there was no equity. The truth was, we had no money to start anything. I thought of what Pastor Dave had told Vernon before we left: "Let God put His vision in your heart." Was this really God's vision?

* * * * *

"J. C. Penny went broke five times," Vernon reminded me when I let fear and doubt enter and questioned what we were doing.

"That doesn't mean that we have to too. Once is more than enough!" I could feel the irritation rising in me.

Vernon was asked to take over a propane opportunity in Fairplay, Colorado, seventy miles away, thinking maybe this would be part of his own company. At least he had an income. He called Mark to come to Colorado to help. I was so excited. We'd been so far apart from him, and I wanted to see God in both our lives. Our son and his girlfriend, whom I still wished he'd marry, were coming to Colorado with her little son. What a blessing! Now Vernon would have some help.

I proclaimed, "The big *D* word wasn't in my vocabulary." Divorce wasn't an option. But more than once, the thought did pass through my mind about taking off down Highway 50—the main thoroughfare through town—as fast as I could and not look back.

When Vernon asked me to drive his old pickup to his office about seventy miles away, I thought about the futility of our effort and how it looked impossible—then the past came up. Was this another dead end? With our cocker spaniel, Jake, along for protection, the farther I drove, the harder I stomped on the gas, pushing the gas pedal to the floor. *I'm giving up everything for this crazy dream! What choice do I have? Left my home, my church—Crystal and her family.*

The old clunker may have felt the same way when it suddenly blew out something in the engine and rolled to a stop on the edge of nowhere. I was stuck out in the middle of a vast high plain in pre-cell phone days, unable to call Vernon or a tow. No cars on the road, no building in sight, just the huge mountains on the distant horizon and a vast expanse of desolate plains with one small road. The next car could be hours away. I gave Jake a pat, thankful for a very protective cocker spaniel.

I wrote a note and stuck it on the window. No way was I going to roll down the window when someone stopped. "Call my husband, Vernon Thompson, at this number and tell him where I am," I scribbled. The next hour seemed endless—no radio reception, nothing. Finally, a car came and was headed down the road that led to the only town between me and Fairplay. There would be a phone there. And Vernon would come.

Eventually his work truck appeared in the distance. Praying for forgiveness, I held back remorseful tears. Any remaining anger turned to guilt when I saw my work-weary husband get out with a chain and walk toward me with concern.

"I'm so glad to see you. I'm sorry you had to come and get me."

"What happened?"

I couldn't confess how my foot had pressed the gas pedal into oblivion. "The engine just stopped going," I lied.

Father, forgive me.

17

God Meets Me in Colorado

When our pastors found out they were being moved, we agreed to live in their home 'til they could sell it. He had been a lot of encouragement to us at a very critical time, and we wished them well. I hadn't been very involved in their ministry—just an onlooker.

In January of 1995, God brought a new pastor and his family to our church who were excited about their ministry. I didn't know what God had planned for me but was inspired from the beginning. On their first Sunday, his sermon was on Romans 12:1–2 about presenting our bodies as living sacrifices and being transformed by the renewing of our minds. *That goes along with that scripture God brought me in the hospital when I had my first surgery. He sent His Word and healed me.*[31] Encouraged to hear God's Word in a desperate situation, I hung on to every word the pastor preached.

The new pastor's wife, Lisa, and I became friends right away. She was friendly and outgoing, fashionable and talented, and took an active part in the church with her husband. I immediately liked her. Although I was twelve years older, I looked up to her as being spiritually way ahead. And she definitely knew more of the Word of

---

[31] Psalm 107:20.

God. *And she is filled with the Holy Spirit and prays in tongues. I want to be like her.*

* * * * *

Vernon's opportunity in Fairplay ended about the same time our new pastor came. Another dead end. I was finally getting substitute calls, which covered our living expenses. I never turned down a call due to Crohn's. Before moving, our former pastor had said he felt God was saying Vernon was to start his own company. A phone call to him confirmed what he had said before—Vernon was to start his own company. But how?

Desperately needing money, we decided to bring our antique furniture back from California to sell. With help from the new pastor and another man in the church, Vernon made the trip to California and brought back everything but the oak glass china cabinet, one of my favorite pieces. He sold it, along with the carved hall tree, to pay for the rental truck.

"They're only things," Lisa reminded me. "That's not who you are."

Wanting to have her kind of faith, I relented without much trepidation, amazed at myself.

Vernon took some of our most prized pieces of furniture to Colorado Springs to sell at an auction. I didn't object, but it wasn't easy. Among them was our English hand-carved oak sideboard. The results were disappointing.

Not knowing how it would happen, I piped up, "God can find a buyer here just as well as in Colorado Springs *and* at the price that we want." He disagreed.

* * * * *

God responded to my faith a short time afterward. Walking down Main Street, I went into the old St. Cloud Hotel simply out of curiosity. The owner had restored the Victorian lobby. Sitting there among the Victorian décor was a modern-looking, shiny white Yamaha piano that looked out of place.

Overcoming my fear and trying not to sound desperate, I spoke up, "I have a beautiful burl-walnut parlor grand piano made in the 1850s in Germany that would look perfect in here." They were very interested and asked to see it.

I wasted no time telling my husband what had happened, and in a matter of days, he had negotiated for some of our nicest pieces. I couldn't resist saying, "I told you so!" Then I told church friends and family how God blessed us by selling our antiques.

The grand piano, the pre-civil war empire couch that had been in my living room, our Chinese mahogany chest on wooden rollers that had been in the Iowa state capital at one time, and the beautiful walnut ball-and-claw guest bedroom set went to the owners of the hotel and for the price we asked for. I was thankful and blessed. God had heard me and responded to my little bit of faith. I didn't waste time telling my parents.

* * * * *

"Oh, no, I hate that you had to do that," Mom said, sounding sincerely sorry when I told her what had happened. She didn't understand. God had heard me and answered my prayer.

Not wanting to sound like a victim, I repeated what Lisa had said, "It's just stuff."

Altogether we collected almost $20,000 to put into the fledgling company. These were only *things* we reminded ourselves, and as our pastor in California had said, "Hold on to things loosely." I began to take my eyes off our hard circumstances and off my husband's struggles, off our failures.

Our son Mark was surprised. "I might have wanted that chest," he said sounding a little disappointed.

"I thought we'd be passing them down too. I'm sorry we had to sell it. But we had to raise money for the company." He understood.

I was amazed myself at how easily I had given up those *things*. But I knew it was God. He cared about me and had heard me.

* * * * *

With money from our furniture, Vernon started his own propane company. Quitting wasn't an option. He knew the propane business from a managerial position but had never been out on the trucks delivering or setting tanks. He didn't let that stop him.

He borrowed a delivery truck and rented fifteen tanks to start one customer at a time in the surrounding areas. Finally, I was getting calls to substitute teach, our only income for living expenses.

Without a tank-setting trailer and equipment, except an old pickup he managed to buy, he started his own propane company in the mountains of Colorado. I rode out with him to keep him company when I wasn't subbing. It pained me to watch him set a tank as he unloaded it by hand and heaved it into place. I didn't have much faith for what he was doing. It looked totally impossible to me. Our daily lives were mostly spent apart, but I went with him on deliveries when possible. It was those times I forgot everything but the beauty of the Colorado mountains as the old Ford cab-over strained to climb up to remote cabin sights for deliveries.

Jumping into the truck beside him one Saturday, I said, "I'll go with you so we can have some time together." He was headed to a campground fifty miles away to fill camper cylinders.

He smiled at me. "Great! Come on." It was painful to see his effort bring in so little money, but the view was breathtaking.

Holding on and wincing at every turn on steep, narrow mountain roads felt like an endurance test. My hopes for a pleasant day were dashed when the truck broke down coming home. That's when the Oklahoma farm boy attitude that he could figure everything out kicked in. He never let these situations get the best of him. I prayed. Somehow we made it home.

* * * * *

Vernon had his eye on a piece of property at the edge of town he wanted for the company. With no money, he made an offer. I didn't know if it were faith or just plain determination. Our pastor walked around the property and claimed it with him, only to have someone else buy it out from under him. Not to be deterred, he told the realtor, "I don't care who bought it, I am going to own that property."

Later the new buyer agreed to sell it to Vernon. The deal went through; although, the price had been raised. *How is he going to pay for it and bring in enough money to pay expenses also?* I questioned, ever the realist.

"It's still a good buy," he said when I expressed my concern.

* * * * *

Without hesitation, I agreed to teach the children at church, something I enjoyed more than anything. Our new pastors quickly put me in charge of vacation Bible school that first summer with their help. We walked the neighborhood giving our invitations and praying. At the end, we saw twenty-five children give their lives to Jesus. *What an exciting time this is going to be. At last, a friend. She really likes me and trusts me with the children.*

Most of all, I was excited when I heard them praying in unknown tongues. I wanted to do that too. Overcoming doubt and fear, tentatively, I began to join in. Finally, several years after being prayed for by Dr. Eby in California, I began to pray like that too. God *was* faithful. I knew if Jesus commanded His followers to wait to get filled with the Holy Spirit before going out, then I needed that power to witness and to pray also.[32] I still wanted all of God I could get even if it meant being called a "holy roller." Whether Vernon did or not, I had to have more.

Putting trust in these two new leaders gave me a sense of peace. They were believing for healing for me and for the propane company to prosper and seemed to have it all together. I looked up to them as the ideal couple and hung on to their every word, trusting that

---

[32] See Act 2:1–4.

they wouldn't steer me wrong. The prayers of well-known evangelists hadn't brought the healing I had hoped for in California. *How is God going to do this?* I thought.

After seeing God move by selling our furniture in this small town, I was eager to learn all I could about faith. Lisa gave me a *Faith Packet*, a collection of scriptures on God's promises that I read and memorized. Since Jesus fought the devil in the desert with God's Word,[33] that was good enough for me.

I could finally fight against this invisible enemy, against the lies and discouragement that had bombarded me, against depression and anger, and all the other thoughts and emotions that had threatened to sweep me away into a heap of failure and regret. The light began to come on, and I began to see which thoughts were not from God: *That's just wishful thinking. No one gets healed from Crohn's. You're just trying to make something happen yourself.*

"Nothing is impossible with God."[34] Your Word says that I was healed by Jesus's stripes on the cross.[35] God wants us to be in health as our soul prospers.[36] "Jesus healed all who came to Him,"[37] I said, affirming God's promises from my packet of scriptures. God *wasn't* the one causing bad stuff to happen to us.

* * * * *

But what about our finances? That was really difficult for me to believe. Substituting became our main source of income. There was no money from the company. Everything Vernon collected had to go back into buying more gas or other things for the company.

"We can't take any money out for ourselves," he answered me when I asked about paying ourselves. "The business is like riding a horse. You can't ride it when it's a young colt. You have to wait until

---

[33] See Matthew 4:1–11.
[34] See Matthew 19:26.
[35] See Isaiah 53:5, Matthew 8:16–17, 1 Peter 2:24.
[36] See 3 John 1:2.
[37] See Matthew 8:16, Matthew 12:15.

it's older and stronger, or you'll kill it." I acquiesced without an argument. He was right.

I never turned down an early morning call to sub. There was always enough money to somehow pay our rent and bills. Physically, I was able to work almost every day, even though the pain was still there in my lower right abdomen. Birthday and anniversary gifts were no longer possible with our budget, but God blessed me in many other ways.

"My God shall supply all my needs according to His riches in Christ Jesus"[38] was the Word God gave me for provision. I taped it on the refrigerator in the little house on Greenwood Street after we exchanged homes with our new pastors, our third move since coming to Colorado. Even the water bugs in that little house didn't overcome my attitude of praise and expectation.

My alarm was set for 5:30 a.m. to get dressed before a call to substitute. Without cell phones, I never knew when Vernon would be home in the evening. His dinner was usually in the refrigerator to be warmed when he came in. Work was the way God provided. When I accepted the calls, God always helped me meet the obligation. Faith for provision required that I do what I could and God did the rest—more than I could have imagined.

* * * * *

God's Word says that many are the afflictions of the righteous, but He delivers out of them all.[39] That was encouraging to know because we had a lot of afflictions. I didn't *feel* righteous. It was hard to comprehend that righteousness was a gift through faith[40]—nothing I could earn. What a revelation!

One such affliction happened when Vernon was driving so many miles nonstop, day and night, in the 1985 Ford cab-over delivery truck. Because he had to keep pressure on the accelerator all the

---

[38] See Philippians 4:19.
[39] See Psalm 34:18.
[40] See Romans 3:22.

time for so many miles in the mountains, the ball of his foot was so tender that he could barely put his weight on it. Even buying an expensive pair of new boots and new socks didn't help.

One night he limped into the house in agony with the pain. Filled with faith by the Word I'd heard and the Holy Spirit, I grabbed his foot and said, "Let's pray for healing. There's nothing impossible with God!"[41] I held his foot as we prayed, knowing that he had no one else who could drive and keep the business going.

"Dear Father," I implored, "we pray for this foot to be healed so that my husband can continue to drive and do the work he has to do. In Jesus's name,[42] and by His stripes, foot, be healed!"

The pain went away, and he went to bed. The next morning when he put his boot on, he said that there was no pain and that the foot didn't fit into the old imprint in the bottom but was changed and healed. Vernon and I were amazed, though we shouldn't have been. God had done what He said He would do. But we were still astounded at the healing. His foot never gave him any more trouble.

Another affliction resulted in a true miracle that happened one night when the delivery truck broke down with a dead starter on a dangerous icy hill on a back road. Without a cell phone to get help, Vernon walked a mile to a customer's house, wading the ice-cold creek to find no one home. Knowing the battery wouldn't even turn over, he made the long trip back in the dark.

As he approached the truck, he prayed, "God, you can put fire in this battery and make it start." When he turned on the starter, the engine roared to life. Finishing his deliveries, he finally made it back to the shop and came home to fall in bed.

The next morning at the office, the truck wouldn't start. With broken pieces of what was once a starter in his hand, the mechanic told Vernon, "There was no way that truck could have started."

We told the story to everyone we knew what God had done for my husband.

---

[41] See Luke 1:37.
[42] See John 14:14.

Then more blessings—Vernon's eyesight improved so that he didn't need glasses, and I didn't go to the doctor for Crohn's disease. I didn't want to. I wanted to be healed by Jesus.

* * * * *

There were many pitfalls—most we avoided. But I succumbed to temptation when allowing myself to feel self-pity for not being able to attend both of my grandmothers' funerals when we were in California. When I found out that my mother's brother had died, I wanted so bad to go and see everyone.

We had sold everything of value except the jewelry Vernon had given me in California. Without telling him, I took the most expensive piece, an emerald and diamond bracelet appraised at more than ten thousand dollars, to the pawnshop and pawned it for five hundred dollars and bought an airline ticket.

I did it without thinking about how he would feel and without telling anyone what I was going to do. All I wanted was my way. I shake my head today that I could do such a thing on one hand and be quoting scriptures for healing and provision on the other.

Nothing I had ever done affected him so deeply. He was hurt and angry. I was sorry, but the deed was done. Vernon used precious money—five hundred dollars needed for propane—to buy my bracelet back, but it was a long time before he was able to let the hurt go and completely forgive me. I repented and was thankful that he bought it back. Later he would tell how he paid for it twice.

* * * * *

Growing in God's Word in the fellowship of Christian women was more than I could have hoped for. I went over and over verses that told me that God loved me,[43] wanted me healed,[44] had put my sin

---

[43] See Jeremiah 31:3.
[44] See 3 John 1:2.

as far as the east is from the west,[45] and wouldn't remind me of them anymore.[46] I wasn't involved in the propane business, but Vernon kept going, putting everything back in the company and even hired a couple of employees. I substituted almost every day. There were times I was tempted to fall into complaining with Vernon being so inaccessible and my frustration rising, feeling alone and neglected. However, I didn't fall into that trap with my heart and mind on God.

I was an eager helper in every project Lisa planned. Still, I never mentioned the abortions to my pastor or her. I had convinced myself that I was okay. But I was also afraid of what they'd think of me. Only Vernon knew, and God, from whom I'd asked forgiveness.

Getting it in my head that God wanted physical healing for me was a struggle. I thought I had been the worst of sinners. Growing up in our little church in Hoskins, I heard prayers for healing ending with "if it be Thy will." I was surprised to find out that it wasn't only His will,[47] but He had provided physical healing for all on the cross.[48] God's Word confirmed it to me. I had a lot of incorrect thinking about healing and about God that had not come from God's Word at all. My mind was getting an overhaul. And I loved it!

---

[45] See Psalm 103:12.
[46] See Hebrews 8:12.
[47] See Psalm 103:1–5, Jeremiah 30:17, Matthew 15:30–31.
[48] See 1 Peter: 2:24.

18

Healed by His Stripes

The doctor's dismal prognosis after my second surgery in California had been earth-shaking but no longer. I didn't deny that the X-rays and surgeries showed I was riddled with abscesses all over my intestines. However, I now focused on what God said, not the doctor's prognosis.

The *Faith Packet* Lisa gave me was my constant companion. Here were the answers to my health, our provision, and all of the doubt and fear I had experienced. When I felt a pain, instead of thinking, *I'm not healed*, I fought the pain with God's Words on healing, believing the source of my illness was the devil.

The Holy Spirit helped me recognize the negative, dismal, discouraging thoughts that had plagued me for so many years. They seemed to be true—everything we had tried in business had failed, and I had almost died of Crohn's disease. Those *were* the facts, undeniably. But God's Word was my new truth. "Incurable" didn't belong to me. Healing was my promise. I remembered the scripture that came to me in the hospital in California. God sent his Word and healed them.[49] That was my promise. I also remembered the word my pastor had told me before my second surgery. This was going to be for God's glory.[50]

---

[49] See Psalm 107:20.
[50] See John 11:4.

I learned the Holy Spirit and the Word of God were more powerful than Satan, a liar and deceiver. The full comprehension of what Jesus had done for me on the cross was yet to come.

Because medical science knew no cause for Crohn's—and medicine offered no hope other than remission—my healing became a spiritual battle.

I prayed, "Your Word, Father, is health to my flesh.[51] Jesus, You healed all who came to You,[52] and You still heal today. You are the same today as You were then.[53] You are Jehovah Rapha and sent Your Word and healed all our diseases."[54] I could go on and on with my newly discovered truths. Almost imperceptibly, my faith increased over the passing months. Without insurance, I was extra motivated to press in and learn all the faith I could.

Faith without works is dead, the book of James says,[55] and I *did* work. I never missed a day subbing because of Crohn's and worked tirelessly in the children's ministry. A pain didn't send me to bed. Instead, I got up, dressed, and was ready for the call to sub. God helped me from being discouraged, because He was giving me strength to keep going each day. He also helped me keep quiet about all the details of my health to everyone I met. I could almost ignore the pain. Rather than giving in to thoughts like, "I'm not healed," "I still have Crohn's," or "This isn't working," I kept going and stood on God's Word as much as I could.

Above everything was a desire to know more about this new life I was living in faith. My hope came from the expectation of seeing God's promises in my life. I began to see Him in my daily activities, in the good things that were happening. I gave Him credit—I was living by faith, by design, and not by chance. I loved what was happening to me and *Who* was happening to me.

* * * * *

[51] See Proverbs 4:20–22.
[52] See Matthew 15:30, Luke 4:40.
[53] See Hebrews 13:8.
[54] See Psalm 103:3.
[55] See James 2:14–26.

I can't pinpoint a day when the healing scriptures became real to me—when they overthrew my unbelief and became more real than the words spoken by the doctor and medical science. When there was no more pain and the hard sore mass in my right abdomen left, it shouldn't have been as much of a surprise as a confirmation. But I *was* amazed to finally experience the reality of healing in my body.

"Vernon, the soreness is gone." I excitedly told him, pushing in on that place on my abdomen that had been so painful and had given me so much agony for most of our marriage. "Feel here," I grabbed his hand and placed it where the hard knot had been. "It's gone."

He felt it.

"My intestine isn't hard and painful anymore! Praise God. Thank you, Jesus!"

Vernon put his arms around me. "When I met you, I told you you'd be healed," he reminded me.

"Yes, you did! And I couldn't see how that was ever going to happen."

I checked and rechecked myself as I got used to my miracle, my new reality: *I. Am. Healed.*

I was overjoyed to be free of Crohn's, but my testimony had started months prior. I had taken myself off the small dosage of prednisone, not something I would recommend, but the dosage was very minimal and hadn't been increased since coming to Colorado. Faith for healing of Crohn's was not dependent on my symptoms and the pain and soreness.[56] Believing for healing came from getting God's Word in me[57] and understanding that Jesus had provided for my physical healing in His covenant with me through the cross—not on my faith making it happen.[58] Faith is just the channel to activate God's promises. My testimony became more fervent than ever.

Something changed when my faith stopped looking to the future for God to move and heal me and, instead, looked to the past—to the cross. Jesus had not only died to save me from my sins,

---

[56] See 2 Corinthians 5:7.
[57] See Romans 12:2.
[58] See Isaiah 53:5.

but his death had also redeemed me from the curse of sickness[59]—by the stripes He took on His body, by the scourging before He was nailed on the cross.[60] That included Crohn's disease.

He was my healer. "By Your stripes, Jesus, I *am* healed," I had declared, putting my hand on my intestine and quoting 1 Peter 2:24. The devil had been defeated. His only weapon was to lie[61] about what Jesus had done for me. Having the manifestation finally was so reassuring of God's truths in His Word. What my husband had believed and told me before we were married had come true.

* * * * *

My expectation for healing had been hard to explain to others, especially to my family back in North Carolina. They had seen how sick I was and were very concerned before I married Vernon. But they knew very little of what I had experienced this past year. When I called Mom to tell her the news, she was glad to hear from me.

"Guess what, Mom, I'm healed—the soreness is gone, and I can't feel the inflamed intestine that was there. It's healed. Jesus healed me."

"That's great, honey. I'm so glad. Do you have to be careful on what you eat?"

"No, I'm great. I can eat anything. I'm healed, Mom. The abscesses are gone. Jesus healed me. The pain is gone."

"Rea-lee?" she said, her voice showing excitement. "I'm so glad. Are you still on medication?"

"No, Mom. I'm off all medication. I feel great. God healed me! I'm not sick anymore. No more throwing up or anything."

"I'm so happy. That's wonderful."

I learned to be careful whom I told, because not everyone was going to believe me. When my faith was weak, a negative comment could leave me discouraged, regretting I had said anything.

---

[59] See Galatians 3:13.
[60] See Isaiah 53:5.
[61] See John 8:44.

Mom was happy for me, but she didn't understand. Only my little church family could truly rejoice with me, because they seemed to be the only ones who understood what had happened after walking through these past couple of years with me.

* * * * *

Just because I was healed didn't mean the devil stopped lying to me that I still had Crohn's. I had fought those thoughts of doubt and the lies that the devil or my own mind had been telling me for years:[62] *You're not going to be healed.* What a lie! *God doesn't heal today.* Another lie.

Now I told everyone, "I've been healed of Crohn's disease. Jesus healed me of an incurable disease." *Don't doubt,* I told myself. *No weapon formed against me is going to prosper.*[63] *The truth sets me free!*[64] The Bible says in Revelation 12:11 we overcome by the Word of our testimony and the blood of the Lamb—so I became an overcomer. The last part of that verse says, "And love not our lives unto death." I would come to know the meaning of that part more intimately years later.

Thankfully, I wasn't close to a lot of naysayers. As much as I wanted to be near my parents and to see them more often, I realized that I may never have been healed if we had stayed in North Carolina. I also stopped wishing we were still in California.

* * * * *

Faith for what Vernon was doing didn't come with my healing, but he was making progress. I wanted my faith to be in God for all my needs, not just health. My focus for my source of provision and healing and everything else was changing. Instead of looking to my

---

[62] See Genesis 3:1–5.
[63] See Isaiah 54:17.
[64] See John 8:31–32.

185

husband and the circumstances, I began to focus on the wonderful scriptures I was learning and on God.

Harrowing details of narrowly escaping tragedy on icy mountain roads were difficult to hear, but it didn't destroy or shake what God was doing in the spirit world for me. When Vernon was late coming home at night, I fought the thoughts that he had gone over the side of a mountain and lay at the bottom of some ravine. We had no communication—no cell phones. Sleep was often uneasy after sending up prayers for him—until he would finally slip into bed beside me, smelling of propane.

There were days I had to fight frustration and anger. Vernon was rarely available when I needed him. Sometimes it felt as if I didn't have a husband. Staying busy in daytime with subbing, nighttime with Mary Kay, and weekends with church gave me little time for anything else. My income paid for our rent, groceries, utilities, and a little spending money. His went back into the company. I was thankful for the sub calls, even though winter mornings meant cleaning snow and ice off my car. *Oh, for a garage again.* Vernon usually left earlier for his day of harrowing deliveries in the mountains or finding the money to pay for gas. As difficult as it was, I never felt desperate, needy, or hopeless—not when I had the promise that God would supply all my needs.

* * * * *

I missed Crystal and her family tremendously and got to visit when they had their first baby, a beautiful boy who reminded me a lot of her when she was born. I didn't even try to explain what we were doing. Mark and his little family were living here, but our relationship was strained after he left the company. Anyone on the outside might have thought we were out of our minds, living in a delusional world. My baby girl had now grown into a happy mother with her own child. Sad to leave, I didn't know when we'd see them again.

We rarely went to the doctor, but when I went for my monthly shot of vitamin B12, I told my doctor that Jesus had healed me, and I was not merely in remission. "I'm healed. Jesus healed me," I insisted. "I'm not in remission. Please put that on my records." I don't think they believed me.

"How is your Crohn's?" someone would ask.

"It's not *my* Crohn's. It's from the pit of hell,[65] and Jesus healed me," I replied with conviction.

"That's great," I would usually hear. But they had no understanding of what I had been through. The good fight of faith[66] isn't easy when everything is fighting against you to keep you sick. It had been years of suffering, of pain, and of discouragement at the setback and surgeries.

Those days of throwing up in the stockroom while teaching were over—just memories I was glad to forget.

My first thought when a sniffle began had always been, *Oh, no, I'm getting a cold,* or *Where's the cold medicine? I must be coming down with something.* Now I would say, "No, in the name of Jesus, that has no right on my body. By Jesus's stripes, I am healed."[67]

Praying for something like that seemed trivial at one time. *But doesn't healing include* all *sickness?* Now I fought every symptom as an attack that didn't belong to me. Sickness is part of the curse, and Jesus defeated sickness and disease.[68]

* * * * *

When I was diagnosed with Crohn's disease, I was far away from God and had no understanding of Him, His Word, or the Holy Spirit. He was still there, even when I was trying to do everything on my own, alone and struggling. He kept me alive with medicine when I was lost,[69] left with two children to raise and then with surgeries

---

[65] See John 10:10.
[66] See 1 Timothy 6:12.
[67] See 1 Peter 2:24.
[68] See Galatians 3:13–14, Deuteronomy 28, Leviticus 26.
[69] See Ephesians 2:13.

when I had no faith for healing and didn't know His Word. I wasn't even acknowledging Him. He loved me when I didn't love Him.[70]

And God didn't give me Crohn's to test me and bring me closer.[71] It came on me for other reasons—my own sin, stress, and unforgiveness[72] perhaps? I believed God turned for good what the devil intended for destruction in me.[73] The prayer our pastor had prayed before I went in for my second surgery came to mind. *My healing is for the glory of God.*[74] *This is happening now!* The scripture Roman's 8:28 no longer seemed to say God was causing bad things to happen for my own good, to teach me a lesson. Instead, as I learned more about God's character and nature, I realized that scripture said the opposite: God was turning to good *all things* in my life—Crohn's disease, losing everything and starting over, and maybe even the abortions.

There is no condemnation for Christians who are not healed.[75] God heals in many ways. I was thankful for what God did for me through medical science. But it wasn't His best, and I wasn't healed. Crohn's surgeries were not fun. I suffered for more than fifteen years. Side effects from prednisone can also be bad. I was told how bad by a lot of well-meaning people, to which I would answer, "God can heal me of those too."

Thankfully I didn't get a lot of negative input from believers in our church. That was because our pastors taught healing, and I was under their teaching—protected in ways I didn't understand. I didn't realize until years later how few pastors were preaching and teaching what I was hearing.

God's power for healing was in me. The Holy Spirit was in me. I was becoming a radical Christian. God was turning a radical sinner into a radical woman for God. I overcame fear and prayed aloud in a

---

[70] See 1 John 4:10.
[71] See James 1:13–18.
[72] See Matthew 6:14–15, Matthew 18:21–35.
[73] See Romans 8:28, Genesis 50:20.
[74] See John 11:4.
[75] See Romans 8:1.

prayer language, or some might call it tongues,[76] and spoke the Word of God over myself and others. No one in my church thought I was crazy. *But what would they think back home?* I really didn't care.

When I didn't know what to pray or how to pray for something, I would pray in a prayer language to fight the enemy—a help in weakness.[77] I also prayed the Word of God. My desire was to grow in everything God had for me.

Praise You, Jesus, praise You, Father. Thank you for healing me, thank you for what you've done for me. I said it and thought it over and over. What a joy I experienced.

* * * * *

Although I didn't fully realize at the time, the old feminist attitude—that God favored men—had tried to divide my husband and me before we came here. Submitting to Vernon by agreeing to come to Colorado regardless of how I *felt* resulted in blessings in my life I hadn't seen or anticipated and wouldn't understand until years later. This town didn't look like a place where I would find healing and be so blessed by God—but it was.

I *did* have to admit that God must have spoken to Vernon and not me. Or maybe I just couldn't hear Him. I had to admit that I was wrong in thinking God wasn't considering me when we came to this small town in the mountains of Colorado. Those were lies. Who would have thought I would receive what I needed from God in *this* place? It didn't matter that we had lost everything. I didn't *feel* poor.

The little stained glass cross I had brought from California stood at my sink as a reminder. "With God, all things are possible." *All* things.[78]

* * * * *

---

[76] Acts 19:6.
[77] Romans 8:26–27.
[78] See Matthew 19:26.

I began to think about the abortions and wondered what people would say if they knew. I got the idea that I needed to confess my past but didn't know how to go about it. I had never been able to talk to anyone. Only Vernon knew, and of course, my ex-husband.

One Sunday, the abortions were so heavy on my mind that I jumped up during praise and worship and said, "I had three abortions!" Somehow I thought I had to confess to be free. I knew that there was no condemnation to those who were in Christ and that my sins had been forgiven, but I needed to tell *someone*. No one said anything. I knew I had shocked everyone, including Vernon. I shocked even myself. I didn't know what to do, so I just stood there, as the worship resumed. I wanted everyone to know—to know me, what I had done, what I had suffered. I wanted my soul to be healed. Somehow my secret had to come out.

Lisa turned around and gave me a hug. Nothing else was said as the service continued. I didn't cry or say anything else. I was too scared.

What have I done? I didn't know what I needed. Evidently, neither did they.

Years later, I came to understand what had happened. Women who have had abortions are either afraid to tell people because of rejection—or they tell everyone, as if saying, "Will you still love me if you know what I've done?"

Until now I'd been unable to sit down with my best friend and talk about losing four children, about what I had suffered. I wanted so bad to be where she was spiritually, but I needed to let the truth out.

Healing from abortions didn't come at that time. I don't believe it was God who wanted me to get up and confess. Healing would have to wait. I still wasn't ready. My confession was a cry for help—to be free.

Years later, I had opportunity to ask my pastor what they were thinking. I was surprised to find they thought from the way I acted that I was already healed. I hid my feelings very well. Pride and fear had kept me a prisoner. I was still in denial, telling myself I was healed but had never let myself grieve for my three babies. My emotions were still protected.[79]

* * * * *

Not everyone felt about our pastors as we did. Some didn't like their faith teaching, and complaints reached the sacred halls of the denomination. Our pastors made the decision to leave rather than to stop teaching what they believed was biblical. We were shocked. Welcome to the reality of churchianity. I couldn't believe what was happening.

When they decided to leave, we supported them. Vernon offered a room in our building for holding services. They decided not to leave town but to restart right here. We loved them as family and started a new church. With God doing so much in our lives through their ministry, we didn't think twice about this move. It was probably a great relief for them, because as we learned later, they had been in a battle with the powers-that-be since they first came. They had kept us innocent of most of it, even the rumor that some had started that I was having an affair with the pastor. *God forbid!* I thought, *I'm ten years older than he is and his wife is my best friend.*

Finally, in 1999, we settled into a permanent building with high hopes for affecting the area with the powerful Word that was being preached. For oversight, we became connected with a ministry out of Texas with the same teaching and vision for evangelism that we had.

"We'll be here a long time," were Lisa's comforting words. "I feel God is telling me. I don't see us leaving."

She must have sensed my uncertainty. I knew I had a long way to go, and I couldn't imagine worshipping at any other church. I had gleaned from her in every area of my life—from my personal appearance to housekeeping and, of course, believing the Word of God for healing. I was confident that our friendship would never end.

---

[79] See Psalm 147:3, John 14:27, Matthew 11:28.

19

The Sad, the Good, and the Ugly

W hen our pastor made the announcement he was starting a Bible college in the fall, I wanted so much to be
included. As part of the course, we would be going
on a mission trip to Ukraine concluding the first year of study in
September 2001. I let out a cheer. "I'm going," I said. *Oh me. What
I've wanted to do for so long. At last! I can give my testimony of healing
and pray for healing for the sick.* Signing up, I trusted the finances
would be there. Vernon agreed.

Juggling Mary Kay with substituting and the children's ministry
kept me busy while Vernon worked hard to gain propane customers.
Excited about my new Mary Kay recruit and the upcoming Bible
college opportunity, I was working on my schedule for the upcoming
summer months when the thought came as if from outside me.

I should call my parents.

Then again, *I should call my parents.*

Mom answered the phone with a troubled voice. Then she said,
"Dad is getting ready to go to the doctor. His back has been hurting,
and he has had a hard time sleeping. I'm going with him."

"How long has he had the pain?" My stomach tightened.

"For quite a while. I can't remember. But it's worse. And he
thinks it's something serious."

Dad got on the phone. "I don't know what this could be." His voice was somber. "But it seems to be my stomach—maybe even stomach cancer."

"I should call my parents" echoed in my mind. *Wow. Thank you, God.*

Something rose up in me. Without thinking, I heard myself utter a brave, crazy declaration: "I'm believing that you're going to be fine and healed in the name of Jesus!" I didn't care what they thought. No way would I believe the worst. "Please let me know what happens." My mind was already going to the people I would call for prayer as I hung up the phone.

Later that day, Mom called.

"Your dad's in surgery for an aortic aneurysm." Her voice quivered. "The doctor doesn't give him much chance to make it."

I heard the words but didn't allow them to sink in and take hold. "No, I refuse to believe that. No weapon that can be formed against him can prosper."[80] My voice was unexpectedly firm and commanding, overriding the fear that threatened to rise up. Mom gave the phone to my brother.

My brother Stan began to give the details: Dad was in surgery and wasn't given much chance to live. "No," I shouted. "He is not going to die. In the name of Jesus, I declare that he will live!"[81] I pushed back every doubt that entered my mind. *Whose report will I believe?*

A few hours later, I was on a flight back home.

Dad can't die—he's only eighty and still working hard on the farm, I thought, remembering the last time we saw him. "I think you're going to make it," he had told us referring to the propane business and our struggle for more than four years. He never mentioned his own health.

---

[80] See Isaiah 54:17.
[81] See Psalm 118:17, John 14:13.

He has to make it through. I was angry—angry at whatever was trying to kill him.

* * * * *

Dad *did* make it through surgery miraculously. My prayer was answered, but he was left paralyzed from the chest down. I returned to Colorado with hope he would be healed and walk again. That summer was a blur. Every day I called to check on his condition. I made one more two-week trip to see him. Dad wasn't getting better, but I still held on to hope for his healing as I started Bible classes in September. Three weeks into the semester, the call came that he had died.

No. Can't be. Not my strong dad. Not him. He's supposed to live to a hundred!

On the flight home, my mind was flooded with memories of Dad—and with questions. Our relationship was restored. He knew I was okay, married to someone who loved me. Still, I couldn't believe he was gone. I had wanted him to be healed. *Why, God?*

Years earlier, I had confessed, "I'm so sorry for being so rebellious. Forgive me, Dad."

"We've forgotten about all of that," he assured me. "We don't even think about that. You need to also."

I had indeed forgotten the past also—both his and mine. Now I knew God's kind of forgiveness, the kind that doesn't bring up the past to us. Dad had been forgiven, just as I had. God commands us to forgive and says we won't be forgiven if we don't forgive others.[82] I loved him, and my memories were without regret.

Vernon had admired Dad and would always remember meeting the handsome Lawrence Keaver in the coffee room at the Lincolnton propane plant where Dad first mentioned his daughter, Candy, and her two children. I had admired Dad so much, but mostly from afar. He was buried in his navy dress uniform with Mom's picture still in his hat.

---

[82] See Matthew 6:15.

Much later, God helped me understand why Dad wasn't healed. It wasn't that God didn't want to heal Dad or wouldn't.[83] Dad didn't believe the way I did about healing. He loved God and believed for salvation through Christ's sacrifice. And what happened was according to Dad's faith, just as the Bible says.[84] I was comforted to know he was whole and healed and with God for eternity. I would see him again.

God was constantly teaching me, and the greatest lesson I got that semester wasn't from Bible college.

"If only I could have held him and told him how much I loved him," I said to Vernon.

"He knew," Vernon assured me. "He loved you and was proud of you."

God had given me a new life and given Dad the grace to start over and live out his life with the love of his family and wife.

* * * * *

There was little time to grieve the loss of my dad. God's call for Bible college was so strong I was able to move ahead with determination that I would not give up. I *was* an overcomer. God helped me through this difficult loss.

Soon I was immersed in studying along with children's ministry, Mary Kay, and substituting. Waking at five gave me an hour to study before a call to sub would inevitably come. Vernon still wrestled with the rigors of the business demands, but the company was growing, and he had his own delivery truck, service truck, and a couple of employees.

That spring, we joined our children and grandchildren on a visit to the farm with Mom. It would never be the same. The one who had planned and kept it was gone, yet his work, his dream remained as evidence of a father and husband who loved his family dearly and

---

[83] See Exodus 15:26, Deuteronomy 28:61, Psalm 30:1–2, Proverbs 3:8, James 5:14–15, 3 John 2.

[84] See Matthew 9:27–29.

gave himself for us. The barbecue pit and shed in the woods, the tennis court, the trees and planters, the barn, the tractor, the little fish pond—all his labors of love. How could I have been so blind to it and ever thought he didn't love me. I was thankful for all God had done through Dad as a strong father who took us to church and called Jesus his Savior. I loved him so much. I trust he knew that.

* * * * *

That year stretched me in many ways, but the greatest challenge came shortly before graduation with our pastor's announcement of a decision that hit me like a punch in the stomach.

"Lisa and I have accepted an offer to minister in a fellowship in Texas where she can minister to the women, and I will be in charge of evangelism, starting with our trip to Ukraine." *How can this be? What will happen to our church? To our friendship? How can they do this?*

Unbelieving, I listened to Lisa's explanation for their decision. *She had told me they would be here a really long time. How am I supposed to act?*

I said nothing. *She must be hearing from God. My feelings must be wrong. Who can argue with God? Why can't I be excited for her?* I did not want to dispute Lisa's conviction that God was in all this and tried to be happy for them. They promised to oversee our church and stay connected. The plan was to meet them in Dallas on our way to Ukraine, where we would minister together. Vernon thought their move was a mistake.

The honor of being valedictorian with recognition at our June graduation was overshadowed by the upcoming move of our friends and pastors.

After a bittersweet farewell potluck, we moved into their double-wide as a rent-to-own home of our own. Surrounded by reminders of them, I felt lonely and forsaken. My thoughts and feelings felt as chopped and jumbled as if they'd been thrown into a mixer. And whenever the mixing paused, I only felt lost. Only my anticipation for the upcoming mission trip gave me any feeling of purpose.

* * * * *

As planned, we met up with Tom and Lisa on route to Ukraine. I had missed them so much and felt straightened up and found when I was with them. Through a Ukrainian interpreter, I gave my testimony of healing from Crohn's disease, prayed for people to be healed, and taught a class on creationism. Vernon was mostly an observer, but his heart was moved to buy a much-needed set of new tires for the Ukrainian pastor's van.

We prayed and a woman with an issue of blood was healed. Hearing about the high abortion rate, I thought about my three abortions. I didn't say anything. *How can I be a witness if I can't even talk about what happened?* This brought on a whole new churning of thoughts that I suppressed while trying to focus on the ministry.

With little warning, Vernon's dad died of a heart attack while we were in Ukraine. We were in a state of shock. There had been no indication he had heart problems. It seemed like a miracle that we made it back to Oklahoma for the funeral on September 10. Almost a year after I lost my dad, Vernon was giving the eulogy at his own dad's funeral.

The next morning came another shock—the attack on the Twin Towers in New York. Exhausted and numb, we headed home the next day on the only available transportation—public bus service. It was a trip to remember, in more ways than one.

Then more things fell down. Tom and Lisa's ministry in Texas *didn't* work out. In the summer of 2002, after a difficult time, they returned to our town to lead our group of weary congregants. We paid their way back and wanted to help them anyway we could. I wanted everything to be like it had been before they left. It wasn't.

We gave them back their double-wide and moved back into the apartments where we started out across from Walmart. I still had hopes of a revival of the Word of God happening as had been prophesied, but we were back where we started. If not for the gratitude I felt for having them back, that would have been a horrible downer. When an office position came up at our business, my husband hoped I would come in and help him. I refused, saying I wanted to pursue Mary Kay cosmetics. Also, I had no office skills. We both agreed to hire Lisa who accepted the offer without hesitation. I was excited to have my best friend working for us.

* * * * *

Shortly after moving back to the apartments, ten years after moving here, a call came from Mom that was life-changing. Her voice sounded excited.

"Candy, I've decided I'm going to do something, and I told Stan, and he's agreed."

"What's that, Mom?"

"I've decided to give you, Stan, and Peter each $100,000 when the sale of the farm closes."

My mind whirled. "Really? I can't believe that. Are you sure?"

"Yes, I'm sure. I've made up my mind. I want you to use yours to buy a house. Nothing else. Stan's going to be sending you a check."

I was stunned. Suddenly we could afford a home. A real home.

More emotions joined the mix. *I will never drive through the gates Dad made, down the drive again, or walk in the woods down to the barn or to the barbecue shed by the creek.* I wanted to hold on to that place forever.

Vernon agreed when I suggested we write our tithe check to the church before anything else. Mom was a giver, and so was I. I knew you can't outgive God, and now I experienced it firsthand.

We found a house under construction overlooking the town with an amazing view. It was more than I could ever have dreamed. I hadn't prayed for a house—just continued to be faithful with the little[85] we had and continued to seek Him and His Word. Wow, first healing and now a new home. God's Word came true in my life: Seek first His kingdom and His righteousness and all these other

---

[85] See Luke 16:10.

things will be added.[86] And they were. I was filled with thankfulness and praise to God. I felt so much love for Him. This was way beyond what we needed. Waking up to praise music in our bedroom overlooking the mountains was exhilarating. I *was* that love letter now—every morning—the one prophesized back in California at our church.

More good news. Crystal and her family decided to move to Colorado to live near us. They moved into our unfinished basement while Ed commuted to Denver starting a new job. I was so happy. Both of my children now in Colorado! I felt so blessed.

* * * * *

For a year and a half, things moved along with our church and pastors. I worked hard with Lisa to start a citywide women's ministry—making flyers, providing decorations, and doing press releases—while Lisa worked for Vernon in the propane business. Things just weren't the same in their ministry, in our church, or in our relationship.

With Crystal and her family in the basement, I was busy in our new home. Mom came out to visit and enjoyed the home we bought with her generosity.

Lisa soon became an administrative assistant at our business. Unexpectedly, when my husband seemed to be pleased with her work, I struggled with jealousy toward my best friend and mistrust of my husband.

Instead of being quiet about it, I let him know how I felt. "All you do is brag on Lisa and talk about how great she's doing. Even to the children," I complained one evening. "I don't like you talking about her all the time." The thought of keeping all that to myself and doubling down on praying didn't occur when these totally unexpected feelings came up.

"I'm just glad it's working out, *and* I don't talk about her all the time." *He's acting as if I am unreasonable and too sensitive.*

---

[86] See Matthew 6:33.

Things didn't seem right. Nothing was the same. But I let it drop. My feelings were wrong, it seemed. I renounced my negative feelings and resumed my peaceful attitude and focused on Mary Kay and our outreach to women.

Every time I thought I had gained control of these unwanted feelings, I would be confronted with another situation. Any mention of my feelings caused an argument.

"I thought we could go to lunch together today," I announced to my husband as I walked into his office.

"Sure, I'd love to. I had asked Lisa to go to lunch today to discuss the budget, but you can join us if you like. It'll probably bore you."

"Sure, I'll join you. No problem," I said, smiling at Lisa at her desk, where she sat in her stylish outfit, slender figure, and long blonde hair. *Argh! Stop the comparison! She's my friend. These feelings are unfounded. He's only interested in his business.* I shamefully repented of this ungodly comparison as we walked out to the car. *Good grief,* I thought. *Vernon is fifteen years older than Lisa.*

* * * * *

I had no one to talk to, and my husband wouldn't acknowledge my feelings. Whether they were justified or not, I needed to be able to express them—just get them out. But I was ashamed—ashamed to admit I was jealous and didn't trust my husband. Also, ashamed that I wasn't spiritual enough to deal with this myself—in other words, too proud.

Another day when I walked in the office, his secretary mentioned she had made reservations for him and Lisa at a motel in Albuquerque for his upcoming trip. *Excuse me?* Vernon hadn't mentioned that part of his trip. He had dreams for a nationwide company, and he said the trip was about acquiring another company. But nothing about Lisa.

I acted as if I weren't surprised, but my head and chest were pounding. I gracefully excused myself before I exploded. *Why is Lisa going with him alone? Doesn't she know how it looks? What about the*

Bible warning not to give the appearance of evil?[87] *Why hasn't Vernon told me? Does he think it doesn't matter, as if she's just another guy?*

I tried taking it to God and controlling my feelings. But when Vernon came home that evening, I let it all out. "You planned a trip with Lisa and didn't even mention it to me? An out-of-town trip *overnight*? And you didn't ask me to go?"

"It's a business trip—don't start accusing me. She's getting training as a manager so I can have someone who can run the business so *we* can get away."

"You hadn't even told me or asked me to go. I only found out today. And you had already made reservations."

"You can go along if you want to. You're welcome to go." *He can't even apologize. Doesn't he see how hurtful it is?* My anger rose above my restraint.

"Oh, sure, as an afterthought. How could you not tell me what you were going to do before you made your plans? Why didn't you ask me first and then decide whether Lisa needed to go?"

He had no answers. There were no good ones. *My best friend and him. Overnight.*

I debated it in my mind, then refused to go. Who could I go to? My intestines churned too furiously to be around either of them. My trust in my husband's love and in my friend was being attacked as never before, and I was being led by something other than faith and God. I was unable to pack and take my place beside my husband. I was on the outside and had been pursuing a Mary Kay career while my husband was sharing his dreams with my best friend.

* * * * *

I had a miserable two days. Thoughts of my first husband and his secretary coursed through me like a reckless speeding car. And I allowed my mind to relentlessly feed on the *what-ifs, it-looks-like,* and *it-seems-like.* Faith and love were hard to find. I struggled to find

---

[87] See 1 Thessalonians 5:22.

scriptures, to find faith, to believe the best, but all the things I held to be true were attacked.

After they returned from the trip, I blew up and let all my emotions out. Again. At least the angry ones. But I couldn't cry. I couldn't tell him how hurt I was, how I felt unloved and unimportant to him.

He yelled, whether out of primal defense or just to shut me down, "Maybe I'll just drop dead, and then you wouldn't have any more problems."

I wanted to agree with his idea, but instead I said something about the consequences of words. Later I asked forgiveness for the way I had reacted. I felt like a failure. I was the one who was wrong—always. I felt hopeless, unloved, and that my feelings didn't matter. I couldn't see my feelings were from lies I was believing from the devil or my own flesh.

A few days later, it all was in my face again. Driving home, I saw Vernon and Lisa at the tank yard together. He was oblivious of me. *More training*, I thought, feeling once again the outsider. Thoughts I couldn't control bombarded my mind. I was angry, hurt, and feeling helpless.

Later that afternoon, I started throwing up nonstop. I called him, afraid and in pain. "Vernon, hurry and come home. I'm throwing up nonstop. I may need to go to the hospital." *Crohn's can't be coming back.* I thought as I cried, "I'm healed. Oh Lord Jesus, help me."

20

The Big "D" Word

ear threatened to overwhelm me as the emergency room
attendant shoved a stomach tube down my throat to stop the
vomiting. *Am I not healed of Crohn's disease?* My faith was as
low as the floor itself. *How can this be? I brought this on myself.* I was
so scared. *Oh, Lord, help me. I'm sorry.*

After the tests results, the surgeon came in. "We're going to have
to see what's causing the blockage."

A third surgery—after fifteen years.

"You're scheduled for 9:30 in the morning."

Vernon and I were bewildered, both thinking this shouldn't be
happening. *How will we pay for this?* ran through both our minds.
But that was the least of my worries.

After surgery the next day, I heard the best news possible: "We
gave you a new connection. There were at least a hundred staples
from the last surgery and a lot of scar tissue causing the blockage." So
it was complications from previous surgeries.

*I won't have to go back on prednisone. The abscesses haven't come
back. I am still healed!* I knew that it wasn't God who was punishing
me with this attack. I had opened the door for the enemy to come
in with jealousy and believing lies. I repented. *Lisa is my friend and
didn't have anything for my husband. He loves me.* I tried to convince
myself.

The physical recovery was more difficult than fifteen years earlier in California. Age *did* make a difference. Another act of mercy—we received financial help for patients without insurance. Again, God provided. I felt so undeserving. My heart was humbled. Emotional and spiritual recovery were more difficult.

Although I had helped in every way possible, Lisa's attempt to start a women's ministry was not successful. Our church wasn't going forward. *Why?* I couldn't put my finger on what had changed.

I tried to put my heart in God's hands the best I could and move forward. I wanted to believe the best of her and my husband. I had been shaken in my marriage and my faith as never before. I couldn't discuss my feelings with Lisa. I wanted to forget everything and trust God and go back like things were before.

* * * * *

Our pastors never let us know the extent of the hurt they had experienced from the broken promises of the ministry in Texas. We had been hurt too. No one talked about what had happened here or in Texas. We all tried to go on as before. I was totally unprepared for what happened next.

I started hearing things that indicated Lisa's favor in our business appeared to be slipping, along with problems in her marriage. Then rumors of her and another employee surfaced. Still her friend, I defended her to everyone.

Then one day in the office I witnessed her interaction with this other employee. It wasn't long before they both left the company in the wake of a huge blowup.

It all came crashing down—their marriage, their family, and the church. With that were dashed all my own hopes for a part in their ministry. The church closed. And Tom and Lisa separated. Both my beloved church and my longtime friends and my mentor, Lisa, were out of my life. It seemed like God's purpose for me had left with them.

* * * * *

The blowup unearthed something else too. My husband owed a huge tax bill I knew nothing about. Somehow he had let it go when he was starting up, never catching up until it snowballed into a monstrous amount. The IRS hadn't caught it either. So Vernon had just kept going. I couldn't believe what I was hearing. *Who else knows? What is the truth?*

"How could you not pay the taxes? Didn't you know the IRS would eventually find out?"

Raising his voice, he defended his actions, "What should I have done? Quit? I was working day and night. I was doing it for you."

"If you were doing it for me, you would have paid it. That is stealing. How are you going to pay that back?"

"Don't accuse me. Are you accusing me of being a thief?"

I knew I had to shut up before things got ugly.

That's exactly what it is. Stealing. And lying. How could he do this? What's going to happen to us? Fear of losing the house and our business—*again*—gripped me like never before. *He might even go to jail.* Then came the anger and the hurt.

Leaving this guy felt awfully easy to do at this point. My faith couldn't wrap around the huge debts we owed. Possible consequences tormented me. Our home, our business—not again.

I was convinced that if we had gone to God together, He would have helped us.

"You kept me out of your life, out of what you were dealing with. We're supposed to be in this together. I could have been praying or maybe had some input. Let's get counseling and some input from someone."

"What pastor is going to understand business? They'd have no idea what to do."

He was completely closed to my questioning and suggestions.

* * * * *

Feeling lost and confused after our church closed, I reluctantly went with my husband to a large church in Colorado Springs. It was an exciting church with a great breakfast and coffee bar and bookstore—programs for every age. But I was hurting, and there was not a single person I knew.

Trying to forget and stay busy, I volunteered at a women's crisis center in town where a friend worked. There was nothing I could do about our business finances, so I tried to leave that to Vernon *and* God. I hoped to be a blessing to the women coming in for help, but instead I got something much different.

In a non-Christian environment at the center where women were coming in with all kinds of complaints, I absorbed their mindset and became more critical of my own husband. We had some heated arguments, and neither of us would back down.

I dug in my heels. *I'm tired of always being the one who says I'm sorry.*

The more I thought about it, the more justified I felt. *I'll be better off alone. He keeps telling me to leave and won't hear me. He doesn't care. How could he keep things from me for so many years?*

Two months earlier, we had celebrated our twenty-fifth anniversary on a cruise to Hawaii. Now I didn't even try to stop our marriage from falling apart. In frustration during an argument, he told me to leave—to get out. After that happened half a dozen times, I decided to file papers for separation.

When we married, I often said that the big "D" word, divorce, was not in my vocabulary. I had said that to Dad when we were going through losing everything. I knew that God hates divorce, and I had been determined that this marriage was for life. Looking back, the progression from woman of faith to filing for divorce was clear.

My hurt feelings were exacerbated by his lack of remorse. He still felt justified in doing what he had done. I had no hope that he would ever change. Then I entertained thoughts about the past—compiling a long list of negatives. I didn't listen to anyone who tried to change my mind. I had no outlet for my emotions. *I'm glad Dad isn't alive to see this. I would no longer be able to tell him that the big "D" word isn't in my vocabulary.* I felt dead and empty inside. Numb.

* * * * *

With encouragement from a friend at the center, I went to an attorney out of town and filed for divorce. Then I had the locks changed on the house, served him papers, and told him to come and get his clothes. No consultation with anyone. I didn't care that he was sleeping at the office on a cot and using a makeshift shower in the employees' bathroom. He never said he was sorry for anything. I didn't see how it could ever be worked out, so I finally convinced myself I'd be better off alone.

The other thing I didn't see was the same old feminist declaration rearing its head—the lies that had so long ago been deeply embedded: *I can make it on my own.*

And I didn't see Satan's plan for destroying us or how I was disregarding the promises I had made to Vernon and to God. My vow, "'Til death do us part, so help me God," didn't give me a pause. I also didn't think about our children and grandchildren. I was done.

Convinced I was justified, I found fellowship in a small church with my friend from the crisis center. The pastor knew me, but I hadn't confided in him about my intention to divorce. The friend even offered to go to the courthouse with me to file. I had told my side of the issues and defended my position against my husband. Vernon attempted to reconcile, but I ignored him.

* * * * *

One day, I stopped by my pastor's home to pick up some Mary Kay products from his wife. He confronted me about the divorce. I was surprised because he knew I had filed but hadn't said anything.

"What's going on with you and Vernon?" he asked.

I told him about the huge IRS debt. He wasn't moved.

Calmly, he told me, "You need to call this off and see if Vernon will counsel with us. If he will, then both of you can counsel at his church too."

You don't understand, I thought. I couldn't talk about my feelings and the hurt and betrayal I had felt and what had happened. But deep down, I did not want to go through with divorce, even though I didn't feel very repentant. So I agreed to counseling.

* * * * *

In our counseling with the pastor and a church elder, I couldn't talk about my feelings. Lisa came up, and once again, the old feelings were there. My feelings seemed to be unimportant. No resolution there. No saying he was sorry. He defended himself.

Then there was the huge tax bill. How was he going to pay that?

My pastor said Vernon hadn't done anything to warrant a divorce according to Scripture. He wasn't a whoremonger nor was he beating me up. I knew divorce was wrong, and I wanted to trust God to work it out somehow, whether I felt like it or not.

The pastor counseled biblically that my marriage was a covenant between God and me as well as with Vernon. My promise had meant, "There is nothing you can do that will cause me to leave you." Jesus would never forsake me and was for my marriage.

My commitment to Vernon, like Christ's commitment to me, was for life whether he ever changed or not. I couldn't disobey God any longer. More than anything, I didn't want to give up God and what He had done in my life.

I agreed to call off the divorce. The truth is that nothing is impossible with God,[88] and our marriage wasn't hopeless. My walk of faith would have to include my marriage. He had been a father to my children when I was in a desperate place, and he declared his love for me. Somehow, all that had been lost in my hurt feelings.

* * * * *

My pastor also suggested I renounce and repent of any involvement in the occult before I came to Christ and married Vernon.[89] We used Neil Anderson's book *The Bondage Breaker* as a guide.

---

[88] See Luke 1:37.
[89] See 1 John 1:9.

"I was curious about the Ouija board and played with it once in college," I confessed. "And I read Edgar Casey's book on spiritualism because I wanted to believe in reincarnation."[90]

"Anything that you showed an interest in, whether you were deeply involved or not, pray and ask forgiveness and renounce your involvement or interest, and shut the door once and for all," my pastor counseled. "As a Christian, you have power through the Holy Spirit to shut any door that was opened to demonic influence."

With each confession, as the Lord brought to memory, I prayed.

"Jesus, I ask your forgiveness for my involvement in tarot cards. I renounce ever having shown an interest, and I close the door to any demonic influence from that in my life, in Jesus's name."

Then I saw "abortions" on the list.

Oh my.

I paused, then took the leap. For the first time to anyone in leadership in any church over the past twenty-five years, I confessed: "I had three abortions in my first marriage." No one said anything. I began to tell about my circumstances in Alaska and my first marriage.

Vernon sat straight and defended me. "She was kicked in the stomach and abused by her husband and didn't want to have the abortions."

I was reminded of the scripture in 1 Corinthians about God not letting you be tempted beyond what you can bear and when you are tempted providing a way out so you can endure the temptation.[91]

I confessed, "That is true. Now I know I could have called my parents. Then I was so blinded and isolated the thought never occurred to me. God would have provided a way out."

I was guarded but relieved when I felt no condemnation from them. No one shook their head and said, "That's the unforgivable sin. Meeting over."

Calmly I prayed, "Jesus, I ask forgiveness for the three abortions I had. I renounce abortion and cast out and shut the door to

---

[90] See Hebrews 9:27.
[91] See 1 Corinthians 10:13.

the design of the enemy on my life."[92] Oddly, I couldn't even cry. But it wasn't about emotions. I had asked for God's forgiveness to myself, but this was my first public declaration and renouncement. The chains were falling.

Romans 8:1 came to mind, "There is no condemnation for those who are in Christ Jesus." No one could condemn me,[93] and no lie of the devil could steal this truth from me.[94] I was a *new* creature in God's eyes,[95] washed clean by Jesus's blood.[96]

* * * * *

I also repented of my involvement in feminism and my tendency to want to rule over my husband.[97] I had not honored and respected the men in my life until this marriage. And I didn't want to go back. The feminist declaration of "I don't need a man to take care of me" had creeped in again with the notion I could go on alone rather than go to God and trust Him.

Vernon didn't want divorce, and he declared his love for me. I don't think he realized how hurtful his telling me to get out and leave—to divorce—had been. He didn't tell me he was sorry. *What if he never does?* Maybe someday. I had myself to deal with, and that was enough.

God led us to a wonderful marriage conference called "Love and Respect" held by Dr. Eggerichs and his wife, Sarah. We held a conference at our church a couple of months after we were reconciled. It was based on Ephesians 5:33 (KJV), "Nevertheless let ever one of you in particular so love his wife even as himself; and his wife see that she reverence her husband." This was the first time I heard of the Biblical basis for respecting and honoring my husband unconditionally and for my need to be loved unconditionally. What also

---

[92] See 1 John 1:9.
[93] See Romans 8:1.
[94] See John 31–32.
[95] See 2 Corinthians 5:17.
[96] See Ephesians 1:7.
[97] See Colossians 3:18, 1 Corinthians 11:3–16.

stood out was their teaching about women needing an emotional release just as men need a sexual release. To be able to release my emotions without fear or without being dismissed was a legitimate need of mine. If only I could. I didn't understand how my trust had been damaged and how it would take time to heal.

* * * * *

With God's help, a lot of work, and another CPA, we survived the crisis that nearly took our business and our marriage down. God's mercy was beyond my understanding, more than I could have hoped in our situation. He hadn't closed the business down and given up on us. Recovery was gradual, and I had difficulty letting go of the past. I needed resolution. The IRS mess remained. I tried to trust God to straighten it out, but I didn't know how He would do it.

Finally, I was able to tell my husband how I had felt, how he had hurt me so deeply. "God says we are not even to give the appearance of evil, and it hurt me—whether anything happened or not. I was so hurt. How would you feel if I had done you that way?"

"I'm truly sorry for that," he finally said. "I didn't want to hurt you. I would never do that again. Please forgive me."

Just that much brought me close to a peaceful resolution. "I'm truly sorry" can be among the most healing words a wounded heart can hear. But he held to his conviction that he had not stolen when he didn't pay his taxes. He claimed that his intent hadn't been to steal. *And how will that fly with the IRS?* I didn't agree. I had to let it go and put it in God's hands. He was in God's hands. I could only pray and forgive. Relief came in a few months.

Through a negotiating firm, he set up a payment plan with the IRS. Vernon was determined to repay his debt, whatever it took. Now I could feel proud of him and more confident that everything wasn't going to come crashing down. And I asked the Lord to help me get over it all completely.

When thoughts returned, I made an effort to rebuke them[98] and not give a voice to them again. I prayed for God's promise of righteousness in our lives...peace and joy. It had been a long time since I had felt real joy. Jesus defeated the world, the flesh, and the devil—and whichever it was, I could defeat it too, with His help.[99] Finally after months, I began to feel close to my husband again.

* * * * *

Our pastors' lives, ministry, and family had been irreparably hurt. I regretted I hadn't been strong enough to speak to Lisa in defense of their marriage covenant. I couldn't believe she was gone out of my life and they had divorced. I felt so letdown with all kinds of feelings—mostly disbelief.

Never again. I vowed that the next time I faced a person or couple in need of such a challenge, I would rise and do it. Tom and Lisa were the ones who had taught me most of what I knew about God. Vernon and I were determined that we would always stand up for marriage covenant with any couples considering divorce. God is a covenant God, and anything can be worked out if both want to obey God and want their marriage to work.

What a disaster it would have been for our children, our grand-children, and my testimony if our covenant of marriage had been destroyed. I was thankful that my new pastor had the courage to tell me the truth about divorce. I attended church but had no desire to do anything in the ministry.

The debt was still hanging over us and seemed impossibly large with no ability to pay without the sale of the company which seemed very unlikely. At least, it was out in the open, and payments were being made regularly. I had no control over this area of my life. God redirected my thoughts and energy to a part of my own heart that I had avoided for many years.

---

[98] See 2 Corinthians 10:5.
[99] See 1 John 4:4.

At that time, I didn't see a connection between the abortions and filing for divorce. But the deep pain I had suffered from my first husband—the abuse while I was pregnant and his taking me to get abortions, leaving me for his secretary—was still rooted in me and had definitely been a factor.

With my secret of abortions finally out, I felt an urgency to find out what God would do if I stepped out and trusted Him with the next step. I wrote the first of many personal testimonies about my abortions and decided to take it to the director of our local pregnancy center. Vernon agreed. I was not prepared for her reaction and what she proposed that day, but I knew it was God.

21

Facing the Pain

66 **W**hat do you think about being our postabortion counselor?" the pregnancy center director asked after hearing my testimony and reading the letter I had written. She was a caring, compassionate woman and sincere about her offer. I saw a door opening without my having done anything but share my story.

Without hesitating, I said, "I would love that. I know God's Word concerning abortion, but what about training?"

"We'll find a training class for you at another pregnancy center. In the meantime, would you volunteer in the office and help us out?"

"Of course." I tried to contain my excitement.

* * * * *

I faithfully volunteered for almost two years before getting an opportunity for training in an eight-week postabortion class in Colorado Springs. *Finally, God will use me to help women!* I would attend as a client, then as a trainee in other eight-week groups. Whatever it took, I was ready, and Vernon fully supported my participation. In the meantime, I was getting bolder telling volunteers and clients about Christ, my healing from Crohn's, and abortion.

Sitting in the group for the first time, I felt confident I would do fine. I'd been studying the Word, been in ministry for years, done a short-term mission, and been healed of incurable diseases. I knew what God said about abortion, had no doubt it was murder,[100] and felt I had repented. But I was apprehensive. This was a new step of faith.

"This eight-week class doesn't promise to be all God has for you for healing," the group leader cautioned. "Everybody is different. You are all very courageous to be doing this, and I know God will bless you for stepping out and being vulnerable. At the end of our eight weeks, we will have a memorial service for your babies. You can name them and bring something like candles or flowers to memorialize them. Some can share a poem or a letter they have written." My mind wandered to what I would bring for them. *What will my feelings be?* I thought.

I looked at our study book. I was a good student. *This won't be hard. Whatever God has for me, I am open.*

* * * * *

"My name is Candy," I said when we each took turns. "And I had three abortions when I was in an abusive marriage away from God." My confession was difficult, but no one was condemning. I was the only one who'd had three abortions. I didn't mention the miscarriage.

Vernon was all-in when I gave him a sheet explaining the effect that the next eight weeks may have on me. He wanted to be under-standing and supportive—a blessing since some women feel they cannot share their abortion with their husbands. As I left Vernon's business to God, God began to put a purpose for His kingdom in my heart. After thirty-five years, it was time for my secret to be fully revealed in the right way, God's way.

Our study guide listed possible effects I may have experienced because of my abortions. Before giving my life to Christ, I could have checked them all, especially anger and depression. When I read that many women suffer grief on the anniversary of their abortion, I

---

[100] See Exodus 21:22–25.

recalled the difficulty I had experienced on Mother's Day at church when the mother with the most children was recognized. With Mark and Crystal, my four in heaven, and Vernon's four, I counted ten. I probably was the top mom. No one knew. *What will they think? How will they treat me if they find out?* I had thought.

* * * * *

I decided to acknowledge the baby I lost from miscarriage. *I have to include you. Shame will no longer bind me from wholeness and healing. Jesus bore that on the cross for me.*

As the memory of that day returned, I found myself weeping in grief and sadness. I could see the small body of my baby in the dorm toilet, flushing it in shock. Now trying to stop my hand from pressing the lever. But the memory could not be changed.

"Candy, why are you crying?" Vernon touched my shoulder.

You have to tell him. I sobbed. *Tell him. Then tell everyone else.*

"I lost a baby in college. There weren't just three. There were four. I had a miscarriage in the dorm." I told him about the horror of the dorm bathroom and the college infirmary.

"Who was the father?" He looked shocked and sounded more accusatory than sympathetic to me.

"A student whom I thought cared about me. I didn't even know I was pregnant 'til I saw the tiny body. It was in summer school. Barbara was my roommate. She helped me, took me to the infirmary."

"Do you still have feelings for him?"

"What?" I composed myself. *How can he think that?*

"No. I'm grieving for a loss." I reminded myself of the new person I was in Christ. "God doesn't hold that against me."

I felt myself getting defensive. I knew my battle wasn't against my husband, but I felt the anger rising thinking about his reaction to telling him the first time about the abortions. On the other hand, I knew Satan was trying to separate and divide by filling my husband's mind with doubts and questions. But it still hurt.

I didn't realize I still saw Vernon as being one of those who stood on the condemning side rather than on the grace-and-mercy side.

But I also didn't see until then that he was struggling too. Neither of us knew where this would end and how it would affect our marriage and our lives.

Would these classes make our marriage better or worse? With God's help, I knew this would eventually turn out good. Through the pain, there were God's promises for healing. I refused to quit.

* * * * *

The floodgate of emotions caught me off guard as we opened doors that had been shut for many years. Early one morning as I lay in bed, half awake, a memory surged into my consciousness: being kicked and taken to get an abortion, then fighting to escape the decision. From deep within me, sobs burst out. I stifled them so as not to wake Vernon, then slipped out of bed and into the living room to watch the sunrise.

Am I supposed to remember all this anger? Where is this all going?

With my morning praise music lifting me out of my pit, I fixed coffee for my husband and greeted him.

"Are you okay?" he asked.

I still had a problem deeply opening up to him and sharing what had happened. *Does he really care? Is he going to condemn me?*

"Yes, I was just remembering the time when I was so far from God, so isolated and hopeless."

"Well, you're not like that anymore."

"I know. I need to be able to forgive completely. I thought I had." My eyes welled with tears. "The hardest part is that he abused me when I was pregnant—when he kicked me in the stomach." The sobs erupted again. I couldn't continue.

"Someone needed to beat him up." Vernon seethed. "That coward. What a louse."

I agreed, knowing I would need help to forgive him.

* * * * *

I didn't realize what an angry person I'd been for so many years. God had been changing me, but I had a long way to go. Anger had plagued me in this second marriage also. I didn't want that anger directed at my husband, especially because he had said, "I can't do anything right in your eyes." I couldn't see my anger's deep origin as being from the abuse and abortions.

Was there more?

There is a righteous anger that God has, but I knew mine normally wasn't righteous. As Vernon and I discussed the events surrounding the abortions, I felt the anger toward my ex-husband that I had shut down so many years before. If we hadn't divorced, one of us may have been killed. We had already murdered, as hard as that was to admit. *I* had murdered. I had been a part of murdering my own three babies. How was it conceivable to forgive him or myself? Without Christ, it was impossible.

To finally confess my sin and acknowledge Christ's forgiveness openly in a group was difficult but a great relief—the only path to true freedom. The devil loves secrets. It's in those dark places away from the light he does his dirty work.

* * * * *

I had lived in denial for almost ten years before Vernon and I were married. I told myself the past should be left behind as a part of starting all over in my new life. Why tell him? I deceived myself. The children I had lost were a part of me I could no longer deny. Jesus didn't condemn me, so neither did Vernon now. God was changing us both. He married all of me: my past, my present, and my future. All covered by the blood of Jesus now that I belonged to Him.

Very few of my friends knew my past. Like so many men and women who have been involved in abortion, I sat in church, afraid of what people would think if they knew. I was in leadership and taught the children, and my pastors didn't know my story. It was a lie to think that most Christians in my churches would have condemned me. Sure, some may have. But not any of our pastors, and not those members who were really friends. Even if they did, Jesus didn't, and

He is the One who really matters. The truth of God's Word continued to set me free[101] in new areas. I wondered, *What will my freedom do for others?*

* * * * *

After Vernon left each morning, I walked into my sitting room that had become my healing room and opened my book to begin. *Help me, Jesus, to do this.* It was only through the help of the Holy Spirit. God wouldn't expect us to forgive if it weren't possible. With Him, all things *are* possible. Even forgiveness of the most heinous acts against us. Jesus said to pray for those who hurt us, and I did.[102]

I meditated a lot about forgiveness and read Christian books on it. I read the Scriptures. *How can I completely forgive?* I didn't feel I had forgiven because thoughts would continue to come up after I made declarations. God doesn't give us any options or exceptions. He commands us to forgive and even says that if we don't forgive, we can't be forgiven.[103] In my own strength, I could not forgive.

The hardest session was writing about Don kicking me when I was pregnant. Abortion is abuse, and what he did had to be the worst abuse of all. A part of me died too. My children were gone. I had lost my hope, my love, my peace, my self-worth, my health, and my soul. But ultimately I had only my own sinful self to blame and the liar and deceiver I had listened to—Satan. I had to take responsibility and not blame someone else or my circumstances. Only through Jesus Christ and His Word could I take an honest look at what had been done to me and what I had allowed and done to please my husband. I had kept those secrets for more than thirty years. I also had to repent for all the things I had said to him, putting him down and criticizing, belittling. I even made a phone call and asked his forgiveness but said nothing about the abortions. He hadn't repented.

---

[101] See John 8:31–32.
[102] See Matthew 5:44.
[103] See Matthew 6:15.

I found mercy knowing Satan had been using him, and he was lost without God. I wrote, "I forgive you, Don. I forgive you for not wanting me and them, for taking me to get abortions, and for the abuse." I prayed he would come to the Lord and also find forgiveness. How could I not forgive when I had been forgiven of so much?

I forgave everyone else I could think of who had a part in my abortions, directly or indirectly: the abortion industry, the government's legalizing the murder of babies, politicians, the doctors who performed the abortions, the hospitals that provided the service, and the US air force that offered free abortions to wives of servicemen.

* * * * *

What about me? How can I forgive myself? I had agreed. I could have refused. I had sacrificed my children to please my husband, to save my marriage, without any hope, in a desperate dark place. Now I know God and His promises. Years ago, I had tried to convince myself abortion was my only option.[104] Anyone would have agreed I was in a bad situation. It looked impossible, with no other choice. Now I had to acknowledge the truth.[105]

In every single case, I could have said no and accepted the consequences. I was afraid—selfish and blinded to the truth that I now know. If I had cried out to God, He would have provided for me and protected me with His lovingkindness,[106] just as He did later when I *was* left alone to raise two children.

I knew the biology. From conception—the beginning of life— forty-six chromosomes determine the adult's every characteristic. Without interruption, a single fertilized ovum from the mother will develop into a baby in nine months. As a science major, I had known the facts, but I still aborted three children. I was without excuse.[107] I confessed my sin, agreed with what God said about abortion—abor-

---

[104] See Proverbs 14:12.
[105] See 1 John 1:8.
[106] Psalm 107:19–20.
[107] See Romans 1:20.

tion is murder—and asked His forgiveness.[108] He forgave me. I had to accept that on faith whether I felt forgiven or not. God says though our sins be as scarlet they shall be as white as snow[109]—washed clean by the blood of Jesus.[110] He remembers them no more[111] and removes them as far as the east is from the west.[112] My response was to love Him who first loved me and gave His life for me.[113] From healing me of Crohn's to now, I had loved Him and worshipped Him with a thankful heart—now even more.

* * * * *

We spent eight weeks in two-hour sessions going through many Scripture verses and sharing experiences and truths about abortions, dealing with emotions, and beginning the process of forgiving, the key to freedom. The abortion chains began loosening. I wanted to believe I would be healed in one eight-week course, but it was only a beginning. It was scary but also rewarding. Jesus had started the process many years earlier—bit by bit and now at full throttle. I could now say I had abortions, overcoming the fear of someone's reaction. I also told about the baby I lost to miscarriage, refusing to let shame dominate me anymore.[114]

Now to a greater extent than ever, I would speak out the truth of what Jesus had done for me. The more I gave my testimony, the less hold the devil had on me. God gave me Revelation 12:11 years before, and now I was going to be the overcomer that verse talks about, overcoming by the blood of the lamb and the word of my testimony and loving not my life unto death. I hoped my new freedom

[108] See 1 John 1:9.
[109] See Isaiah 1:18.
[110] See 1 John1:7.
[111] See Hebrews 8:12.
[112] See Psalm 103:12.
[113] See 1 John 4:19, John 3:16.
[114] Isaiah 61:7, 2 Corinthians 4:2, Isaiah 54:4.

and deliverance from the lies and deception[115] would inspire others to also be free.

* * * * *

Abortion also stole my feelings of love.[116] I hadn't understood why it was hard for me to *feel* love for my children and for my husband after having three abortions. Now it became clearer. My feelings had been shut off to the babies I had aborted. Instead of the normal love I should have felt, I felt nothing—just anger toward my husband and deadness toward everything around me. Or I felt fear. That carried over to my second marriage at times when depression and anger would come upon me, even as a Christian.

I wanted all my feelings back—my emotions were being healed. Jesus's love for me was restoring what Satan had stolen from me. Instead of being liberated, abortion had stolen my love. But after I came back to Jesus, I had felt a sincere love for the children I taught, for my family, and for other Christians at times. When I sang to Jesus at church, I was enraptured with His love. I had also loved God and many others without all my feelings being there.

I wanted to *feel* a deep love for my husband and trusted God to take care of that too, knowing that God's love wasn't based on feelings[117] nor should my love for my husband be based on his performance. The Bible says that in the last days, the love of many will grow cold.[118] With so many getting abortions, I can understand how that can happen.

* * * * *

The list of effects of abortion is long. Temporary psychotic breakdown and depression had both afflicted me. None of my doctors at the time ever gave me any warning about these effects. Now

[115] See Jeremiah 9:6, Proverbs 13:5, Ephesians 4:29.
[116] See Romans 1:28–32.
[117] See 1 John 4:17–19.
[118] See Matthew 24:12.

my mind was being renewed with the truth. I proclaimed, "I have not been given a spirit of fear but of power and love and a sound mind,"[119] That was my promise for sanity I claimed as my mind was still being transformed and renewed by God's Word.[120] I was not afraid of another episode in the psychiatric ward.

Through the years since *Roe vs. Wade*, as more information is gathered, the list of abortion's detriment to women's health has grown. Physical, emotional, psychological, spiritual, relational—on and on the list grows as more women come forward.[121] If I hadn't turned to Jesus, where would I be? Jesus's promises and covenant for health are mine and for anyone who turns to Him.[122] I believe in my case that Crohn's disease came from all of the pushed down emotions from the abortions and abuse—the sin that weighed so heavily on my soul. My body turning on itself—self-hatred? Guilt? Unforgiveness? When I turned to Jesus, He healed me and replaced all of that with His truth and love.

Because abortion is such a political issue, women are not being told the truth. Our class was based on the truth of God's Word. Most fundamentally, abortion is not a political issue or a personal choice issue. It is a spiritual issue. Only God can give life, and only God can take it away. Abortion is murder; it is sin. But there is a remedy. God's Word says, "If we confess our sins, He is faithful and just to forgive us and cleanse us from all unrighteousness."[123] Now I am free. What a blessed hope. Only with His love and truth could I ever be healed and truly liberated.[124] And I will see my lost children again. All four.

* * * * *

---

[119] See 2 Timothy 1:7.
[120] See Romans 12:2, Philippians 2:5–8.
[121] See Romans 6:23.
[122] See Isaiah 53:4–5.
[123] See 1 John 1:9.
[124] See John 8:36.

I felt anticipation with some angst before our long-awaited memorial service at the end of our study. I asked God to help me find something to commemorate the four children I had lost. It was also a celebration, a celebration of their lives and God's promises for me—His promise that I would be reunited with them, just as King David looked forward to seeing his dead child.[125]

Looking for something commemorative for the service, I found bouquets of orange and yellow lilies and four plaques with crosses and the words *faith*, *love*, *hope*, and *joy*—one for each child. Then I picked out a favorite song and planned a dance of praise for my presentation. A letter, poem, craft, song, candles, flowers—all were suggestions for commemorating our children at the service.

Vernon was the only spouse there—the only man. He really *did* care. And seeing his genuine love drew me closer to him.

"Thank you for bringing me and for being here," I said.

He smiled and hugged me. "I love you. I hope you know that. I wanted to do this for you."

Vernon had helped me name my babies: Peter John, Mary Hope, Joseph Paul, and Sarah Noel. Our leader gave me a certificate to commemorate each life. They were real and with Jesus.

Completing that eight-week course was the beginning, not the end—the beginning of my deliverance out of the pain and lies of abortion into the light and love of the truth of God's Word. Someday I would have a great testimony to share with other women.

Once again, Jesus assured me, "Don't be afraid. I am with you. You will not fear what man can do to you."[126] You are an overcomer. Then I thought of the Word He gave me years earlier. "And they overcame him by the blood of the Lamb, and by the word of their testimony; and they loved not their lives until death" (Revelation 12:11, KJV). If I loved my life, I would want to protect myself from any criticism and please man and not God. I did that before—feared man rather than God.[127] I will never do that again, never.

---

[125] See 2 Samuel 2:23.

[126] See Deuteronomy 3:22, Matthew 10:28.

[127] See Acts 5:29, Proverbs 29:25, Galatians 1:10.

22

The Alder Wood Boxes

I t was just a routine pap smear—until I got the results. Abnormal cells called for a biopsy. Vernon went with me to hear the results.
I braced myself and heard the doctor say, "The cells are precancerous from HPV. You need to have surgery of the cervix, or you will have full-blown cancer within a year." I knew this was an attack from the pit of hell, but I was still scared.[128]

HPV! What could have caused it? Those past relationships—way back to the years before my first marriage in college?[129] Whatever, it's from the devil. I feared both how Vernon would react and how to deal with that dreaded word—*cancer.*[130]

I didn't want to accept what the doctor was saying. "We'll be in touch," I said, taking her information for an appointment with a surgeon.

As we drove home, I turned to Vernon. "After being healed of Crohn's disease, I want to trust God with this situation too. I don't want to have surgery."[131]

"All right, if that's what you want," he conceded tentatively. His voice showed his concern.

---

[128] See John 10:10.
[129] See Roman 8:1.
[130] See John 8:44.
[131] See Romans 10:17.

To the doctors and many others, I was taking a chance. To me, it was not chance. It was faith. Chance was believing that surgery would get every single cell and that it would not come back. Chance was years of wondering if they got everything and trusting medical science that only knows remission.[132] Faith and trusting God was knowing that every wayward, abnormal cell would be healed and every virus eradicated—by His stripes on the cross. No remission.[133]

I called the doctor's office.

"Hi, this is Candace Thompson. I'm calling to let the doctor know that I have decided not to have surgery. Please cancel my appointment with the surgeon. Thank you."

It was done. I was relieved. Now for that good fight of faith.[134]

* * * * *

I asked for prayer at church.[135] No room for pride. I believed healing, just like salvation, was provided for me through Christ's sacrifice on the cross. The prophet Isaiah said Jesus took our infirmities and carried our sicknesses,[136] and Matthew said that Jesus went about healing all that came to Him.[137] I believed He still did today and hadn't changed.[138]

Later I had all sorts of condemning thoughts that could only have come from the devil, telling me that HPV was from past sinful relationships, and cancer was the consequence I deserved, so God wouldn't heal me. Part of that was true. I did deserve to die, but Jesus had already done that for me. I was no longer guilty,[139] and healing was available to me just as much as to any other Christian. Lies and deception didn't work on me this time.

---

[132] See 2 Corinthians 5:7.
[133] See Hebrews 11:1.
[134] See Matthew 21:22.
[135] See James 5:14.
[136] See Isaiah 53:5.
[137] See Matthew 15:30.
[138] See Hebrews 13:8.
[139] See Psalm 103:12.

God reminded me of His promises: *You are redeemed by the blood of the Lamb*[140] *and no weapon formed against you is going to prosper.*[141] *You are forgiven, and God remembers your sins no more.*[142]

Many scriptures came to mind on healing.[143] I stood on His promise for healing—not easy when day after day there was an abnormal discharge on my underwear. I kept the symptoms from everyone, only casually mentioning them to Vernon. Talking about the symptoms and the prognosis tore down my faith. Declaring God's promise for healing regardless of symptoms increased my faith, so I stood on God's Word, not the medical facts nor my observations. I also remembered Deuteronomy 28:1–15 about the blessings that were promised for those who obeyed God's commandments, even more so as a recipient of the New Covenant through Christ's blood.

* * * * *

In the winter of 2010, I attended two more series of postabortion classes in Colorado Springs as a trainee to help other women. Vernon drove and waited for me. God bless the guy. I didn't miss a single class. Driving eighty miles roundtrip to each of the twenty-four classes was his labor of love.

Excited that I would possibly lead classes at the center and train church leaders in the area, I continued volunteering. Nothing materialized. Every door shut to postabortion healing—even at the pregnancy center. Sad to say, no church in our town did this sort of thing. Our church was small, and any postabortion ministry would have to be an outreach.

I still had mornings when tears would hit me. I wondered if there would ever be a time when I wouldn't be covered in sadness. Denying my babies and trying to forget what had happened for so many years had left me with very little—even the dates that would have been their birthdays. I had no good memories or anything tan-

[140] See Ephesians 1:7.
[141] See Isaiah 54:17.
[142] See Hebrews 8:12.
[143] See 3 John 1:2.

gible from any of my four children I had lost. Hoping that might be part of my sadness, I mentioned to Vernon that I would like to have a box for each child for mementoes.

* * * * *

One day, Vernon brought home four perfectly matched boxes of red alder wood and proudly set each box on the carpet. I was overwhelmed. Kneeling on the floor, I opened one and looked inside. Running my hand over the smooth finish, my mind already was going to the contents that each would hold.

I hugged him. "Thank you so much. I love you. They're perfect."

His arms held me tightly. "I love you too. I love you more than you could ever know."

"I know." Nothing felt better than his arms around me.

I examined the four empty boxes. The corners were tongue and groove, and their lids were crowned with a small curved molding along the edges and fitted with brass hinges and fit snugly on the boxes. There were no latches. They were larger than I had imagined—more than a foot long and half a foot deep. The natural finish of the red alder accented the grain of the wood flowing around the darker knots, giving the boxes the finish of fine furniture.

I know it hadn't been easy for Vernon to watch me go through the pain of the previous year. He had hoped it would all be gone after my classes, and he tried to understand. Do you ever completely get over the loss of a child? Of four? His natural instinct was to console or fix me, but he didn't know how. Watching and loving and being there without condemning had been a process for him too. I later found out he had paid one hundred dollars for each box. This man who had true compassion and love for me was fully together with me on the most important issue in my life.

* * * * *

I assembled my tributes and expressions of love: four ceramic plaques with jeweled crosses, certificates acknowledging their lives, handwritten letters, clothes, and toys. The letter to each child expressed my love as their mother. I had written a letter to each one in our classes. Thinking about my losses, I was flooded with the pain of my own empty arms that ached for the children who were not there. The smell of a baby's soft skin and the thought of their little faces nudging mine—only for a brief moment—was too painful.

My grieving was no different from the loss of any child, regardless of age. They were part of me and couldn't be denied, brushed off, or easily processed—regardless of how they had died. Aborted or miscarried, I would always be their mother. Abortion couldn't change that.

* * * * *

Peter's plaque had the word "Faith." I wasn't ashamed anymore. *Faith is the assurance of things hoped for.*[144] *I will see my son again,*[145] I thought as my eyes teared. It was okay to cry. In his box, I arranged tiny white tennis shoes, socks, and a little matching newborn romper. Last went in the little toy I bought for him. Holding his certificate, similarly written for each child, I read the words:

Peter John Thompson
waits in heaven nestled securely in the arms of Jesus.
This child lives forever in the hearts of
Vernon and Candy Thompson
Parents (adopted by Vernon)

At the bottom was Isaiah 40:11 (NIV), "He tends his flock like a shepherd: he gathers the lambs in his arms and carries them close to his heart; he gently leads those that have young." *He's with Jesus, safe and happy.*

I need faith now more than ever, I was reminded. *It's not about feelings.* And the tears came. *But I have to stop denying the pain.* I had

---

[144] See Hebrews 11:1.
[145] See 2 Samuel 12:23.

forgiven the young man who was his father. The pain of the circumstances was gone, and shame would no longer rule me. Giving myself permission to cry and letting myself feel the loss wouldn't have been possible years before because of that horrible guilt. It would have been unbearable. Now grief was possible.[146] Jesus was with me now. I knew how much He loved me and had forgiven me. The sin of those circumstances was wiped clean, no longer attached to his life or mine.

* * * * *

Mary Hope, you were my first girl. I couldn't face what I had done. I wanted you so much but didn't stand up for you. I love you so much. Who do you look like? Do you have blonde or brown hair? Everything for Mary was pink: a pink giraffe, a pink romper, and pink newborn slippers with sparkles. "Hope" is on her plaque. *I will see you again— that is my hope. Just as King David knew he would see his child that died, I'll hold you and love you as your mother. The promise is there will be no more tears.[147]* Tears wet my face for the little girl I never got to see. I know you have forgiven me and don't hold anything against me.

"Jesus, please tell Mary Hope I love her, and someday we will be together," I said aloud. *I can love her without feeling guilt. I can love at last!* Perfect love casts out all fear,[148] and Jesus is the One with perfect love. He doesn't remember my sins, and neither do I.[149]

* * * * *

I placed the plaque with "Love" in the box for Joseph, whose namesake was Mary's husband, Joseph, Jesus's stepfather. He was willing to take on his wife's scorn and circumstances, disregarding what

---

[146] See Psalm 34:18.
[147] See Revelation 21:4.
[148] See 1 John 4:18.
[149] See Isaiah 43:25.

others said about her and raised her child as his own.[150] *That* was love. I thought about Vernon. *He's standing with me and unashamed of me.*

"Joseph Paul, I love you, love you." A warm peace came over me, pushing out everything else as I arranged the little teddy bear, blue romper, and little white tennis shoes for tiny feet. As I squeezed his little bear, the tears started again. *Would you have been a little ballplayer like your brother, or would you have been a famous doctor or a preacher for the Lord? Are your eyes brown like your mother's? You are not gone forever. You were created to love and praise the Lord for His glory and to be like Jesus. There will be a joyful reunion someday for us. I love you with all my heart, my sweet little boy.*

* * * * *

The last box was for Sarah Noel, named after my beautiful mother, Sara Magdalene, and after the great matriarch Sarah, who believed for the promised heir along with her husband Abraham, the father of faith. "Joy" was on Sarah's plaque. *You are not forgotten. I love you and someday will hold you. I know you are not sad—there are no tears in heaven with Jesus.* "Now faith is the assurance of things hoped for, the conviction of things not seen."[151] *I have faith that I will see you and know you and have joy at our reunion. No more tears with Jesus.*

Are you dancing before the Lord like your mother, singing praises to Him as I love to do? You're no longer my child of sorrow but of joy. Someday we will dance together. I put the little dark-haired doll in her box, along with the certificate and the plaque with her name. God promises that I will have joy here on earth as well as in heaven.[152]

* * * * *

---

[150] See Matthew 1:18–25.
[151] See Hebrews 11:1.
[152] See Psalm 30.

Feeling both comforted and emotionally spent, I put the boxes on a shelf in my closet. Then I remembered something I once heard: "They have an eternal purpose.[153] They are not just gone forever." I wondered, *How will they be used for Your kingdom, Father? My testimony? Peter John, Mary Hope, Joseph Paul, and Sarah Noel—you're waiting for me, and until then I will not be ashamed to speak out the truth and what Jesus has done for me and for you.*

Later I discovered that the red alder tree hadn't always been considered good for making fine furniture and cabinetry and was once referred to as a "trash tree." The reddish-brown inner bark was used by the Native Americans as a dye because damage to the outside of the tree exposed the red layer underneath, appearing to cause it to bleed.

These four beautiful alder wood boxes were made from a tree once considered useless and undesirable, a "trash" tree. *When injured, they bleed, just like You did, Jesus, rejected and scorned, shedding Your blood—for me—on Golgotha, outside the city gates with criminals.[154] These boxes hold my heart, just as You do.*

* * * * *

For a year, I patiently and consistently stood firm in faith for healing of HPV cancer just as I had for Crohn's disease. The symptoms gradually went away. When I went back for a yearly Pap smear, I received confirmation of my healing—no abnormal cells. Praise God! All symptoms were gone. Another testimony! By Jesus's stripes, I had been healed once again.

How would God turn this for good?[155] I wanted women to know when they repent, God not only forgives, but He will also take away the effects of sin when we believe. There was no shame associated with it, just as with the abortions. *Jesus bore the shame for me.*[156] "There is no condemnation." I said, remembering Romans

---

[153] See Jeremiah 1:5.
[154] See John 19:17.
[155] See Romans 8:28.
[156] See Hebrews 12:2.

8:1, "No condemnation for those who are in Christ Jesus." That one Bible verse brought me more healing than the many hours in the psychiatrist's office. I was thankful my husband didn't condemn me or criticize me for the stand I was taking. He was standing with me.

I took the alder wood boxes to the pregnancy center to share what God was doing in my life, spoke at their annual banquet, and attended a pregnancy center conference where I gave my testimony on abortion. To say I was disappointed about the postabortion program at the center was an understatement. My dream was to train women to do postabortion healing groups in their churches, but there wasn't an open door for that anywhere. God must have another plan.

* * * * *

When I was struggling to make sense of what God was doing in my life, the door to help someone opened unexpectedly while having lunch with a lovely woman I had met in a local women's political group. "I'm volunteering at the pregnancy center as the postabortion counselor. The Lord has healed me of three abortions," I said without fear of being judged.

She checked the surroundings for potential eavesdroppers and almost whispered, "I had an abortion when I was in high school. My mother took me. For more than forty years, I've had nightmares about babies crying."

"Oh, I'm so sorry. That is terrible." I took her hand. "God doesn't hold the things we repent of against us. He says we're new creatures and forgives us when we ask. I just finished my training for postabortion and named my babies and had a memorial service." And I told her their names.

Before we finished, she had agreed to go through the eight-week postabortion healing class with me—just the two of us in my home. We faithfully went through the eight-week study, named her baby, and held a memorial service. I was so blessed. She understood that God wasn't punishing her—it was Satan lying to her. She was able to forgive her mother for taking her and the high school boyfriend for his part.

And I thought, *If it's just one, that's all right with me.*

God blessed me and encouraged me at a very low time through this friendship. The time and effort I had spent in classes hadn't been in vain. The hours of training had also been for me—for my personal healing. And whether it would be used in our pregnancy center or not, it would not be wasted. God was faithful, and I would go wherever He led.

* * * * *

Passionate to get out what God was teaching me on abortion and feminism, I began to write. The pastor who had counseled me to call off my divorce was not shy about preaching against feminism and abortion. Vernon's enthusiasm encouraged me. My first article exposing abortion and feminism was published in the *Sangre de Christo Sentinel*, a small weekly newspaper in Westcliffe, Colorado. It wouldn't be my last. "You're a good writer," Vernon said. "You need to write a book so you can reach more people."

After three years, I resigned from the pregnancy center. "I believe God is leading me to write a book so I can reach more people with my testimony," I said to the director, fighting the thought that I had failed. But I knew the abortion classes had been for me as much as for others.

So I wrote articles on abortion—some political, but many from my personal experience—and I started my book. More tears flowed as I put into words the hurt and pain of my past and the losses I had experienced. Speaking out at any opportunity, I was determined to be used by God.

However, instead of book tours and speaking engagements, my life seemed to be headed in a different direction—one I had never imagined and one that would present the most difficult challenges of our marriage *and* the most rewarding.

23

Giving Up to Gain

W hen Vernon's mother died in November 2007, we inherited part of the Thompson farm in Oklahoma—the old house, dilapidated sheds, and thirty-five acres. We were separated at the time. His mother had called me before she died to tell me that Vernon loved me, and she believed we would someday be ministering together. How I wanted to believe her. I thanked her for calling.

After finishing the basement in our home in Colorado and completing the landscaping, Vernon started a herd of Angus cattle at the farm, hiring a farmhand to help. His vision for our future seemed to be taking us in the direction of *Hee Haw* and *Green Acres* with land and cattle, back to the home place where he was born. My heart wasn't in this vision, but I tried to accept what I couldn't change.

Our children were doing well. Crystal and Ed had bought a house of their own and relocated near Denver with their two boys. Mark was doing well with a business of his own; he and Sherry had three sons and were active in their church. I wasn't ready to leave Colorado, our family and friends.

Our first Thompson reunion at the farm was a year after Vernon's mother passed away in the fall of 2008. A large group of Vernon's family was there—children and grandchildren, cousins, and even two great-grandchildren. It was a great beginning with a hay ride and cookout in the yard of the old house. *Someday they all will be here*, I thought, wishing my two children and their families had been there.

* * * * *

Vernon was almost seventy still running the company and now trying to start another dream with retirement seeming to be beyond reach. I didn't see how all of this was going to work. *What about priorities? What about our kids and the church? Our new home? Our debt?*

And there was Sam. Sam was our only investor, an elderly Christian, who had saved the company with loans and investment capital years earlier.

"What about Sam?" I asked. "Are we paying him back?" I had stayed away from any involvement in his business but knew enough to be concerned.

"I'm paying myself back what I put in the company. Sam will be paid back when the company sells." I had to let it go and tried to stop worrying about something I couldn't change. However, I *did* pray, "Thy will be done, thy kingdom come in our lives, as it is in heaven.[157] In our business, I ask you to bring about righteousness, peace, and joy[158] and guide and lead my husband to be in your will in everything he does."

* * * * *

Still it was hard to put my heart into the farm with so much money and work it would require. In the unspoken desires of my heart was a yearning for oneness, to be a helpmeet, a helper suitable for him,[159] who was bone of his bones.[160] Sometimes I was more of a thorn in his side, especially when I questioned how he spent money on the farm. I didn't know how to be that woman, and he didn't know how to let me be the woman God had created me to be.

---

[157] See Matthew 6:9–13.
[158] See Romans 14:17.
[159] See Genesis 2:18.
[160] See Genesis 2:23.

My input on our business finances or the farm were mostly ignored or rebuffed; however, I managed our modest household expenses with an income from the company, paying all the utilities and groceries, as well as tithing on what I got with social security. We never lacked for anything. I even had extra to help others. *I am so blessed. Thank You, God, for all You are doing in our lives and what You have done for me.* I loved my life with friends at Bible studies and women's Christian conferences. Vernon encouraged me to be involved in local politics and volunteering. With Mark's family nearby, I had the joy of being a grandmother as well.

When Vernon hired a friend to start remodeling the farmhouse while keeping the cowherd as well as the propane business in Colorado going, it seemed as if I were on the outside with little input about the details of our lives. When the "friend" left with the house half-finished and half-covered with plastic, Vernon wouldn't give up the dream—to be a rancher with more land and cows to provide for our retirement. It wasn't my dream. And I didn't hesitate to tell him what I didn't like about the farmhouse, especially when parts were exposed to the elements and invading vermin.

* * * * *

At the farm, I struggled to put into action what I had learned about his need to be respected and praised. When I had repented of feminism and wanting to control Vernon, I didn't realize I would be tested. I didn't want to be that nagging wife described as a continual dripping on a very rainy day in Proverbs.[161] Another verse says it is better to live in the corner of a housetop than in a house shared with a quarrelsome wife.[162] I didn't like what God was showing me about myself. My flesh wasn't as dead as I had thought. But what about him? He's not considering me—again.

"That's all I *am* thinking about," he retorted when confronted, angry I would even think that.

---

[161] See Proverbs 27:15.
[162] See Proverbs 21:9.

Promoting the *Love and Respect* video series we had watched together during our reconciliation, I quoted Ephesians 5:33 in my articles. "A man's greatest need was unconditional respect and a woman's, unconditional love," I wrote. As his helpmate, I was to deeply honor and care for him, reverence and edify him.[163] He, in turn, would love me as he loves his own body, as Christ loved the church and gave His life for her.[164] It sounded easy, but putting it into practice in these circumstances was a challenge. *With God, all things are possible*, I reminded myself once again. *I can do all things, all things through Christ—another promise.*[165]

* * * * *

It *was* easy to be kind and respectful in the comfort of our beautiful mountain home. However, it was a different scene at the farmhouse On winter visits, the fireplace in the living room kept the temperature above freezing, barely. I could feel the tenseness in my jaws as I walked in the front door. We spent most of our time in our large bedroom with a gas fireplace. To my repulsion, unwelcome vermin left traces of their visits on our old sectional couch, and insect invasions tested my resolve.

The problems threatened to cloud my mission to expose the lies of feminism and abortion and their true effects on women. I complained, then repented—no clear victory. I was tempted to disrespect, complain, and be anything other than submissive, encouraging, and uplifting. I prayed, but my heart wasn't in Oklahoma. *How can the farm be in God's plan for us?* I asked.

However, as I watched Vernon sweep up the dust and debris and bring in wood to start a fire in the living room, my heart softened and I repented—again. He never complained, even when our toilet pipes froze and he had to carry water from the creek to flush it. Gradually, I overcame the opposition in my spirit and the fif-

---

[163] See Ephesians 5:33.
[164] See Ephesians 5:25–29.
[165] See Philippians 4:13.

ty-five-degree kitchen temperature to fix us a warm breakfast. Once more, I had overcome. I was his partner—wherever this was leading. The negative thoughts died without being given life through my tongue. They were the enemy to my marriage and my relationship to Christ. Winning this battle for this visit unfortunately didn't end the assault on my feelings permanently. God was teaching me how to defeat this enemy within through the Holy Spirit, His Word, and the accountability I had in my fellowship of believers. I got no sympathy at our Wednesday night Bible study whatsoever as I related all the trials I had endured.

* * * * *

For years, Vernon poured money into the farm. More cows and upkeep. "More debt from another big dream" was a thought I had to put down more than once. I dealt with anger when he bought more land. *More debt when we still owe our investor and a huge tax bill.*

"We'll pay those when we sell the company," he always replied to my questioning. I felt left out. He knew I'd object if he told me his plans to expand. It seemed as if nothing had changed—at least with him. I tried to remain calm when I saw a new expensive tractor in the field as we drove into the farm on one trip. Still it hurt. Trust had been damaged already, and this didn't help. *I am not a victim, and Satan isn't going to use this to defeat me. Cast down thoughts that oppose God and my husband,* I told myself. My victories over my emotions and thoughts came as I learned to control the weapon that had served me so well before I came to Christ—my tongue.[166]

Feminism would have had me angry and walking out of the marriage. But submitting in the Christian sense didn't mean I was to be like a doormat or dog on a leash. Fortunately, we were fellowshipping at the church where I was getting the truth about feminism and trusting God. Ephesians 5 speaks of mutual submission where the husband's part is to give himself up for the wife the way Christ gave

---

[166] See James 3:3–10.

himself up for the church.[167] How would that work with Vernon—or with any man? Changing my husband by what I said or did wasn't possible. I prayed and tried to honor him.

* * * * *

On a positive note, Vernon *did* encourage me in my writing for a conservative newspaper and helping with prolife initiatives that came up on the ballot. My passion for getting out the truth for God's purpose in my life kept me from focusing on things I could not change. Vernon liked my bold stand against feminism and abortion.

God blessed me in many ways through my husband, meeting my needs and providing trips back to North Carolina to visit family when my mother had to be put in a nursing home after a severe stroke. He never complained about the money spent or my time spent away. As long as I didn't complain, grill him about the tax debt or how he spent *his* money, my husband was a happy, positive man. He was driven to make sure we were provided for in our retirement. I found out early in our marriage that Vernon was an entrepreneur— he had a gift. But his drive for money had led us down some difficult paths.

* * * * *

Almost seven years after the tax situation, the business suffered another setback when a manager was fired and other employees quit. A series of events in the business resulted in Vernon leaving our church. I was devastated. After saving our marriage, I had hoped this was where God was going to give us a place to find our purpose in God's kingdom with support for my testimony. I was already writing a lot, and my testimony of rejecting feminism and abortion was going out in weekly articles. We also had a testimony of covenant and marriage.

---

[167] See Ephesians 5:21–33.

I didn't want to leave the people who knew me and go somewhere else in this small town. I wasn't a spiritual vagabond, as had been described in John Bevere's book *The Bait of Satan*, and I wasn't offended. When I didn't leave with him, he was very angry and accused me of all kinds of lies. "You care more about them than you do me." Any defense only made things worse.

I need the true teaching I am getting, I thought. What I didn't get was anything negative about my husband and marriage. I stayed, convinced I was in God's will. Vernon believed it was God's will for him to leave. I was submissive to Vernon in our home in every way possible, but I wouldn't leave where I felt God had me for what He wanted to teach me.

When things looked very difficult at the business, God brought a Christian couple who had the skills and desire to do a good job. They proved to be a blessing. Taxes were being paid back, and payments to our investor became regular. Dropping by the office became a pleasure. Our new manager, Lynn, became a close friend. With our taxes, mortgages, notes, and loans being paid down and with the help of a CPA, *and* prayer, our financial situation improved.

* * * * *

In his late seventies, Vernon was still going into the office five days a week and sometimes Saturday. Although he seemed to be in good health, he sometimes had difficulty breathing when walking in our mountainous neighborhood. While on a trip to Oklahoma, he went to the emergency room with chest pains and was admitted for a possible heart attack.

Two days after the 2016 presidential election, Vernon had cardiac surgery with a stent in one artery that was 99 percent closed. Another was 100 percent closed, but his heart had grown natural bypasses around it. I prayed in the Spirit God's Word on healing, "No weapon formed against my husband is going to prosper," and much more with the support of my church. God gave me peace through it all. I was sure God had His hand in saving him, because for a couple of years, we thought the chest pain was from the altitude and had been diagnosed as possibly asthma. We were thankful for the good care and successful surgery he received and the good prognosis.

* * * * *

Absentee ranching was difficult, and the cows required a lot of work and money. There was always a vet problem, an employee problem, an equipment problem, or a pasture problem begging his attention. He was leasing another acreage for more pasture and more cows. The day he had to shoot an injured cow was the day he decided to make a big change.

"I'm going to sell all the cows." He looked down, almost tearing. "And the equipment I don't need. I'll just raise hay to sell for income and tax purposes. I'm giving up my dream. We'll use the money to finish the house." And then he said, "I just want to spend my time with you."

I. Was. So. Happy. But I remained calm. "That's wonderful, honey."

"This is really hard."

"I'm sorry, honey." I tried hard to commiserate and hugged him tightly.

"All I want is to take care of you."

These were words I had wanted to hear. God had answered my prayers. Vernon wasn't as agile or as confident as he'd been twenty-five years earlier. Neither was I.

"I want to die on the farm, not in Colorado," his voice was almost urgent. These were words I *didn't* want to hear. His parents were buried in a small graveyard adjacent to the farm. I knew that's where he wanted to be buried with me beside him. Sometimes I felt like I was already dying, unable to see what God was doing. But when I submitted without continuing to argue and trusted God, our time together improved.

* * * * *

On our next visit to the farm, Vernon sold thirty cows to get the foundation laid on the house for the south addition. We would have a welcoming fireplace and a spacious, glassed-in sunroom with a swing. We sat down with the house drawings and worked out the details with consideration for each other's opinions. Vernon agreed to cut down the size of the house. Still it was 3,300 square feet. I struggled with his vision of a large home at our age.

"I'll have help for you cleaning it!" he tried to assure me when the negative was getting to him.

Peace eluded me as I watched the framers and roofers starting on our plans. I battled feeling close to God at times or close to my husband. One reason was the debt we owed to our one investor and Christian friend, Sam, who had saved the company with loans years earlier. The company was making payments on the loans, but our ninety-seven-year-old friend's health was rapidly failing. It was a concern to both of us when we heard the news that he had recently become blind. When Vernon mentioned putting our Colorado home up for sale, I balked, reminding him about the cows and equipment we were going to sell to pay for the farmhouse. On our next trip to the farm, the subject of selling our home came up again. This time, I agreed.

"We can put the house up for sale after Christmas in January. We could live in the fifth wheel while in Colorado. But all the equity has to go on finishing the house," I said. "We are not going to spend any on the business or the farm." I was adamant. He agreed.

"In the spring when the landscaping is greening out would be the best time. That would give us time to get everything ready," Vernon added.

"God can sell it any time—even in the winter," I piped up, remembering how God had moved years before when we sold our furniture.

We agreed to list it after Christmas.

However, that was not God's plan. After hearing about Sam's worsening condition, my heart was heavy. On our next trip to the farm, I suggested, "Let's use the equity from the house sale to pay Sam back."

Vernon shared my concern. "All right, that is fine with me."

Did he really say that? Praise God. "I know God will take care of us and provide what we need for the farm if we do the right thing." My heart had changed. It was God's will to use the equity in our home to pay this man who helped us when we were desperate. Repayment had been sporadic at best. Now we had an opportunity to redeem ourselves with God and with this man and his family. My heart was so thankful. *This has to be you, Father God. Thank you.*

Two weeks later, Vernon answered the phone to hear a local realtor make a surprising proposal: "I have a buyer who wants a house in the $500,000 range and wondered if you were interested in selling." We were amazed. Without listing it. In November before Thanksgiving, with Christmas coming in six weeks, we had an interested buyer. A few days later, there's a contract. Closing was set for December 28.

"This has to be God," I said. Vernon was astounded. Within two weeks of agreeing to pay our debt to Sam, we were showing our home. He agreed. There was no other explanation.

* * * * *

Surrounded with boxes and packing material, my heart sank when I heard my brother's voice. It was Mom. As I listened to the report of pneumonia and sepsis, I realized he didn't give her much hope. She had rallied so many times, why not now? There is a time for healing and a time when a person's body wears out and they depart this earth. Her time had come. *God, I don't know how all of this is going to come together. Please help us and give me peace and joy at this time.*

We flew back to my hometown for her funeral and took time honoring the woman I had come to admire so much and love. She died eighteen years after Dad. Even in the nursing home in her limited condition, she had poured out her love to all of us and to others.

My memories were good, especially my trips back every three or four months to help take care of her in the nursing home. Expressing my love had been difficult at one time but not when she needed it the most. I bought her pretty clothes and jewelry she still enjoyed and fixed her face and hair. Gone was the guilt of a foolish, rebellious daughter who had judged her as less than a role model and not honored her as the most precious gift God could ever have given a daughter. *Oh Mom, I love you so much. If I could only be half as loving as you were.*

God helped me write her eulogy and give a tribute during the service. Even though I knew she was with Jesus and that she had lived a long, good life, I would miss her so much. She was a wonderful mother. She loved. She forgave.

* * * * *

With a check for $250,000, Vernon and I smiled at each other as we walked up to Sam's door two days after Christmas. I never doubted our decision nor God's involvement. Tears ran down Sam's cheeks as he and his wife thanked us. He had recently become blind, and they were moving to assisted living after the first of the year. *Thank you, Father God. You will supply all my needs as always. I love you.* I felt free—peaceful as I wiped tears away and climbed into the truck to finish packing.

Miraculously, with the help of a dear friend, we were out of our home and in our fifth wheel with everything stored at the office by the deadline. We were tired and stretched to the limits physically and every other way, but I was thankful to God for selling our home, even if it meant moving into a fifth wheel while we finished our home in Oklahoma. It was God's will.

I hadn't seen myself responsible for the debt to Sam. I hadn't been a part of the transactions. It was Vernon's problem, not mine. Not true. His decisions affected me and involved me whether I agreed with them or knew about them. The cries of my heart to be one with my husband were being answered, but not as I had anticipated. Giving up what I had considered my right, the right to determine how the money my mother had given me would be used, was another step in a long journey of surrendering to Christ the things I had held on to for security.

Giving up most of our equity to pay on our debt to our friend was something I had never anticipated, but it was the right thing to do. Giving up a house and furniture twenty-five years earlier had resulted in great gains in my life, and I was certain God would do even greater things as we celebrated the new year in our fifth wheel and wondered what 2019 would bring.

24

Liberated by Love

Going from a 4,500 square feet home to our fifth wheel was not easy and stretched me in ways I hadn't anticipated, but I can honestly say I never looked back. I was pleased for the couple who bought our Colorado home.

"I never thought I'd live in a home this nice," the wife said.

My same thoughts fifteen years before. I never regretted our decision to sell it. But I joked to my friends that "the fifth wheel is smaller than my master bath and closet together." To those who had bets about my endurance, I said, "You don't know my God. Nothing is impossible with Him." But I did have my moments.

"I'm sorry you're having to live in this fifth wheel. I know it's not easy," Vernon said one evening, watching me struggle to make things work in our crowded quarters and not complain. His sincerity touched me. I hoped he would know that my love didn't depend on how much he could give me.

Giving up my home this time was different. God showed me how the attachment of things was much less than with our first home. I held on much more loosely. Material things weren't my identity.

"It's amazing how quickly God moved to sell our home. If only we could sell the company and the land without me having to advertise it and go through all the paperwork and redoing numbers."

"God can bring a buyer for the business without even trying to sell it, just like He did with the house," I said, wanting to walk in faith.

* * * * *

At seventy-nine, with the company needing less oversight, finishing the farmhouse became Vernon's priority. Trips to Oklahoma became more frequent. We went from winter into the heat and humidity of summer with one-hundred-degree temperatures and no central air. Driving the seven-hundred-mile trip up to four times a month and living out of a suitcase were the least of our challenges. Our excitement grew as we saw the brick finally going up.

At the farm, away from everyone on 150 acres, we had little choice but to make every effort to get along. We were together driving long distances, dead, weary, tired, and having to deal with flats, transmission problems, pulling heavy loads in all kinds of weather. God protected us in so many ways I lost count. Every time we returned, I had a testimony of how God saved us from some catastrophe. My friends were all amazed. They were hysterical when I told them that some of my favorite clothes blew out of the back of the truck and were somewhere on the plains of the Oklahoma Panhandle. I finally was able to laugh.

Back in Colorado, there seemed to always be a challenge with the fifth wheel. Gray water, black water, potty problems, shower, air-conditioning. Vernon was always working on something. Overcoming the temptations to be irritated and complain, I was so thankful for his patience and persistence to keep everything operating and comfortable.

* * * * *

I never regretted using our equity to pay the company debt, even when finding the money to finish the house was difficult. Finally, the house was bricked in, tight and secure. The old brick and stone we picked out was rustic and inviting with red windows—lots of windows.

The farmhouse was really amazing. I looked at the large living room divided by a sixteen-foot fireplace that had once been the four main rooms for a family of seven. Above on the south end was where my husband had slept for most of his first eighteen years. Vaulted ceilings of tongue and groove pine with wainscoting of beetle-kill pine from Colorado gave it a rustic, warm feeling. *Maybe it's going to be worth all the expense and hassle to keep part of the old house.*

A warning came to mind as I admired the progress—reminding me of the past. *Our lives can't be consumed with material things like in California*, I thought. *I need a vision for a purpose beyond a place for our comfort and enjoyment. All of this has to be for something greater than ourselves—for God's kingdom.* Without a purpose, all of this effort would be empty and joyless. *I am not the same woman I was in California.*

Most of our family had probably given up on seeing our house finished and wondered if we would ever be free to finish our dream at the farm or if I would ever finish my book. Our reunions and hayrides had lasted a few years and then fizzled out. The house had sat untouched for several years. Now once again, the funds were limited with the business needing so many things. After six months in the fifth wheel, we still weren't near finishing. Surprisingly, I was managing quite well—even going to the laundromat once a week. Determined my situation was not going to get the best of me, I held my tongue as I struggled with loads of groceries, clothes, and tight quarters on all sides.

* * * * *

In mid-September, an unexpected call came from a man who had looked at the company more than two years earlier. The company was running better than ever before and making more profit. The time seemed right when we heard the long awaited words, "We're ready to make an offer, and we believe that we can put a deal together."

Through no effort of our own, we had an offer. Another God thing? Unbelievable. *After so many years, is this actually happening?*

That same week, I was speaking at an interdenominational women's simulcast conference held in our town. I was excited about the opportunity to share my testimony of abortions and the devastating effects of feminism on my life, both controversial and highly emotional issues for women.

Vernon helped carry the four alder wood boxes in and set them up. I asked God to help me with the right words and started without any notes. This was the first time I had shared my heart and my precious mementoes with a group of women I didn't know.

I began with my rebellion as a young woman in college. "As a young woman, I rejected God's plan for me. I was pulled into the feminist rhetoric about equality, refusing to submit to and honor a man. Believing those lies led to an abusive marriage, to three abortions in an ungodly marriage, an incurable disease, and finally divorce. Instead of being loved, I was discarded and rejected—a failure in every way, left to raise my two children alone."

Telling about my past wasn't easy, but I wanted to make sure the women understood the true nature of feminism and abortion.

The account of me repenting, my marriage, and how I was delivered out of the terrible lies to be healed of Crohn's disease brought tears and a depth of emotion I hadn't expected. I spoke through tears of joy to the group.

"God's Word brought truth and deliverance from the lies I had believed. He gave me a new identity and a new mind. There is no condemnation to those who are in Christ Jesus.[168] That one scripture did more for me than all the hours in the psychiatrist's office."

I went on to tell about how God brought Vernon into my life and how being in God's plan had finally brought blessings and the love and value I had dreamed of as a young woman.

"God has really been working on me, and I've repented of wanting to rule over and control him. I want my husband to be the man God created him to be."

---

[168] See Romans 8:1.

Toward the end, I walked over to the boxes up front—the four alder wood boxes. I had placed them in a row with the lids open, waiting until last to tell about the babies I had lost. I began with the first baby I had been ashamed to acknowledge, the one associated with my sin in college, the one I had lost by miscarriage—Peter John.

"Jesus has forgiven me and set me free from the guilt and pain of the past. He promises that I will see my babies. There was nothing to remember them by. I had never held them or been able to tell them I loved them. I wanted to show they were real babies, my babies, whom I was able to love and finally look forward to seeing again, so I named them and collected some things for each one."

I held up the pink slippers for Mary Hope. There was the little doll for Sarah Noel and the tiny tennis shoes for Joseph Paul.

"A little white romper and shoes for Peter John and the plaques with their names. They are not gone but are with Jesus."

I wiped away the tears as I passionately declared the truths I knew that had set me free. Others in the room cried with me. God gave me the words I needed—words that were setting us all free.

Afterward, a woman came up to me crying. "That's the box that meant most to me," she said, pointing to Peter's box. "I lost a baby by miscarriage when I was young after my husband left me pregnant. I have always felt that it was my fault and have never told anyone until now." She was weeping.

I hugged her. "It wasn't your fault," I assured her and prayed for her. We both were crying. *Thank you, God. I do have an important story.* Many said they were interested in reading my book when it came out. I was encouraged so much. Vernon had always encouraged me to reach more women through a book.

* * * * *

After three months of negotiations, the business sold. Vernon's heart was to be free after twenty-five years—free of the responsibility of running a company.

Was it really twenty-five years since that cold January day when we drove in pulling our Olds with a U-Haul truck? I could never have imagined what God was going to do in our lives.

On the day of signing, Vernon and I were like two school kids being let out for vacation. I felt true excitement and anticipation for our lives that I have rarely experienced.

* * * * *

So many things happened that once seemed impossible. Our debts could be paid off, and we could finish the house. My book had been sent to the editors of Trilogy, and after so many years, publishing was becoming a reality. My patience was tested through another winter in the fifth wheel. I was certainly going to appreciate a home again and eating something other than frozen dinners and packaged salads. Vernon and I prayed together more often, mostly for our family, our marriage, and our country.

What was supposed to be only a few months in the fifth wheel had turned out to be eighteen months. On one trip to the farm, we found a church and started going together. One Sunday while visiting, during praise and worship, I felt so much closeness and togetherness in this important part of our lives. I smiled at him as he raised his hands and sang boldly to one of the songs. Others smiled at us as we worshipped together. *We must be the liveliest white-headed couple in here,* I thought, amused and thankful for our renewed zeal for God.

When a young man whose wife had divorced him came up to us after the service and began sharing, Vernon eagerly witnessed from the heart about covenant. After praying with him, we left encouraged that God had turned the pain of our past for good.

I also came to realize Vernon was my ministry first and foremost—not to make him into what I wanted him to be but to serve him and to respect him. I wanted to be the best wife I could be with no aspirations to be some great postabortion minister or a famous writer. We were together at last, giving our testimony to whoever would listen for God's kingdom. There were so many people getting divorces and abortions needing to have hope and experience God's love. Now, walking across a stage with a microphone, speaking to thousands of women with my husband in the background didn't fit my vision of success. There was no secretary helping him with the business part of our lives. Now we were doing it all together.

I wanted my husband to be the man God made him to be—a leader who heard from God, who couldn't be tamed into some submissive lackey who backed off and let me lead and call the shots, and who cried easily and had a feminine side. Vernon *would* back off if I insisted on my way. "You take over and do it," he would say. It wasn't in his makeup to fight a woman. That's when I knew to let it go. I had learned to pray before it got to that point.

* * * * *

We have great influence as women and can use it for good or evil. I have witnessed so many couples experience financial disaster because the husband let his wife take over. One such example was a Mary Kay director, a hard-working, talented woman who was making lots more money than her husband. I wasn't surprised when I heard they divorced after hearing her brag about not letting her husband buy a gun he wanted.

Equality sounds good, but two heads in any organization spells confusion and failure. God says in His kingdom that there is no male or female. That's in the Spirit. However, there *is* a created order in our relationships to others that has never changed and has nothing to do with credentials and all to do with an orderly placement for a purpose in God's kingdom. Only in the right submitted order to authority can any Christian, male or female, ever hope to attain anything in God's kingdom. The husband is the head and submitted to Christ, serves his wife in a wonderful tender caring way, loving her as his own body. In turn, she willingly submits to his headship.

The glory of God is revealed by those families who exhibit and demonstrate godly order to the world. The church should be different from the world outside where women are competing with men in every area. The blessing of being able to carry, birth, and nurture the next generation was given solely to women. It is an awesome responsibility and great honor, challenging and the most rewarding of anything we can ever accomplish. Nowhere is there the potential of matching fulfillment. Not in the board room, not in the operating room, not in the halls of academia or in the pulpit—nowhere.

* * * * *

Moving from the fifth wheel to our new home was a freeing feeling I will never forget. The large spaces, bright lights, and sun-filled rooms were overwhelming. Walking from one end to the other was like taking a hike compared to the confinement of the camper. Thrilled with our new home and being together, I found that I enjoyed our daily ride into town running errands and discussing plans for the day and being his helpmate. We need each other more than ever in these later years.

When God had Adam name all the animals, Adam saw that they all had mates but him. God made Eve for him—the perfect companion as his helpmate, bone of his bone, flesh of his flesh, a suitable partner for life. Then God brought her to him.[169] What a gift that must have been to Adam. The same is true today. What a blessing when your husband can see you as a gift from God to be loved, cared for, protected and provided for to the point of giving his life for you. That is who he was created to be. But the greatest love is God's love—perfect and pure, never ending. His love was so great that He died so we might live with Him forever. He alone can meet all our needs. Giving my life to Him was the best decision of my life with eternal consequences. I trusted Him as my Savior, and He has given me everything, both spiritual and material, that I need for life and life abundant.

When I read the 1 Corinthians 13 verses on love when we got married, I had little concept of the unconditional love described by Paul—the God kind of love. God *is* love, and only He can love us perfectly. In order to be liberated *to* love, I had to first be liberated *by*

---

[169] See Genesis 2:18–25.

love—God's love. Only His love could wipe away the condemnation and fear, the hurt and failure from the past. Only His love could enable me to receive His forgiveness and give me the courage to face the future as one of His. Only His love could free me to forgive others and myself completely.

* * * * *

When the Covid-19 virus hit the entire world, I saw clearly what a blessing to have sold our business and our home prior to that time. I was thankful for the time we had to say our goodbyes. There were friends and Mark's family we would miss but vowed to stay close. Mark's life as a father, a Christian businessman, and elder in his church was one of our greatest joys. Crystal and Ed were empty nesters with two sons earning college degrees in Colorado universities. Just thinking about where we had come from and what God had done in all our lives was humbling. I am so thankful that they too have overcome what Satan would have meant for evil in their lives and are believers today. Together, we have eleven grandchildren and now seven great-grandchildren from our six children. And I have four waiting for me with Jesus.

When I turned seventy-six, Vernon was the one who was there looking into my eyes with love and appreciation. Being told that I am beautiful at my age was certainly nice to hear. He told me I am beautiful inside and out. Coming from the person who knew me better than anyone, who had watched me struggle, who had seen me at my worst, was a great blessing. Finally, I was able to believe him.

"I'm amazed at how much you've changed. God is really doing great things in you," he told me.

Yes, He is, I thought. *I am truly liberated—liberated to love this man and to receive the love he has for me—without having to change him.*

Pleasing Vernon was important, but I wanted to please God above all others. He honors covenant and marriage, even for those women who may be married to unbelievers. Honoring a man who is an unbeliever and is difficult to live with may be hard, but he also may be won by the obedient wife who can trust God as she blesses a man who has done little to deserve her respect and honor. Submission is an act of obedience to God and isn't dependent on a man's character or behavior. God will give the grace to accomplish great victories of the soul seen by few but highly praised by God. The truth of God is freeing, liberating.

One day, I caught Vernon looking at me as if admiring me as I worked in the kitchen fixing breakfast. "What are you thinking?" I asked, smiling at him.

"That you are the most wonderful woman and that I am blessed to have you as my wife."

Tears filled my eyes as I walked over to his chair and gave him a big hug. He had been doing that a lot lately. *Our later years really are going to be our best. a farm again—our farm.*

Our new home quickly became a blessing for others. Had it really been twelve years? The warmness, the peace, and comfort were what I wanted in our home—a retreat and respite for others. Was all of this really mine to steward and manage? To enjoy? I started cooking special meals again with expectations of many gatherings and untold blessings *and* with Vernon's help—surprise of all surprises. He was eager to help and learn his way around in our beautiful kitchen.

My heart was full of gratitude when our Oklahoma church asked us to do a video of my testimony of abortion and healing for a Sunday service and women came up to me afterward and thanked me. Although Vernon didn't say a lot, his affirming presence beside me was monumental. I wasn't alone. In other ways, God showed me how He was going to use what He had done for us to liberate others, to see them healed and delivered from the lies of Satan. I remembered the prophecy Vernon had received before we left California— that he would be a pillar in the church and speak terror into the powers of darkness. And me—a love letter. One in purpose, one heart for the lost, for the hurting from abortion, and one for saving the lives of God's precious ones, our most vulnerable, the unborn. All of the previous years were a preparation for the years ahead. Deep in my heart, I tucked away those things God had given me that were more precious than gold,[170] His promise to complete those things that concern me[171]—my relationship with my husband and my children, speaking out for the unborn, telling the truth about feminism, sharing the good news of Jesus Christ, and above all my relationship with Him. He promises to finish what He began in me, making me more like Him 'til I go to be with Him.[172] He will never give up on me. He knows the deepest desires of my heart—He alone. Nothing is impossible with Him. Nothing.

---

[170] See Psalm 19:10.
[171] See Philippians 1:6.
[172] See Romans 8:29.

EPILOGUE

I pray that those who have read *Liberated by Love* have been liberated by the Spirit of God and that many have given their lives to Jesus Christ. He says if you confess with your mouth that Jesus is Lord and believe in your heart that God raised Him from the dead, you will be saved.[173] He will never forsake you and loves you so much that He died for you and wants you with Him now and forever. It's a wonderful journey, and He will never let you down. Find a life-giving, Spirit-filled church where learning God's Word is more than a religious activity and the people love you as Christ loves you. Start reading the Bible and praying to God and find out your new identity and all the promises that you have inherited as a child of the God Most High. Find out how His forgiveness through His shed blood wipes away all your sin and gives you a new life. I will be praying for you and would love to hear from you. I love you and so does God. You can connect with me through www.liberatedbylove.org and at thealderwoodboxes@yahoo.com.

---

[173] See Romans 10:9.

CPSIA information can be obtained
at www.ICGtesting.com
Printed in the USA
FSHW011557260221
78978FS